Design Review

INDUSTRIAL DESIGN 24th ANNUAL

Design Review

INDUSTRIAL DESIGN 24th ANNUAL

Compiled and written by Barry Dean

Whitney Library of Design, an imprint of
Watson-Guptill Publications/New York

The Architectural Press Ltd/London

To Eliot F. Noyes
(1910–1977)

First published 1978 in New York by the Whitney Library of Design,
an imprint of Watson-Guptill Publications,
a division of Billboard Publications, Inc.,
1515 Broadway, New York, N.Y. 10036
ISBN 0-8230-7156-1

First published 1978 in Great Britain by The Architectural Press Ltd.,
9 Queen Anne's Gate, London SW1H 9BY
ISBN 85139-167-2

Manufactured in U.S.A.

First Printing, 1978

Contents

Foreword

With this, the third volume of *Design Review* published in book form, it seems fair to evaluate the direction and content of the series. One might assume after reading the jurors' comments over three years that design is in an unhealthy condition. There has been much harsh criticism of what their peers have produced and relatively little praise. With all this "negativism" one might even ask if such a review is worth the effort. We submit, however, that this is not negativism in the usual sense, but is a reflection of the jurors' approach to the review and of their standards.

True, the jurors are looking for excellence in design, but their approach is not a superficial one, more appropriate for a picture/caption presentation. Their effort is to analyze both the good and the bad and to include their reasoning in the *Design Review* text. Beyond evaluation of specific projects, the jurors are encouraged to probe influences and trends as well as suggest remedies for the perceived ills.

The intention of this labor is not only to recognize the best that is being produced but also to provide a sourcebook for the practitioner as well as the manufacturer/client. Feedback from readers of the first two volumes indicates a desire for even more of the same. We believe a cursory glance through these pages will attest that we have not ignored this wish.

Among those whose special efforts have made this publication possible are Sarah Bodine and Susan Davis of the Whitney Library of Design and the editors of *Industrial Design*.

George T. Finley
Editor
Industrial Design

Introduction

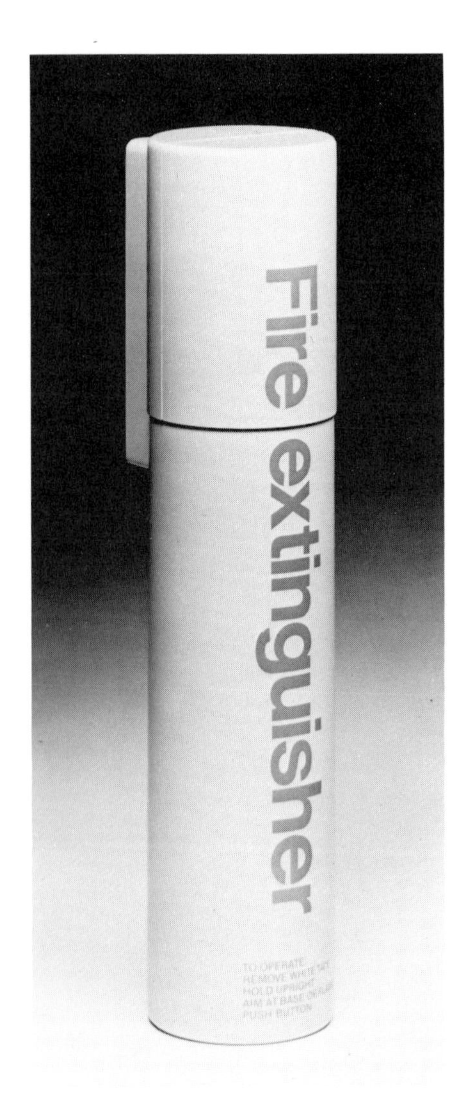

The jurors felt that the Gillette Captain Kelly Fire Extinguisher is an example of styling which obscures the critical function. Manufacturer: The Gillette Co., Boston, MA; consultant design: Morison S. Cousins + Associates, Inc., New York, NY.

Interpreting the 1977 Design Review is similar to reading a radar screen to forecast the weather. A cohesive picture of the results is only revealed through the coordinates that map out the relationships of individual elements. These elements include the diverse scope of work submitted and those designs selected, the comments and insights of jurors, and those political, economic, social, or technological forces which come to bear on the designer's perception of his work.

While comments of this year's jury panels, as well as the products and projects selected and discussed, represent an uncertain and perhaps clumsy groping to turn a significant corner in the dark, there is still a strong sense that the traditional coordinates which previously gave definition and context to design are in the process of strong and articulate permutations.

As yet unforeseen consequences to American design and the design professional are becoming evident in the form of new government legislation, research and studies supported and encouraged by consumer-advocacy groups, the development of updated standards and criteria in many areas affecting design.

The forces which bear most heavily on today's design seem to be external (i.e., consumer groups, safety legislation); certainly it is about time that design was acknowledged more formally by both government and the public. Yet designers seem to be uninvolved in helping to form the directions and ethical standards that they must deal with. Though the Industrial Designers Society of America (IDSA) is officially involved in developing contacts with government agencies, such as the new office for cultural resources in the U.S. Department of Commerce, as individuals, designers aren't as of yet noticeably involved in the activities and trends which seem to be surfacing and affecting changes in lifestyle.

As has been noted in earlier volumes of this review, the giant steps of innovation and change associated with design have slowed to a state of refining and formalizing the ground broken in recent years. Though there is little going on within the profession of controversial note, designers are literally getting down to business. Small manufacturers and design-oriented companies are recognizing the importance of design as never before. No doubt the seeds for future directions are being planted in a call for maturity from among the ranks of the design profession: through the development of concrete standards, revision of design education, and the kind of individuality and craftsmanship not evidenced in the majority of design work produced today.

The Latest in Form vs. Function

In the nuts and bolts area of human factors and the concern for the product's function—areas where the designer has made a positive albeit less visible contribution—the real accomplishments have been overshadowed, if not distorted by marketing's attempt to capitalize on them.

The soft-sell approach, seen, for example, in the style of the more subdued ads for European luxury car imports, is recognizable not only in the hype surrounding contract and residential furnishings, but in technical literature for equipment and instrumentation which uses statements about human factors research and development as a marketing tool.

In the consumer marketplace, "functional abilities" and "good design" are the passwords of current trends in retailing. However, the smooth, clean-lined casings designed to surround the mechanical workings of some consumer items have brought products with critical-use functions to a dangerous state of overrefinement for the sake of successful styling.

The Gillette Captain Kelly Fire Extinguisher, selected in the 1976 Design Review, was used as an example of styling which neutralized a critical function. David Pasenelli, juror on the Environmental panel, stated:

"I found that fire extinguisher very disturbing! As a designer, I like it very much, because it's a very refined design, very pure, and it looks like a good use of materials. It succeeded in design terms very well. But that form says nothing about being a fire extinguisher. In fact, it is so overrefined that there is nothing left to tell you about danger, to communicate with you directly when you are under extreme stress.

"I think that designers need to distinguish, as they proceed through a vocabulary of forms that become more and more refined, between those things that are designed as decorative items, or decorative and functional items, and those that have a critical use. . . . And the Gillette fire extinguisher was probably one of the most blatant examples that I've seen of that. I find it disturbing that it became so neutral."

The fact that the more appropriate qualities of Hewlett-Packard's Line Clip (page 97) were so quickly appreciated early-on in the Equipment and Instrumentation judging was indicative of that panel's cautious search to dig out the purest and, in a sense, the least aggressive wedding of form and function. The jury often placed the responsibility, as well as the blame, on designers to convey esthetics in an ethical context.

Is this the reaction of a profession whose unavowed principles are easily overlooked by management in favor of confidently posed marketing attitudes? Or could it be the gathering of forces for a period of refinements and maturation when "less is more" will become something other than stylistic idiom?

The line clip's lack of self-consciousness produced this reaction in Robert Gersin: "Exactly! It's not the kind of thing that you would say has been done by an industrial designer. But maybe that's a positive aspect." Gersin continued, "Maybe it has to do with what you're expecting. It reminds me of the high-voltage electrical towers designed by the Dreyfuss office [Henry Dreyfuss Associates]—sculptured forms. And I thought at the time, 'My God, what's wrong with a very simple, plain telephone pole' as opposed to this rather elaborately designed thing. They may be all right as shapes go, but I just don't think they added anything. In many cases there's nothing wrong with a purely functional form!"

The Place of Humor in Design

But, in some cases, form has followed function into a deadly state of sterility, producing products out of touch with a sense of humanity. Rarely is there a sign that fun exists in the design disciplines. Yet humor and warmth are also important human factors. It is just these qualities which, when integrated into design objects, can illuminate the familiar and transcend the industrial qualities of mass-produced goods.

The lack of humor and warmth pervaded discussions by all the Design Review juries. For example, the Contract and Residential panel found a few designs among the entries which they felt deserved mention, despite some objectionable design aspects, because they illustrate a sense of humor or delight in areas which are most accessible to an exploitation of these qualities.

For example, though the panel thought the Sackspot, designed for use in direct spotting or indirect lighting, to be a fun design, they found the idea old hat.

While the Mighty Push Pin was designed "to avoid the dangerous aspects of previous spindle-type noteholders," one juror's response to that phrase on the entry form was, "People who would swallow that line would wind up stabbing themselves to death!" Though all agreed on this point of safety, the jurors found the quality of the pin's concept genuinely cute.

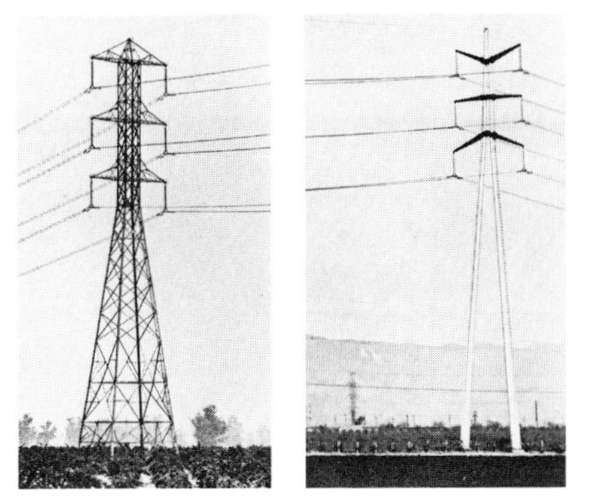

High-voltage transmission towers, before (left) and after (right), redesigned nearly 10 years ago, raise the question: Is design input inappropriate when form is 99 percent function? Manufacturer: Southern California Edison, Los Angeles, CA; consultant design: Henry Dreyfuss Associates, New York, NY.

Certain product areas (such as this example of lighting by Sackspot) lend themselves easily to applications of wit. Manufacturer: Plus Designs International, Inc., New York, NY; consultant design: E. Kevin Schoffer, designer, Lee A. Tamaccio, packaging, Laurence Tamaccio, photography, Sara E. Green, graphics.

Though meant to be light-hearted, the design of this desk accessory, The Mighty Push Pin, makes a dangerous point, according to the jury. Manufacturer and designer: The Colossus Corp., New Haven, CT.

When the Consumer Products jurors began to resolve their opinions on an injection-molded comb for detangling (page 59), designed by the office of Morison S. Cousins + Associates, as an accessory for Gillette's swivel hair dryer, a debate arose over the place for humor in what are basically functional products. Following are excerpts from that dialog, sharpened by the fact that Morison Cousins, who abstained from voting with the panel on this one, was able to provide a first-hand rebuttal to the pointed criticism from other jurors:

Cooper Woodring: I think we get awfully concerned that everything has to be so serious.

Freda Diamond: I think it is serious. I don't think it's that functional.

George Finley: It's a schizophrenic approach. You're basically talking about a serious problem, yet on the other hand you say, 'Make that a fun product,' and that would interfere with the proper resolution of the problem the product is designed to solve. That is not a very good position to be in!

Morison Cousins: I believe the comb itself may perhaps be the best nonhandmade comb you can buy, because of the design of the teeth. That really was an engineer's design. Because we looked at it from the point of view that your hand can really hold onto an incredible variety of forms, we had a lot of freedom to deal with the comb in a more human manner.

Richard Penney: I think that we as a jury have to look at certain products as to their influence and base our judgments off of that strength while overlooking some of the little things. Does this comb signify a particularly new statement in combs?

Woodring: Its significance is its insignificance—the fact that there's this cute little thing given away with the product.

Diamond: But you see, that's my basic objection. It's not a 'cute little thing'—you're saying it's doing something. If it is doing something for the woman who will be attracted to the fact that this will take the tangles out, then it doesn't have to be 'cute' or anything else. It has to function! And the words 'cute little thing' are inappropriate for something that is supposed to be functional.

Cousins: I tend to think that we underestimate the hand's ability to be very adaptable, and sometimes we get overly concerned about comfort in certain situations. I would think that if you spent 15 or 20 minutes combing your hair you might run into that kind of problem, but not in the handful of minutes that you are using it. But we're really moving away from the issue here. We contend that a lot of problems exist in product design today because—one of the reasons why it isn't advancing—there is an excessive tendency to deal with everything seriously. And, in fact, there are certain instances where you don't have to. That is precisely why that statement is there in the comb.

Penney: I think that is something that ought to be considered as designers, particularly in this country, come to a point of accumulating a vast amount of design input. We have assimilated very well what significant designers in other countries have done. Yet what we are doing, slowly but surely, is distilling all of it down to a point where it has little or no interest, and very little significance in the marketplace. Looking at the larger picture of architecture, which has always influenced design and very often has been a forerunner of things that happen in design, the movement is going towards a functional, decorative direction. The Italians are just beginning to do it. Sometimes it looks difficult and tortured, but they are addressing that point. And I think we here in America better begin to understand it.

Woodring: I think the comb may be significant from the point of view that if we had to justify everything we did, every penny and nickel, everything would be pretty dull pretty fast. And we're rapidly moving in that direction. Perhaps I didn't make myself clear before when I said the significance is in the insignificance. The fact that a designer was able to get a client like Gillette, which is very cost-conscious, to include this little attractive thing—I called it 'cute' though maybe that's the wrong term for a product like this—is significant. It's a nice extra. There's no way that you could ever justify it.

Penney: I think it's actually the beginning of turning toward another direction in design. And the world is struggling for that right now. Not that the comb has solved the problem entirely, or even given us a significant point of departure, but I share the feeling with a lot of other people in this field and outside of it, that it's a way things are going to turn. Hopefully we are going to turn away from "wood graining," which has been for the exact purpose of "humanizing" a design. Supposedly the customer wants this. Well, these little things—whether they be fun, decorative, or whatever else you may want to call it—may accomplish that and give some new life to industrial design.

Diamond: There is a time for humor and wit, but I think that something mechanical and functional is nothing to laugh about. It has to be easy, it has to be easy to maintain. . . .

The panel decided that a comb should be sent to each juror so that its functionality could be personally tested. Satisfied with the way it handled, the majority selected the comb for the Consumer Products category. Finley, however, maintained his opposition.

Generic Packaging: A Trend toward the Consumer-Advocate Future?

In graphic design as well, the lack of wit and warmth, or the sense of sterility which results, is related to a plethora of uninspired, spare, Swiss-influenced solutions in Helvetica that are proliferating to the point of creating visual boredom.

In view of this generic packaging could become one of the consequences of consumer-oriented forces affecting significant change in the standards and scope of graphic design and the design profession in general. The Visual Communications panel discussed the possibility that generic packaging—the straightforward expression of what a product is with absolutely no frills—will predominate in the foreseeable future. In the past year, for example, two Midwestern supermarket chains announced successful initial attempts with generic packaging, which passed on to consumers the savings from considerably lowered advertising budgets, and plans in the near future to change over retail outlets in other regions.

The Aldi-Benner chain, based in Burlington, Iowa, asks its customers to bring their own shopping bags—a tradition of European shoppers—to stores where generically labeled products are displayed on plain shelves with no fancy fixtures.

Meanwhile, the Chicago-based Jewel chain has reserved a special department in each of its stores for the sale of generically packaged products, claiming price cuts from 10 to 35 percent on national brands and up to 20 percent on house brands.

Though it is not strictly generic packaging, the redesign of the Fisher Nut Company's product line indicates the evolution in this direction. Some of the Visual Communications jurors at first thought the packaging looked like anything but food—like hardware or film developer, perhaps. "It's shockingly clean for a food product. We always say we want to see nice, clean packaging, and then when you see it—it's too cold. You're

Will designer-less packaging become part of the solution for a consumer-oriented future? Generic grocery products distributed by Jewel Food Stores, Division of Jewel Companies, Inc., Chicago IL.

Though it was designed, this Fisher Nut Company packaging series indicates a possible evolution towards generic labeling. Manufacturer: Fisher Nut Company, St. Paul, MN; consultant design: Design West, Irvine, CA.

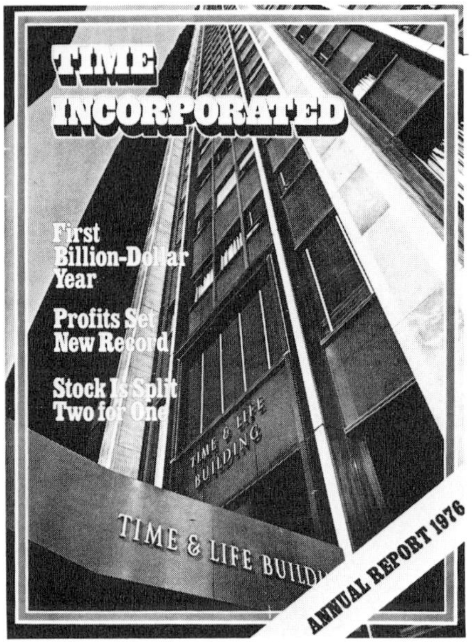

This 1976 take-off on *Time* magazine's format was lauded by the panel for its uniqueness among annual reports. Time, Inc., New York, NY; staff design: Leonard Wolf.

going to put this in your stomach, not hit a rock with it!" commented Penny Johnson.

Speaking both as a consumer and a graphic designer, Chava Ben-Amos talked about the emerging trend: "Then we can admire what they are doing, that they are not trying to mislead. But this kind of packaging is not a 'beautiful' thing. I love opening a new package when it's a beautiful package, when it gives me all kinds of ideas about the product. When I go to the supermarket and look at something, I buy as much for the packaging. Sometimes I buy for the package more than the product. So we won't be judging beautiful package designs anymore. It will probably come to that."

Attempting to make light of what would amount to a serious financial loss for many graphic designers, Jack Odette retorted, "Designers could stop wasting their time doing packages and do more important things. . . . God help us if the day ever comes!"

Speaking with less emotion, Robert Salpeter added, "You know, on the other hand, if it comes to that—supermarkets going towards generic packaging—I think the client instead of the design ought to be commended in that the name, in this case Fisher, recedes into the background and the generic name is in the foreground. You also have to look at it from the point of view of 'on the shelf.' Right now all the other peanut companies have peanut-company-looking jars. This one, by default, is going to stand out. You know there are things that are more important than graphic design on packaging. And generic labeling could very easily be one of those things."

One panelist noted an inconsistency in what otherwise was a fine example of the transition to generic labeling: "There's a failure of nerve when it comes to 'Fancy Nut Topping' and 'Fancy Mixed Nuts.' The typography changes to Optima from Helvetica, equating fancy nuts with fancy typeface and run-of-the-mill nuts with Helvetica." If generic packaging succeeds with the consumer, and its economy of cost certainly suggests that the odds are in its favor, then more pragmatic criteria for design would surely result.

The Effects of Economics on Design

In this context, the Visual Communications panel thought the 1976 annual report for Kimberly-Clark Corporation was a harbinger of things to come. The design consists almost entirely of layouts of financial descriptions and listings. There are no photographs and the few simple illustrations are limited to charts. When one juror quipped, "This is not visual communication," another quickly responded, "They may only use words, but they had to design with them."

However, the 1976 annual report for Time, Inc. was lauded for its execution of a lively and clever concept, a take-off on *Time* magazine's style and layout consistently carried all the way through the report to a back cover featuring a full page ad. Considered by the jurors to be a unique and less studied departure from what they had been seeing, they insisted that note also be made that "Although the concept is true to the visual like a rock, it's not really good typography. Yet, it tells the whole story of the corporation in the language of the corporation. Perhaps 'good design' would have been self-defeating to this concept!"

Economic considerations also strongly influence the design of annual reports, sometimes creating hardships for the designer. Penny Johnson noted, "One person could have done four-fifths of these things. They're so similar. Very nice pictures, pretty good printing, organized, nice borders, same layout—all the things you're supposed to do. But, except for one or two, nothing to make you say, 'Oh, isn't that nice!' "

Annual reports are especially difficult to do because they have to pass through so many different hands and be approved by so many people. This provoked Chava Ben-Amos to comment from her experience doing reports, "Everybody has their own opinion that they put into it. Some people want to have it much sparser; others want to have their pictures in it. You start with a beautiful dummy, and slowly the company takes all the pictures out and puts more copy in. Suddenly, costs start skyrocketing and they start taking everything out. The paper gets cheaper. . . .

"In most companies there isn't just one person who's in charge of the annual report. If there is one person, he's low on the totem pole and doesn't have much say. That's what he's there for. The best annual reports are the ones, I find, which were designed outside of the company—that went out to a design firm and were written by outside sources. They are presented like, 'This is it.' "

In general, the jurors on each of the Design Review panels agreed that a lot of the work they had seen during the judgings was repetitive—"just designers talking to designers." The question was raised during the Environmental session of whether or not the profit motive was at the bottom of it. David Pesanelli commented, "There was one office that had three or four exhibits, and they were basically the same exhibit regardless of what the content was. Maybe what's showing up as design is a solution that clients can relate to and will pay for without a lot of hassle."

Judith Stockman asked, "I wonder if the economic situation has had an effect on the corporate client, whether corporations are much less willing to try out very daring solutions or something new because the market is tight and they are afraid that they might lose that fragile growth potential." To which Pesanelli responded, "I'm sure that's in there to a degree. But depth comes from people. And designers often lack depth. It's just not there. While it isn't garbage, the maturity that we want isn't there frequently. That maturity isn't there within the designer. And I don't think that economics is necessarily the door. Good designers do good work. It is as simple as that."

Plagiarism and Designer Ethics

It's been said that originality does not exist for the individual in the sense that it's a collective process of discovery and assimilation by society. Inventions can, and have been, developed at approximately the same time at opposite ends of the earth. In the book, *Man and His Symbols,* Carl G. Jung discusses "genuine, if unrealized, recollection," and gives the example of a musician who has heard a peasant or popular tune in childhood and finds it turning up as the theme of a symphonic movement he is composing in adult life. Jung also documents the unwitting plagiarism which occurred in a famous book, written almost word for word out of a story read in childhood by the book's well-known author.

Today design, especially the visually oriented disciplines, is a frequent contributor to the fast-paced and overly saturated communication media. As a result, it is often difficult to discern "who did what first," as was the case with the controversy over the NBC logo a couple of years back. Nevertheless, it was the unanimous decision of the Visual Communications panel to award a "Shame on You, Plagiarism Is a Disgusting Thing" citation where appropriate.

The issue first arose when the jurors reviewed the newly designed trademark for Off-Track Betting (OTB) in Connecticut. The similarity to the New York OTB symbol is so obvious that at first glance the panel thought both had been designed by the same designer. Finally, they decided that the Connecticut symbol was too contrived, in comparison with the simplicity of the earlier-designed New York mark, for it to possibly be the work of the same designer.

A call to the Connecticut design firm which submitted the symbol elicited a considerable degree of

Jurors were reminded that some design solutions are complex and difficult when credit is given or blame is placed, as in the case of Connecticut's OTB logo, which is obviously reminiscent of the earlier New York City OTB logo. Client: American Totalisator Company, Inc., New York, NY; consultant design: Industrial Design Consultants, Farmington, CT.

The New York OTB logo was designed before the one for Connecticut. Client: American Totalisator Company, Inc., New York, NY; consultant design: Rudi deHarak.

surprise. Everyone in the office claimed they had not actually seen the New York mark while in the process of designing the symbol for Connecticut. They were aware of its existence and vaguely assumed that the New York mark used lower case lettering.

Though they should have, they never visited any New York OTB parlors. Their office submitted several solutions to the architect in charge, and this is what was eventually chosen. Coincidently, New York-based American Totalisator Company, Inc. was also the client for both New York and Connecticut OTB parlors.

Whether or not the OTB case can be rationalized as a contemporary example of Jung's "genuine, if unrealized recollection" (a fleeting glance on the TV screen or in a newspaper or magazine) or as a case of poor research technique, the jurors were adamant in their condemnation of plagiarism.

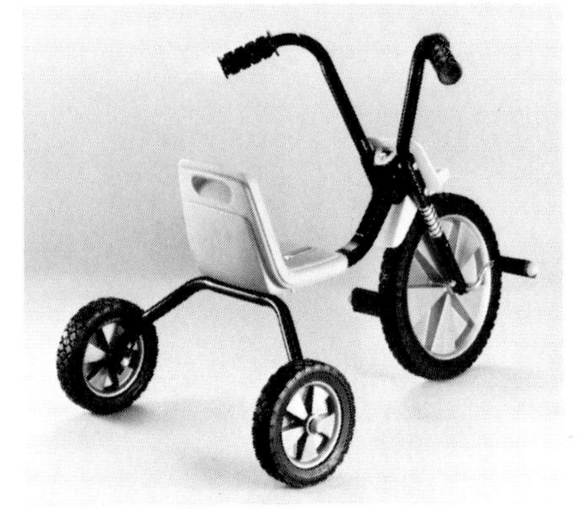

Safety is an especially important issue in the design of playthings for children; note the specially designed wheels on this Radio Flyer Tricycle. Manufacturer: Radio Steel and Manufacturing Co., Chicago, IL; staff design: Mario Pasin, Fred Michelau; consultant design: Deschamps Mills Associates, Ltd., Bartlett, IL.

Another issue related to designer ethics involved children's toys. On the question of whether it was safe or not to operate, the Radio Flyer Tricycle with wheels specifically designed to prevent children's fingers from being caught was voted in (page 41) by the Consumer Products panel, while Weirdwands, which at first received a general yes vote, was decided against.

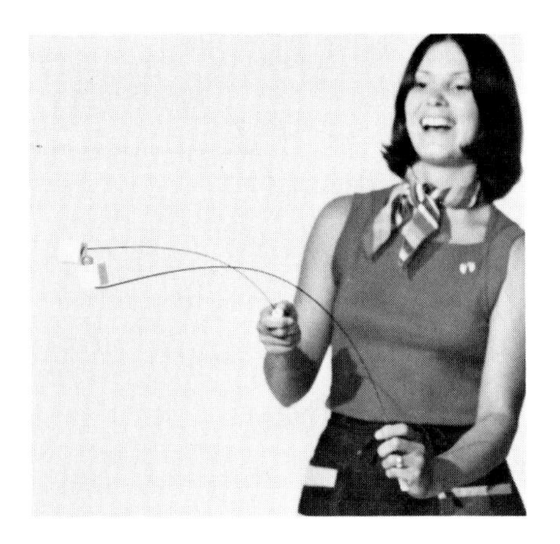

Jurors would have selected this toy design by Weirdwands if they hadn't felt strongly about its inherently hazardous qualities. Manufacturer: Weird Products, Ltd., Stowe, VT; consultant design: Huston Associates, Burlington, VT.

Weirdwands was designed with the intention of developing motor control capabilities. Though the panel initially thought it was clever, they were concerned that the toy, with an overall length of 39 in. (a full meter), was too unwieldy and presented a definite built-in hazard even though otherwise it was a well-designed product. It was even felt to be too unsafe for use in a controlled or supervised situation. Cooper Woodring tied up the discussion when he said, "The government position on product liability is that the designer is responsible for anticipating misuse. And this is a classic example of that."

Why Some Good Ideas Just Don't Make It

Manufacturing costs are often a restraining influence in the development of thorough safety standards, human factors research, as well as ethics. Though they found it to be "ugly as sin," the Contract and Residential panel made meritous notice of the Series 9000 seating system, designed to meet the needs of mental health institutions, because it made the effort and solved many of the problems. "Perhaps no one has ever addressed themselves to that properly because there's not a big enough market for it. It's a low-cost market that most manufacturers can't even compete with."

The Rollback operational chair and stool didn't fulfill the first priority of seating—chairs must seat people comfortably. And though the panel appreciated its esthetic resolution and lauded the concept, they had to vote no when it came down to function. The problem, they asserted, is that the chair and stool, designed to be nonrestrictive and encourage movement, exemplifies the type of design where the concept is its only reason for being.

Peter Buhk compared this design to the Ergon chair of a few years ago. The concept is basically the same for each design. While the earlier version's backrest was deliberately shaped for turning at different angles, the Rollback stops short of providing good back support.

It was not so much its lack of esthetic appeal that kept the panel from selecting the Swing Along crutch and walker. Robert Gersin exclaimed, "It's the only inventive idea in the whole damn bag of stuff. I think it's beautiful—like an old airplane, a lighter-than-air-craft. It's so refreshing to see something that hasn't been messed up with design for its own sake."

Some of the other Equipment and Instrumentation jurors expressed concern about the rockers possibly hooking into objects on the street, under fences, or around doors, as well as difficulties getting in and out of small spaces. Another concern was the inaccessibility of the small-sized knob used when converting the walker into crutches. The panel thought it looked difficult to get at and perhaps impossible to turn with gloves on. "We have no way of knowing the function of any of these objects. We don't know if an IBM computer works, either. We have to buy a lot of it on faith and make judgments presuming that it works. The designer's done it about as purely as he would a bicycle wheel, and I think that deserves some merit, too."

If the Ob/Gyn examination chair system is any indication, woodgrain (i.e., simulated) is something doctors seem to like, but exactly the type of esthetic that turns off many designers. Yet, our environment is polluted with the stuff in growing numbers, from the external housings on kitchen appliances where real wood is functionally inappropriate to the interior panelings of autos where the luxury of beautiful wood detailing has given over completely to the economy of plastics.

Gersin commented, "I think the chair is a very well resolved functional device. It's just not terribly attractive. Although it looks like an old Barcalounger, it's a more humane device than any that I've seen recently in offices and hospitals. Nevertheless, from a human engineering standpoint it's very well resolved, far more considerate of the patient."

Situations may occur where human engineering has been taken to its extreme. The structure of the Foregger 710, an anesthesia control center, is a case in point that caught the panel's eye because of its flexibility. Human engineered for the anesthesiologist, the design incorporates accessory tracks at the machine's corners, providing organizational capabilities. Though they admired its sense of accessibility to the components, the panel did not feel it was the proper resolution. Gersin summed up his

Would the design of products for the handicapped be more advanced than this Series 9000 Seating if manufacturers didn't consider it to be an unprofitable market? Manufacturer: InterRoyal Corp., Plainfield, CT; staff design: Roland A. Benoit.

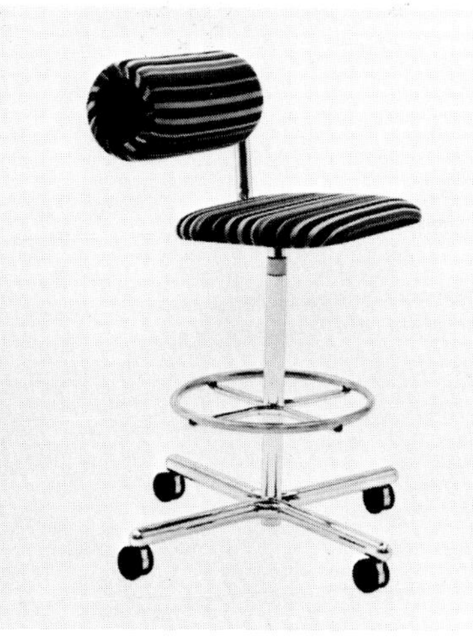

Jurors felt that the function of the Rollback Operational Chair was overpowered by the concept. Manufacturer: Herman Miller, Inc., Zeeland, MI; consultant design: R. Wilkes & Company.

Introduced in March 1976, the Ergon Chair is promoted as the first ergonomically designed chair produced in the U.S. after seven years of research. It was cited by the jury as a successful precursor to the Rollback Chair. Manufacturer: Herman Miller, Inc., Zeeland, MI; consultant design: William Stumpf.

Though problematic detailing exists on the Swing Along Crutch and Walker, the panel appreciated the "lighter-than-air-craft" feel of the crutch and lauded the designer's exploration of a vital but often overlooked area of design. Manufacturer and designer: Channing Wallace Gilson, Los Angeles, CA.

viewpoint when he said, "My reaction was that this type of product tends to be chaotic anyway. There are so many diverse functional elements tacked on to this. There should have been more effort put into integrating them as much as possible. It has the feeling of a lot of things piled on, stacked up and hanging off." The panelists predicted that we would probably lose our ability to adapt if the environment ever became this accessible and flexible.

The panel rejected the use of simulated woodgrain on an otherwise well-resolved design of the OB/GYN Examination Chair. Manufacturer: I. E. Industries, Minister, OH; staff design: John Oldiges; consultant design: Simpkins Design Group, Snowmass Village, CO.

The Varying Role of Esthetics in Design

Among designers the debate is on as to whether it is more challenging to design for the 95 percent function/5 percent esthetics of capital goods where form always follows function or consumer products where esthetics—and sometimes function as well—most often represent the combined interests of manufacturer, market research, and perhaps, the end-user.

In the area of Equipment and Instrumentation, it is not always apparent if form wedding function is the result of a shotgun marriage, a passionate affair, or a formal agreement. Confirming past Design Reviews, there were literally only a handful of entries in this year's Equipment and Instrumentation category with a ratio of 99 percent esthetics to 1 percent function. Though the majority weighed in at the other extreme with typical counts of 95 percent function/5 percent esthetics, a sizable number average around an even 50/50.

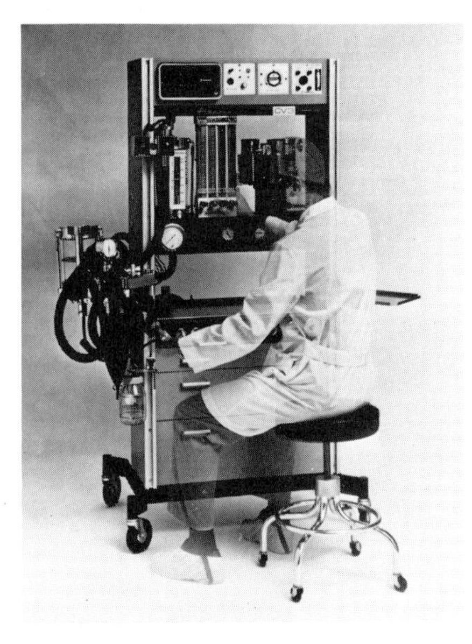

Should the diverse functions inherent in this type of equipment, Forreger 710, have been integrated better; are they too flexible here? Manufacturer: Air Products & Chemicals, Inc., Allentown, PA; consultant design: Manalog, Princeton, NJ.

Of course, in regard to how a product functions for its end-user, as well as its competitive ability to convey unique properties within its own market, this seemingly insignificant "5 percent esthetics" is often the deciding factor between success and failure.

In the other areas of product design, esthetics tend to be much more in cahoots with marketing. In comparison with the versatility of the consumer products market, product design for contract and residential furnishings is apt to be of a more refined, sleek caste that translates into higher bottom lines for costs and less skittish, more substantial and restrained innovations. That results in an overall sense of slowly evolving traditions as opposed to the vogueish trends of consumer products.

In the contract and residential field luxury and comfort are wed through arrays of finely textured fabrics that wrap around clever, sometimes smug and elitist conceptual gymnastics in the name of convenience. With architecture at its heels, the visual poetry of engineering and design is expressed with elegant, sexy lines trained in human factors to behave like a respectable seat or a self-sufficient workstation. "Classy, classical, classic" evoke sentiments in the realm of contract and residential furnishings equivalent to those stirred by the "good, better, best" equations familiar to consumer product terminology.

It is certainly of interest to note why the Mies van der Rohe collection, carefully reproduced by Knoll, did not fare well with this year's Contract and Residential panel. Believing in the capabilities of mass production to bring better quality designs to the majority of people who would otherwise not have access to higher priced, low-production products, the jurors voted a unanimous no. The panel could not forgive the well-known fact that these Mies reproductions have been beset with manufacturing problems from the time they were first developed. The question was raised whether or not the seats would be produced today if they hadn't been designed by Mies van der Rohe—implying that the underlying desire on the part of the manufacturer was perhaps to gain the recognition of a dying elitist market. Why not a $500 Barcelona chair? A brief comment summed it up, "It's basically elegant—and amazingly uncomfortable!"

Examples of Inappropriate Marketing

When the Consumer Products panel judged the design of the Polavision instant moving picture system, they went against the odds of tradition in more ways than one with a final no vote. Anyone would assume that the classic teaming of two experienced specialists like Polaroid—often regarded by designers and others as a concerned and caring, technologically design-oriented firm—and the office of Henry Dreyfuss Associates, which has handled every Polaroid photographic project since 1960, would have a far better chance than most of producing a highly marketable design. Yet, due to the recent promotion of home video recorders and the public's growing interest in home computers, this product is suffering from what could be called a marketing jet lag. Though its function is distinctly different, Polavision's low-keyed design must compete with these other, flashier products as part of the home entertainment market. Perhaps the remedy would be five meaningless dials, ten nonfunctional switches, and a digital readout that lights up when spoken to!

The system's three simple components are a camera, viewer, and a phototape cassette of 2-min, 40-sec duration, which develops instantly as the cassette is being automatically rewound the first time it is inserted into the home viewer. Polavision's total cost is $699. The panel's comments ranged from "its design is direct but old-fashioned" to "it is a very safe design, in its idiom, very well done," and "there is a great dichotomy between the excitement of the product's concept and the design of it." Cooper Woodring almost balanced the scales when he said, "You can probably argue in favor of safe, sane design in anything that revolutionary. In so far as if it's going to sell—because of its revolutionary qualities—the last thing that you would want to do is tag on a high-risk design. But that is not a good enough reason to select it for a design review."

In a somewhat similar vein, though their consumer products and packaging have been cited by the Museum of Modern Art in New York, the American Institute of Graphic Arts (AIGA), and the Design Review, GAF's lines of cameras, films, and color print papers have been discontinued due to the intensely competitive market situation with Eastman Kodak's amateur photographic lines.

Marketing high technology, the Hewlett-Packard Company, according to *Business Week* magazine, boosted its design budget by more than the 15 percent growth in sales it recorded the year before. But the Consumer Products panel still didn't select the Hewlett-Packard HP-01 Wrist Instrument. Although the technology impressed them, the panel couldn't swallow the price, ranging from $650 for stainless steel units to a gold-filled

The panel questioned whether or not the Mies van der Rohe Collection caters to "good design" or represents an attempt to market elitism. Manufacturer: Knoll International, Greenwich, CT; staff design: William Stephens, Richard Hopkins.

Will the revolutionary concept of Polavision succeed in competition with high-technology home video recorders introduced to the consumer market at the same time? Manufacturer: Polaroid Corp., Cambridge, MA; consultant design: Henry Dreyfuss Associates, New York, NY.

model for $750. One juror commented that "These 'technological' products are thought not to need good design."

Questioning its human factors, the complex wristwatch was sent on to the Equipment and Instrumentation panel, where the comment was made, "Human factors? As technology, it's impressive—as industrial design, it's very ordinary."

To the contrary, another juror found the form pleasingly clean and handsome. The central issue, though, was just how comfortable and convenient it really is to manipulate the six different functions incorporated into the face of the watch: time keeping, date keeping, stopwatch, alarm/timer, continuous memory, 200 year calendar. Questions were raised about the degree of error in calculation due to scale, the amount of pressure applied to the wrist when calculating, the consequences in various circumstances of having only one hand free while utilizing the wrist instrument—for instance, when holding a telephone.

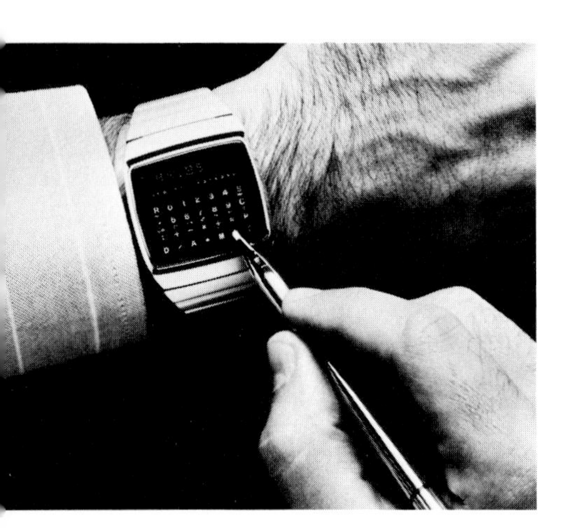

This consumer-oriented product, the Hewlett-Packard HP-01 Wrist Instrument, was rejected by two separate panels for marketing high technology with a high price tag. Manufacturer: Hewlett-Packard, Palo Alto, CA; staff design: Allen Inhelder, Edward Sater.

Another example of inappropriate marketing, this time with technology that didn't measure up to its price tag, is a series of five battery-powered quartz alarm clocks. Though the least expensive was selected because it offered a simple, efficient solution (page 89), the Contract and Residential jurors criticized the other four units for being too slick, overly designed, and expensive for the type of mechanism they offer. It appeared to the panel as if the casings' esthetics were meant to compensate for the mechanism, as well as conceal it.

A number of times the panels decided to block the selection of a particular product because, though they might agree it possessed good esthetic qualities, they felt it was really just a groundbreaker for new, but unnecessary, areas in marketing. A case in point is the developing market for individual task lighting in the office environment. The Eyeshades task lighting lamp, developed specifically for a furniture system, can also be purchased separately. One comment stated the panelists' objections simply: "My concern is that it's very costly for doing the same kind of job that a Luxo lamp does quite well. And although it's handsome, is that reason enough for it being what it is?"

At the other end of the spectrum are those products that fulfill the requirements of both the manufacturer and the end-user well, only to have their sense of good design killed by a marketing decision, for instance, executing a casing in a plastic, simulated woodgrain finish.

This was brought home to the Contract and Residential panel through Rubbermaid's submission of an easy-to-assemble, injection-molded plastic fernstand with a smooth matte finish and integral color. The suggested retail price was $12.95. Since a sample had been submitted along with the entry, the jurors were able to do some first-hand testing.

They found that it solved all its structural and mechanical problems very carefully: the modular pieces assembled easily with a good fit at the joints, and it was reasonably stable. Yet, everyone was hesitant to select it. "The real problem is that we are responding to it as a decorative item, and the problem it solves is a very mechanical one," explained Noel Mayo.

"You look at it and respond to a shape reminiscent of bamboo. That's what is offending me. My memory says it should be made out of bronze bamboo, and that's what I relate to. If Joe Colombo did it you'd love it! And he has done a coatrack just like that. It becomes higher using modular parts. You can stick umbrellas in it, hang coats on it, and shift them all around."

During the discussion on wit in design among the Consumer Products jurors, Cooper Woodring expressed his concern over how differently manufacturers may interpret adding humor and warmth through their present vocabulary of materials and marketing: "I think the only danger in the type of statement the [Gillette] comb makes is that that's how Rubbermaid arrived at the cannister it entered into the review. That's what that 'woodgrain' knob does, in their opinion. They could justify that with the same argument—that cannisters are too serious, it needs design on it, put on daisies and make it pretty."

Manufacturers and Retailers Increasingly Recognize Role of Good Design

If the 1977 Design Review is any indication, smaller-sized design offices and those manufacturers consciously striving for well-designed mass-produced products are taking the lead in good design. The fact is that of the majority of work rejected by the panels, the designs that were the real losers are still represented by the larger corporations.

A growing interest in design and the services of designers was evidenced last year by a number of newly formed design staffs among manufacturers. Among these were the selection of 17 architects and designers for Formica's new design advisory board to aid translation of materials into end products; the establishment of Mobil's first in-house design staff, which will coordinate with outside consultants; and a design center formed at Samsonite to serve day-to-day design efforts.

Though the 10-year-old, nonprofit Research and Design Institute in Providence, Rhode Island, closed early in the year due to a lack of financial support on the local and federal level—and there are still no definite plans for the much-discussed national design center—awareness of industrial design on the part of the federal government, especially at the Department of Commerce and the National Endowment for the Arts (NEA), has never been stronger.

The IDSA has been a quiet catalyst in the government's emerging

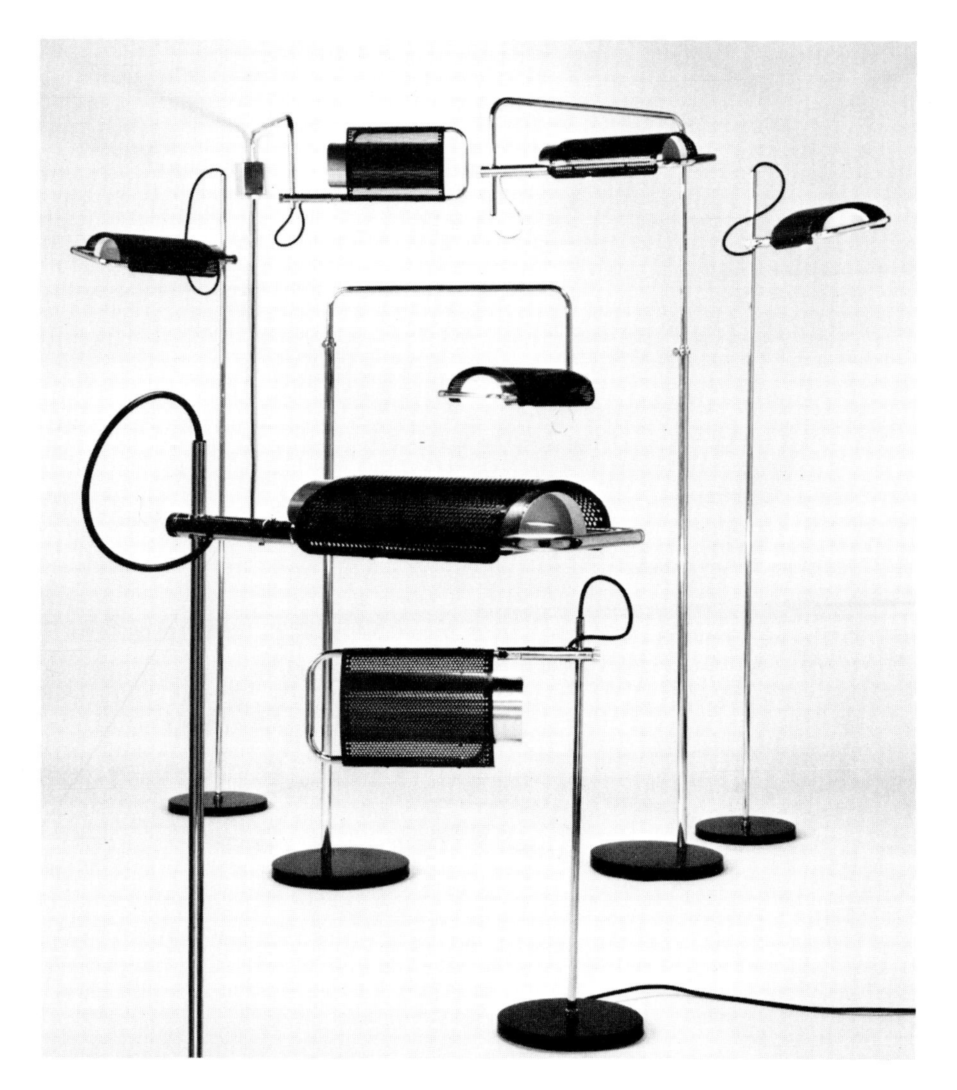

Though the jurors appreciated its design attributes, they rejected this task lighting system, Eyeshades, because they felt that its creation of another market was unnecessary. Manufacturer: Koch & Lowy, Inc., New York, NY; designed and developed by: George Nelson & Company, New York, NY.

The jurors wondered if the design of the Rubbermaid injection-molded plastic fern stand would be interpreted differently if it were designed by Joe Colombo? Manufacturer: Rubbermaid, Inc., Wooster, OH; staff design: Peter M. Berend, William D. Taylor, Richard D. Dilyard, Howard J. Vaeth.

Some manufacturers genuinely feel that simulated woodgrain, as shown on this Rubbermaid cannister, infuses warmth and other human qualities into their products. Manufacturer: Rubbermaid, Inc., Wooster, OH; staff design: Peter M. Berend, Richard D. Dilyard, William D. Taylor, Alan E. Willard.

awareness. Last year IDSA submitted a proposal to the Department of Commerce, outlining ways in which the department can assist American business in achieving competitive market advantages through industrial design, including business and public awareness efforts and research into user needs. The efforts of NEA have included lobbying to establish an industrial design classification within the Civil Service, support for accreditation of industrial design schools which meet minimum standards, as well as consideration of proposals for establishment of a national design center.

In a March 13, 1978, *Business Week* article entitled "Industrial designers win new clout and status," it was reported that executives are busy "looking for consultants and in-house designers who have track records in business." The article mentions Rubber Queen, a competitor of Rubbermaid, Inc., as "typical of a swelling number of small manufacturers that are making greater use of industrial design to develop new and improved products and corporate identities so they can keep up with their big national competitors."

The optimistic report continues by stating that "The design push by smaller companies is just one of the new developments that are sparking a boom for industrial designers. These specialists had been adjusting to a 10-year slump in demand for their principal services by diversifying into graphics, packaging, interiors, and corporate identity programs. Now, however, manufacturers are again seeking their advice on products ranging from radios and toasters to bulldozers and softball bats, drawing on their expertise in form, function, material, color, and esthetics."

In stride with this news, an extremely heavy retail emphasis on "good, better, best" design has taken a welcomed stronghold in the consumer marketplace. Small manufacturers like Heller Designs, Inc., with its inexpensive line of well-designed bakeware (page 69), are holding their own and then some. Hopefully, as good design becomes more profitable, the retail marketplace will make more room for higher quality products than it has in the past.

Large, established retailers, such as Macy's Department Stores and JCPenney's, have already recognized and committed themselves to design, respectively, through a reorganization of selling space into specialty boutiques centered around well-designed products and by nourishing the importance of its in-house design staff.

Conran's, a retail outlet for British industrial designer Terence Conran, opened its doors to the American public in 1977 in midtown Manhattan stocked with a careful selection of simple, clean-lined household furnishings and kitchen accessories with rather modest price tags. Subsequently, two more retail stores opened their doors to bring better design to the public with reasonably affordable prices. Chains of small-sized stores such as Pottery Barn and Workbench have been quietly doing this kind of retailing for years now. Perhaps it is not too bold to predict a foreseeable end to the marketability of simulated woodgrains.

Housewares, especially centered around the kitchen, are the focus of many retail efforts to sell better designed products in volume. And products with multiple functions have become a trend in and of themselves. Among the entries was cookware that steams an entire meal in stackable containers attractive enough to serve at the table; varied combinations of broiler, oven, slow-cooker, defroster, and toaster; coffeemakers that also grind the beans, as well as dispense water at the proper temperature for tea; and, of course, the highly marketable food processor that takes the place of 5 to 15 different kitchen gadgets as it chops, grates, mixes, shreds, whips, slices, kneads, blends, and purees—doing each job with ease in a matter of seconds.

Overall the Consumer Products panel favored multifunctional products for their inherent qualities—the innovative capabilities for which they exist—economy of space, reduction of energy output, and lowered costs. Costs are lowered in comparison either with purchasing a conventional and expensive appliance like an oven—as is the case for the compact, countertop broiler/ovens—or in comparison to spending seemingly small amounts of money buying single-purpose utensils and gadgets one at a time—when a multifunctional processor would probably cost about the same or less. One juror, though, voiced the opinion of the more wary or less adventurous, conservative consumers when he said, "The more things a product does is in reverse proportion to how well it does any of them."

New Resources Influence Environmental Design

Marketing techniques and methodology become a valuable tool to the designer and the client when successfully harnessed and incorporated into the work process. The work of Stockman & Manners, the New York consulting office of Environmental juror Judith Stockman, is influenced by a design philosophy strongly rooted in marketing.

Stockman did the preliminary design studies for a proposed 70,000 square foot (6,500 square meter) convention center in midtown Manhattan: "That was very exciting to do because it was so city-oriented. Our hopes were that the restaurants' facades would become a sampler for people coming to New York, perhaps for the first time. We wanted to promote the idea that the convention center is really going to provoke tourism. We felt that these spaces should be designed in such a way that they would provoke people to go out and explore the city.

"For example, instead of a cafeteria, we would create a whole street festival with little booths so that people would go here for one kind of ethnic food and there for another kind. We found that, from the point of view of servicing people, it's very efficient. Because people didn't have to wait in lines the whole process was much less dehumanizing—not having to go through that terribly institutional kind of fast-food situation. Its design and conception was meant to give the sense of a mini-city. All the promotional graphics and hangings were designed to get people out there to try the real thing."

The three other designers who made up this year's Environmental panel also have their own consulting firms and are actively engaged in putting theory into practice in areas of environmental concern. David Pesanelli's firm, based in Washington, D.C., has been using behavioral consultants of one kind or another for approximately the last seven years: "For the last three years we've worked with one environmental psychologist in particular. He's very warm and not into jargon, quite far away from the laboratory and very people-oriented. We have a very compatible relationship with him. He approaches a problem the same way we do, starting with words and abstractions and diagrams of words, meanings of words. When we began working with him, though, we found that the client didn't want a psychologist in the project. So we'd put him in for a few hours. Now sometimes he's in a project for weeks at a time."

When another member of the panel asked why clients didn't want the psychologist involved, Pesanelli responded, "Six or seven years ago I would get responses like, 'I came to you to do this project, don't you know what you're doing? Why do you need this other consultant?' I think some were also a little afraid that in a face-to-face meeting the psychologist might see through them a bit. But that never really happens. Actually, the psychologist is helpful during meetings, keeping them on track.

"We may have a client who has spent a year internally and with other consultants putting together

Food processors, like this one by General Electric, have been leading the trend in housewares over the past year towards functional, well-designed products for the kitchen. Manufacturer: General Electric Co., Bridgeport, CT; staff design: O. E. Haggstrom, M. C. Hauenstein.

some kind of package that goes out to the public. The level of the audience may only be the fifth-grade reading level although the material is of a grade thirteen level. And they simply can't do it. In other words, the client operated out of their own level and experience, making all kinds of assumptions about the public. Hopefully, the psychologist's role is to help us define problems more from the perspective of the audience, rather than just problems we find that we'd like to solve as designers.

"We've found that the psychologist is as effective in a print/graphic project, if it's a system of some kind that has to be handled and used, as he is when it comes to planning a total environment and doing a bit of predicting on what the responses might be. He's also very helpful if we have to go in and do a survey and analysis first. He prepares the questionnaires and tracking studies, those kinds of materials which help you understand how the public is performing in a particular kind of environment, also how the staff may be performing, and whether their transactions are happening easily or with great difficulty. He sets up all those behavioral tools that we're now relatively conversant with as designers, but which aren't really our area."

Bruce Burdick's recent work utilizes computer access systems in museum planning. Memory banks can be used to involve visitors in much deeper levels of participation than they would ordinarily choose on their own.

Burdick explains, "We're working on one that uses three languages to talk to people in. You determine your language as you begin to work with the computer. Roughly, the computer is really looking for what your interests are, perhaps your grade level. Then it adjusts the language. It has a couple of languages to experiment in with you, seeing how you will stay with it. The depth of understanding determines the language. As you move throughout the exhibition, it continues to ask you questions. You have opportunities of doing different things with the computer—making certain statements, answering questions. It continues to watch which ones you answer and which ones you don't, which ones you ask and which ones you don't ask."

When Burdick, who did initial research with an associate by attending computer school, was asked what possible influences the use of computer systems may have for the traditional museum exhibition, he replied, "All of us have keys to a library, but none of us have keys for the museums that are around. Museums only present what they are working on or what they think the public should see. It's entirely different than your access to a library. I think the best thing that can happen is to turn museums around so that they are giving you the keys to them, in a sense.

"Museums are essentially thought about on the order of the curator versus your understanding of what you personally encounter. The computer allows people to establish their own agendas. For instance, a natural history museum will usually have a hall of vertebrates and a hall of invertebrates. It won't usually address the fact that that's the curator's own order for his understanding of the subject; it may be of no value to you or your understanding. A computer used in this situation can be like having a curator go along with you, to do the things you are interested in. I see a renaissance in the utilization of museums, much like a library."

Pesanelli interrupted to say, "One of the problems with museums today is they have such a low rate of people paying attention to a particular experience. First of all, you don't know how large the museum is or how long it will take to see the museum in any particular quantitative terms. So you go slowly in the beginning, and you rush toward the end. Could a computer help the visitor plan a day or an hour?"

Burdick answered, "That is one of

the traditional problems with museums. I think the best way to treat a museum is like a kind of magazine, the way you can just thumb through a magazine, put it down and then return to it. Of course, that is what visitor centers in museums are about—to give a person that thumbing type of experience. One of the important aspects of using a computer is that it is not a limiter. It's an extender.

"People think the computer is going to tell them what to do. Not true. What a computer may do is make a recommendation. But it will always show you what is on either side of the recommendation. One of the best things about going to a library is you often find when looking for a particular book that the books on either side of it are more interesting, and you didn't even know about them. That's what a computer can do very significantly. It can tell people what's on either side, and see if you bite at that. If you bite, then it will open up the doors on either side of that bite."

Innovation in Exhibition

The disciplined art of exhibition has come a long way from the opening exhibits in the Crystal Palace of mid-19th-century England to the outpouring of money, time, and talent that produced a tremendous flourish of activity during the American Bicentennial. Reflecting this surge, last year's 1976 Design Review documented, through 60 percent of the entries selected for this category, the abundance of innovative experimentation which yielded great strides in the state of the art. Of this year's 16 Environmental projects, 50 percent are exhibits.

The conceptual directions and technological advances which exhibition and environmental designers have assimilated in the past few years have dramatically influenced the face of art, history, and science museums across the country. Yet stirring up curiosity and sparking interest among audiences through contact with sophisticated techniques of the film and television industries was beyond the traditional ken of curatorial display.

In the face of rising costs and economic setbacks museums slowly made nervy policy changes, often with the financial backing of government, corporate, and other outside funds. Many for the first time encouraged outside design consultants to bring in the latest structural systems, clever multimedia effects, traffic flow concepts, and brightly colored environmental signage and graphics to once-hallowed and musty halls. These nearly forgotten public institutions were brought full-force into the last quarter of the 20th century, producing a renaissance of public accessibility as information about science and the arts or the history of you-name-it began to be conveyed in the upbeat language of the communication media which the public could understand.

The Latest in Environmental Design

Much has happened generally this past year in the field of environmental design and its related concerns. The Accessible Arts exhibit, produced by the National Arts & the Handicapped Information Service and sponsored by Bristol-Myers Company and the National Endowment for the Arts, was created as a model for designing other exhibits and developing criteria to serve as an example of arts accessibility for designers, museum administrators, and arts officials in response to the special needs of the handicapped public.

In relation to the environment itself, cities across the nation are slowly getting facelifts in the form of extensive restoration and renovation of existing sites, spurred by the slow-down in the building industry. Likewise, the "visual pollution" that billboards and junkyards have created along the nation's highways is being reluctantly done away with under the Highway Beautification plan. There are only a quarter of a million billboards left!

On a bright note, the Cooper-

Hewitt Museum of Design, the Smithsonian's National Design Museum, opened in late 1976 with an exhibit, MAN TransFORMS, which explored the design process and delighted the public doing it (pages 158-159). The museum has since sponsored exhibits about subways, 200 years of architectural drawings, and the intriguing "Place, Product, Packaging," which investigated commercial institutions, such as fast-food chains, gas stations, and airlines, which project a total environment by coordinating the look and presentation of a product with the look and presentation of a place.

Environmental graphics designers consolidated interests and influence this year when they created the nationwide Society of Environmental Graphics Designers. The society has already established criteria appropriate for soliciting design services as well as criteria for identifying responsive suppliers.

Davad Rice, the fourth juror on the Environmental panel, is chairman of the Organization of Black Designers (OBD). Founded in Detroit, Michigan, in September 1975, OBD is currently raising funds to aid those Black women and men entering design schools and those already there. Another of the organization's projects is to compile a directory of Blacks already in the various design professions. Rice raised the question of how to get more Blacks and other minorities into design schools: "The first priority is communication. There are still many Black youngsters who have never heard the words 'designer,' 'architect,' or 'engineer.' There's been no family or professional history extensive enough to make these words an ordinary part of their vocabulary.

"Those of us in the design professions should feel responsible for getting at least one other person into our particular discipline, if we value our profession at all. There's a tremendous amount of design talent in the Black communities across this nation, and as professionals we have a responsibility to see that as much of it as possible is directed and nurtured to maturity. We all gain by doing that."

The Environmental panel was also concerned with the fact that there is not much cross-fertilization among designers from other disciplines. The jurors postulated that that situation began in the design schools themselves. "I think we're too isolated," said Stockman, "and there is much that we can learn from each other. I remember feeling so frustrated when I was in school. I was in the Environmental Design program, and each time I expressed curiosity about other areas of design—graphics, product design—I would get my hand slapped."

Bruce Burdick, who agreed that he suffers from the lack of real graphic training and cannot work without a graphic designer, continued by saying, "How many schools try to still keep their departments separate. I think it stems from instructors not wanting to appear foolish in front of each other, because they'd be intruding into each other's field, in a sense, showing their ignorance if they ever really started working together.

"We experience the same thing in our office when we bring in a consultant from another discipline. It takes a long time to get someone to stop protecting their own realm and begin to focus on the problem. Sometimes we won't even bring consultants together. We keep them working separately, and instead, we keep introducing to them individually what each has said or developed. Because we know that it will be a stand-off if we ever bring them together. We are too afraid of intruding on each other's territory."

Why Mediocrity?

After a discussion of the projects and products, the issues and the trends which are currently affecting designers, we are left with the role of the designer as an individual. Noel Mayo's rhetorical questions speak to that point: Why do so many of the mass-produced designs today continue to be of mediocre quality? Is it because the designers are incapable? Does it mean that people don't really want anything more than that? He answered his questions by firmly pointing the blame at the level of inarticulateness in the design profession. "Because a designer, in effect, can't communicate clearly, he ends up allowing the marketing people to tell him what he has to do," Mayo concluded.

Summary

Though the volume of submissions to the 1977 Design Review expanded, the percentage of well-designed work selected by the panels remained constant. Of a total 553 submissions this year, 112 were selected by the jurors. Total submissions were up 32 percent from last year; yet, total selections, up an equivalent 30 percent, remain in a consistent ratio of 1 to 5, or 20 percent of the overall number of entries submitted. In statistical terms, the Equipment and Instrumentation panel was the most discerning group, selecting only 8 percent of all work judged. The panel judging Visual Communications came in next at 17 percent of a total 180 pieces of work. Though they are the smallest in total submissions, both Contract and Residential and Environmental panels managed to choose a whopping 24 percent of all work seen. The most liberal group was Consumer Products. This panel picked 35 percent of the 120 products they evaluated.

Consumer Products

Ford Fairmont and Mercury Zephyr Models
Master Ice Scraper
The Pacesetter III Electronic Cruise Control
Sparkomatic CB Equipment
Sparkomatic Auto External Speaker
Arthur Fulmer Generation II Travel System
The Eclipse Slide Mount Rack and Pannier System
Radio Flyer Tricycle Model 312
Largo 5 Meter Sailboat
Pro-Tec PTH 3000 Hockey Helmet
AMF VOIT Compound Archery Bow
Night Lighter Quartz-Halogen Hand-Held Spotlight
Q-Beam Outdoorsman Fluorescent Lantern
20-, 12-, and 8-Liter Jugler Thermoses
GEI Pocket Pak Portable Water Purifier
TAG™ Modular Travel System
Polaroid SX-70 Telephoto 1.5 Lens
Falcon Print Positioner
Falcon Print Cutter
True Pointer Pencil Sharpener
Sentry Survivor Fire-Safe Deposit Box
Koss CM/1030 Loudspeaker
JCPenney Two-Motor Lightweight Vacuum Power Foot
Norelco Gotcha Gun™ 1200 Hair Dryer Model HB1777
Gillette Supermax® Swivel Hair Dryer
Accessory Comb for Gillette's Supermax® Swivel Hair Dryer
Rincon Soft Lens Disinfector Model SJL 100
The La Costa Spa Shower Bar
U.S. Borax Powdered Soap Dispenser
Airwick "Stick Ups"
Norelco HB1115 Food Processor
JCPenney Slow Cook Broiler Oven
Waring Steam Chef™
JCPenney Drip Coffeemaker
Norelco Super Juicer™ Model HB1110
Copco Cast Aluminum Cookware
Corning Ware® Grab-It® Bowl
Heller Designs Bakeware
- 8-in. Square Cake Baking Dish
- 1-qt Casserole with Au Gratin Cover
- 2-qt Casserole with Au Gratin Cover
- 9-oz Custard Ramekin
- #509 Pie Plate

In Consumer Products, as in each of the categories this year with the exception of Environmental, we see a significant increase in the number of entries submitted. Out of 122 entries sent in, 42 were selected by the jurors, compared with 22 selected out of 85 in 1976. Although the general consensus was that the panel would like to have seen an even greater number of selections to consider, they seemed to agree with Morison S. Cousins that "good taste is, thankfully, intruding on design."

Members of the jury panel were Morison S. Cousins, Freda Diamond, George Finley, Richard Penney, and Cooper C. Woodring.

Left to right: Cooper C. Woodring and Morison S. Cousins.

Left to right: Freda Diamond and Richard Penney.

Morison S. Cousins

The firm of Morison S. Cousins + Associates, of which Morison Cousins is president, was formed in New York 15 years ago. The consulting office enjoys a diverse practice in the design of products and packaging for varied markets. In recent years the office has become increasingly involved in design for large consumer markets, bringing a high level of product design and communications to the American consumer. A member of IDSA, Cousins has served as director of the Package Design Council, chairman of the New York Chapter of IDSA, and chairman of the IDSA Bronze Apple Award Committee. Cousins was co-designer of the Gillette Promax Compact Hair Dryer selected by the Museum of Modern Art, New York, for its design collection. Many of his designs have been selected in past Design Reviews, as well as by Packaging Design and the American Institute of Graphic Artists (AIGA). His office's work has appeared in various design-related publications and has been exhibited at the Brooklyn Museum and the Smithsonian and in several of the world-traveling exhibits of the U.S. Department of Commerce. Cousins graduated in 1955 from Pratt Institute, Brooklyn, after which he attended the College of William and Mary for graduate study. Prior to forming his own firm, Cousins worked as a designer with a major truck manufacturer and a noted New York consultant.

Freda Diamond

In an article entitled "Designer for Everybody," *Life* magazine once had this to say about Freda Diamond: "Millions of U.S. homes profit by her good taste." Diamond is an internationally known designer and home furnishings consultant with her own New York-based office, Freda Diamond Associates. Besides her role as designer, Diamond serves as a style and merchandising consultant to department stores and manufacturers as well as government. It is Diamond's abiding philosophy that taste and style have no price tag. Over the years she has pioneered this principle, working to bring taste and style to the mass market. Some of Diamond's past and present clients include Libby Glass of Owens-Illinois, General Electric, Regina, Continental Can, as well as department stores across the country—from Hess's of Allentown, Pennsylvania, to G. Fox and the May Company of California—and as far away as Greaterman's department store in South Africa. In her work with manufacturers Diamond reaches out to all phases of distribution from fine department and home furnishing specialty stores to syndicate stores, trade associations, mail order houses, supermarkets, and premium users. On two separate assignments for the Japanese government, she acted as design and merchandising advisor for the Ministry of International Trade and Industry. Diamond advised on ways and means of developing and adapting indigenous Japanese design for the American market. She has also worked in a similar capacity for India, Israel, Czechoslovakia, Italy, and most recently the Dominican Republic. Diamond's work has been cited for good design by the Museum of Modern Art in New York, the Toledo Museum, the Akron Museum at the Akron Institute of Art, and the Avery Museum in Hartford, Connecticut. A member of the Industrial Designers Society of America, the American Society of Interior Designers (ASID), and the National Home Fashions League, Diamond was chosen in 1974 to receive the highest honorary degree from Cooper Union in New York, of which she is a graduate. Listed in *Who's Who in America,* Diamond was at one time a member of the Cooper-Hewitt Museum Advisory Board and is a past chairman of IDSA's Consumer Affairs Society. Author of *The Story of Glass,* Diamond lectures frequently at universities on industrial and decorative design.

George T. Finley

Editor-in-Chief of *Industrial Design* magazine for the past three years, George Finley is a member of the Board of Directors of Design Publications, Inc., the new parent company formed during the last year to bring the magazine under new direction. Finley has written about a broad range of design-related subjects including product design, urban planning and transportation, packaging, graphics, and exhibit design since joining the magazine as assistant editor in 1969. Under his direction the magazine has pursued what is best described as a business-oriented approach to design, relating the function to broader interests and needs of the corporate world. Human factors has also received considerable attention during his tenure. Participating in each year's selection of design work, Finley has served as a member of the Visual Communications panel for the past two years. Lecturing widely about industrial design and the role of the magazine, Finley has been a guest speaker at numerous schools, colleges, and institutions. Last year in California the Society of Art Center alumni appointed Finley one of the judges for their Eighth Annual International Exhibition open to all alumni. Finley is an affiliate member of IDSA as well as a member of the American Society of Magazine Editors and the Advisory Board for the Design Management Institute of the Massachusetts College of Art.

George T. Finley.

Richard Penney

For the past 10 years Richard Penney has operated his own consulting office, Richard Penney Industrial Design, in New York. His product-oriented firm works in three main areas: graphics, architectural, and industrial design. In the area of product design, Penney is very involved with research and development for clients in both the U.S. and Europe. Among his past and present clients in the U.S. are Sperry-Rand, 3M-Linolex, JCPenney, The Conde Nast Publications, GAF, Calvin Klein Cosmetics, Inc.

and in Europe N.V. Philips and ITT International. An officer of IDSA and a member since 1967, Penney graduated from the School of Design at Syracuse University in 1960. After graduate studies in design and painting at Columbia University, he worked in the New York office of Peter Schladermundt Associates. For a year Penney worked in Europe—in Italy, France, and Denmark. Upon returning in 1963, he went to work as a staff designer for Henry Dreyfuss Associates, New York. Until 1968, when he opened his own office, Penney worked on various accounts, including Bell Labs, AMF, and American Safety Razor, as well as on the management of design programs.

Cooper C. Woodring
Cooper Woodring is manager of product design for the JCPenney Company. Each year his department designs about 300 products in the areas of furniture, sporting goods, toys, housewares, appliances, electronics, lawn and garden, photography, personal care, hardware, and automotive equipment. For a "significant contribution to the stature and recognition of the design profession in the United States," JCPenney received the Award for Advancement of Design from the Industrial Designers Society of Amerca in 1974. In 1966 Woodring's work received one of four awards given by the IDSA for the "Best Product Design of the Year." His work is represented in the Product Design Group of the Museum of Modern Art's Permanent Collection in New York. Woodring has written magazine and newspaper articles, and lectures at universities and design schools. Before coming to work at JCPenney in 1969, Woodring began his career in 1962 with two years as a designer for F. Eugene Smith Associates in Bath, Ohio, and as an instructor at the Akron Institute of Art teaching industrial design and model making until 1964. Woodring then worked for five years as senior designer for B.F. Goodrich Company, where he was responsible for product design in the B.F.G. Tire Company and the B.F.G. Research Center. Woodring graduated as an industrial designer from the University of Kansas and holds a master's degree in design from Cranbrook Academy of Art. A member of IDSA, he has held numerous positions in the New York Chapter, including membership on the Board of Directors since 1975. Woodring is also a member of the National Society of Literature and the Arts since 1974 and an active participant in numerous community activities in Plandome, Long Island. In 1976 Woodring was the American representative to Designworkshop sponsored by the Hong Kong Industrial Design Council and the Hong Kong Department of Trade.

The jury panelists had this to say about the entries in this category.

Moderator: What are the considerations involved in the selection for this category?

Finley: Those considerations that we feel are important include appearance, human factors, manufacturing, materials, cost—both manufacturing and retail—and how well the design satisfies the stated requirements or needs of the product. Also we try to consider what the designer's input was, how he or she specifically improved a product.

Woodring: Are we judging an item against a broad spectrum of products, or are we judging an item against its competition in turntables, for example. In other words, it may be an excellent design when considered among other consumer products, but it may only be average against specific competitors. Generally, all turntables are above average in terms of design, and likewise all appliances are below average.

Finley: We have to judge an item in terms of the competition and, of course, in terms of its design.

Diamond: Another consideration is if something is very nice, but there are millions of them. What do we say? A no vote sounds as if the item is bad design.

Woodring: I think a no vote is justified because the item doesn't improve the state of the art of design.

Finley: There is a question which is perhaps broader than the *Design Review* which a lot of people have raised—and that is, can we afford as a society to go on limitlessly making products of any kind with the most specific functions.

Cousins: I think it's terrific to keep on going. Unless you do some of those things, you don't get some of the other things accomplished. Unless somebody had thought to have disposable erasers, nobody would have thought of having disposable syringes. For instance, disposable razor blades came before disposable scalpels for medical use. I just think that probably you can't have one without the other. No one can say, "We're just going to develop and produce the good things." Somehow the other things are part of it all. I would say we have to continue, but at a reduced cost.

Diamond: But we don't know what reduces the cost. You will find very often that when you reduce the cost, you are taking something out of it somewhere.

Moderator: What do you feel about the quality of what exists today in this country?

Penney: Better and better. The nice thing is that it's filtering down into simple, everyday products, not only the special items like cameras and things that have always been high in cost. We see this reflected in what we chose here in this review.

Diamond: The concept of design is becoming much more important to the manufacturer. It used to be primarily a function of price. But manufacturers are becoming much more conscious of the appearance of a product, and not purely from a decorative or clinical point of view. There have been tremendous strides made in design. There has also been a plethora of trivia, which is unfortunate, and I just don't see the end to it. Unless we think in terms of more multipurpose products we're just going to design ourselves, from that point of view, out of the market. At some point, the consumer is just going to quit. There is just too much designed for too many limited, specific uses. We have to figure out a way to broaden the base.

Cousins: A certain amount of good taste, though, is starting to merge with design. Obviously, design has existed for quite a number of years, and I think good taste is thankfully intruding on this. The savvy marketers are starting to recognize that, and in the next five years design will really happen in the consumer market. There is a lot of evidence of that in retail environments—the kind of merchandise that mass marketers are willing to carry in their stores. The only trend I can see from what we looked at here is that products are getting a little cleaner. The next trend, and it will be five years before it really starts to show itself, is going to be in products that are a little more whimsical. This will be not because the product lacks seriousness, but in recognition that everything doesn't have to be ultra-serious for it to be totally functional. The most disappointing thing is that the handicapped don't seem to be considered in anything that anybody is doing in terms of everyday consumer items. We're going to start to do that, too, in the next five years.

Diamond: You have to spell out "handicapped" more specifically.

Cousins: Almost everybody is handicapped. That ranges from the loss of limbs to the fact that one has their vision corrected, which is a very simple thing to deal with and we're not dealing with even that very simple thing—not to mention some of the more serious problems. I believe that we really can do that. One of the things I'd like to see is designers themselves having more fun at what they're doing. I think they have turned design into a deadly serious business. The end result is that the profession is not as exciting or well-rounded as it could be for the designers. In that case it's not going to be exciting for the marketing people, and so won't be exciting for the consumer either.

Moderator: Do you see design as a service profession?

Cousins: I consider it a service profession now. I'd like to see it move into more of a profession of innovators, where they are creating something that is very, very exciting. People will use the service because of that, as opposed to the fact that designers just do one more job like accountants.

Diamond: What do you think about the use of designers' names in the two-dimensional field or designers who were never associated with a particular product area but are now going into new products?

Cousins: It's great for them, and it's a clear indication of how industrial designers have to some extent failed. In actuality, I think it's going to turn out to have a pretty good influence.

Diamond: In bed appointments, manufacturers have almost run out of designers with a recognizable name, so they come out with a line and tack it onto celebrities' names instead. I wonder if the consumer is going to react negatively to this at some point. We're really watering down and denigrating the role of the designer.

Woodring: I don't see it that way. I think that being designed by anyone is better than not being designed at all.

Diamond: As I understand it from other designers, most celebrities have very little to do with the product they endorse. Most of the products are staff or house designed. The famous name may help to encourage excitement or romance for the product, but is it a lasting contribution, and will it in the end help the designer?

Finley: I wonder if that trend doesn't relate to what Morison has been saying about the need for whimsy. But I think it's better described as a desire for some kind of personality in products.

Diamond: I think "whimsy" is the wrong word here. Closer to it is a term you all use—the human aspect—which to me is very funny because we have always been designing from that point of view. Everybody does. But I do think that there's been a certain sterility in some aspects of design and maybe that is why they are going out into other fields, to bring more romance into design.

Woodring: I think that's clear in what Penney and Morison have said about a lack of excitement or fashionability. We've already mastered human factors, materials and cost accounting, and all those essential but mundane things that the consumer today expects. These are not qualities that we ought to be judging. They are exactly the things that we ought to throw a product out for if it fails in any one of them. Just having those things alone is not good enough any more. Forty years ago we looked at a product and questioned whether or not it worked. Today that is taken for granted. It works because it exists. Now the most important thing obviously becomes, "Do I like it? How do we judge this?" We do it visually. Like the psychologists have been telling us for 20 years, 80 percent of everything we perceive is visual.

Moderator: When you look back on these entries, do you feel that you would like to have seen a wider selection?

Diamond: I was a little disappointed, generally.

Woodring: There were more things that I didn't see than I did see. And I don't think it's because they're not out there. It's just that they weren't submitted. There are whole classifications of just exquisite design in ski boots and athletic equipment, and so on. I didn't see as much of it as I would like to have seen.

Penney: I'd like to come back to the question of whether or not the future portends well for the professional designer, with the intrusion of personalities and people from other fields entering the design marketplace. This reflects, specifically in this country, a very serious problem in design. If we look at design in Europe, the name and personality of the designer have become a very important marketing tool for themselves and their clients. All the way to the consumer. They buy because Mario Bellini designed something for them. That phenomenon just has not occurred in this country among industrial designers. My feeling is that what is happening through some very clever and very intelligent promotional people in this country is people who are not designers are jumping headlong into a gap, a void, which we have failed to service and attend to ourselves.

Diamond: Is it because in industrial design we limit the scope of the definition of industrial design? We used to have this discussion many years ago. The word "decorative" in design was a dirty word. Then it happened at one point that Mr. Lowey did a line for Rosenthal, I believe. It was a very beautiful shape, but it wasn't until his office, or perhaps somebody else, put a rose on it that it really began to sell. After the word "decorative" fell out, it became "graphics." And then graphics became very respectable. I think that we have to broaden the base of what we consider industrial design to be. If you design for industry on a mass production basis, then it ought to be a little bit more all-inclusive.

Finley: There is also a hang-up about what "professional" means. To me, professional means to do your job well, to have good standards, to have quality as a primary concern. I don't think it means you don't dirty your hands with less than serious problems, like the appearance of something. Styling, for example, is considered a dirty word.

Diamond: In my own field, I became involved with the decorative design end while working for Lightolier. It's terribly important that the product be decorative, good looking, and even pretty. I think these are words that we all should realize and accept because that's what we're talking about.

Woodring: One of the most important things that is happening in design, other than the quality aspect, is the availability of it—the quantity of it, in other words. I have a theory that goes like this. Each person is a consumer, and each consumer has some invisible level of design tolerance at which he or she will not buy something because they find it offensive. Your level would be different than mine, but regardless, we each have our own personal level. Consumers are aware when a company markets a new product. Once the product falls below this imaginary line, it starts to inhibit or cut off its market share because it's below the invisible standards. What happens if the manufacturer wants to be safe and conservative and go up a little bit in design? Though I, the consumer, will not buy below my standard—it is a hard line—there were other things, as a consumer, that I will purchase that are above my standard, above what I was looking for. In other words, there is nothing on the up side and a hard line on the bottom.

Diamond: Don't you think that is our job, to upgrade that taste level?

Woodring: The restriction on our ability to do our job in the past has been that the businessman did not understand that. So he did not demand of us that we design in good taste, or in many cases he insisted that he not get that high a level. We were always capable of doing more than he would accept. Now the opposite is true. He is beginning to recognize and realize the real value of better design. He wants to be safe and conservative, and that means better design. That is a major breakthrough.

Diamond: Absolutely, but also years ago, before we had certain technologies, let's say, in dinnerware, it was very difficult to make a perfectly plain white plate that didn't blister or whatever. If you had to select a perfectly plain white plate, you were left with many seconds. So then what would you do? You'd get a great big decal with a big cabbage rose on it and sell a second. Then you would say, "For that price level, that is what people want." With the advent of World War II, we learned how to make a piece of pottery without the crazing, without the amount of blistering. We learned to make a furniture joint. There was a time when we had to take two pieces of furniture and span them with what we called the "waterfall front"—simply because we didn't know how to get that joint together level. When we learned how to do these things all the editorials said, "Isn't it marvelous how the consumer's taste is improving." It didn't improve at all, the technology improved! We were able to give the things to them. I think we make a great mistake when we underestimate the taste of the mass consumer. They are waiting for good design. And now we're able to give it to them more easily.

Woodring: There is hope yet!

Ford Fairmont and Mercury Zephyr Models

Designed for the typical American consumer, the mid-sized Ford Fairmont and Mercury Zephyr reflect a growing interest in automotive efficiency and economy. Built on a 105-in. (266.7 cm) wheel base, the twin Fairmont and Zephyr models are available with four-, six-, or eight-cylinder engines. Weighing under 3,000 lb (1,360.8 kg) with refined aerodynamics, this lightweight, fuel-efficient performer delivers between 15.5 and 30.9 mpg (6.6 and 13.1 km/l) using a four cylinder with a manual transmission. Lightening holes in inner panels, much thinner doors, and aluminum bumpers were used to reduce weight. Overall length, wheelbase, and width have also been reduced, with enlarged interior and cargo space. Retail price for the Fairmont ranges from $3,589 for a two-door to $4,031 for a four-door wagon. The Zephyr model begins at $3,742 for a two-door version and goes up to between $4,814 and $4,983 for its four-door wagon.

Materials and Fabrication: Options include 200 cu in. (3.28 l) 6 cylinder at $120; 302 cu in. (5 l) V8 at $319; automatic transmission at $368 including radial-ply tires; power steering at $140; power brakes $63; air-conditioning for $465. Extensive wind-tunnel testing netted an improvement of ½ mpg (0.21 km/l).

Manufacturer: Ford Motor Co., Dearborn, Michigan.
Staff Design: Eugene Bordinat, Jr., vice president, design.

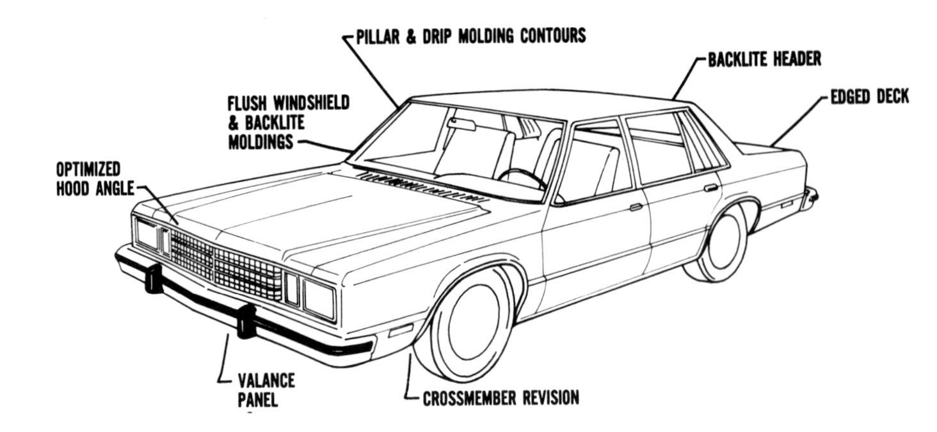

Master Ice Scraper

Weighing only 4 oz (113.4 g) with a front cutting edge angle of 60° to the horizontal, the Master Ice Scraper limits the stress required while lowering the risk involved in removing ice, snow, or frost from automobile windshields. While other similar tools rely on various wrist-hand angles which are not well suited to applying force, this scraper is held in such a way that the force and shock impacts of ice removal are absorbed by the heel of the hand, directly in front of and in line with the wrists and forearm bone so that sprains and pulled muscles can be avoided. It can be used effectively by children as well as adults and by both sexes. Influential in the design approach was the manufacturer's desire to sculpture this tool esthetically so that it could better accomplish its human factors objective. Retailing from $.90 to $1.25, the scraper measures 5.7 x 3.4 in. (14.5 x 8.6 cm), with a maximum thickness of 1.1 in. (2.8 cm) at the handle end.

Materials and Fabrication: The product is injection molded in high-impact styrene with a simple "open-and-closed" mold and no moving cores. A high-gloss finish in orange, green, blue, or yellow is molded in for good visibility in car or if dropped in snow.

Client: Mastermotive, Inc., Savage, Minnesota.
Staff Design: Peter Hemp, product engineer.
Consultant Design: De brey Design: Robert De brey, consultant designer, human factors, form, engineering; Kent Macintosh, assistant designer, graphics; Eric Rivkin.

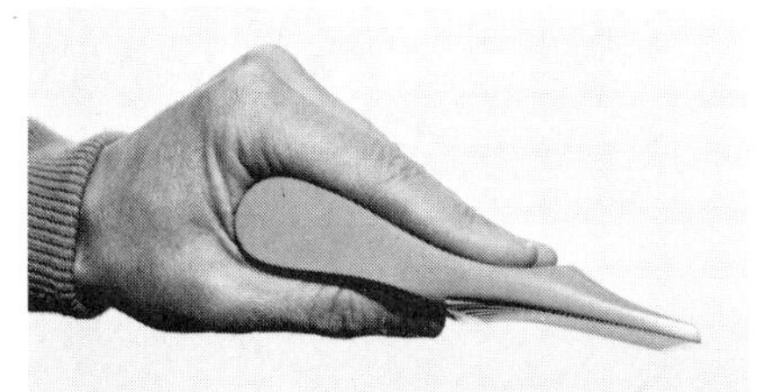

Top, finger pad

Bottom, thumb pad

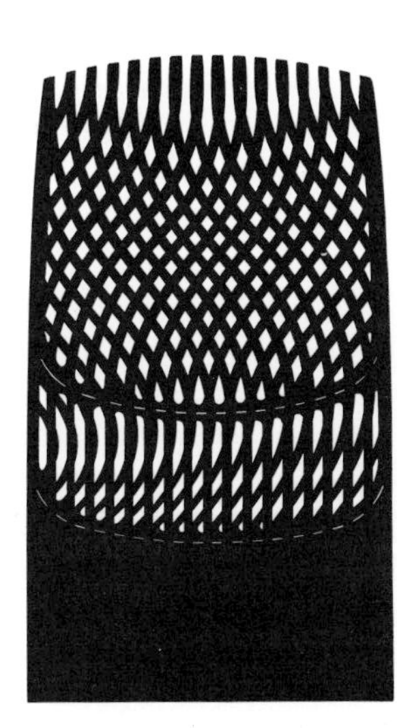

Composite structure

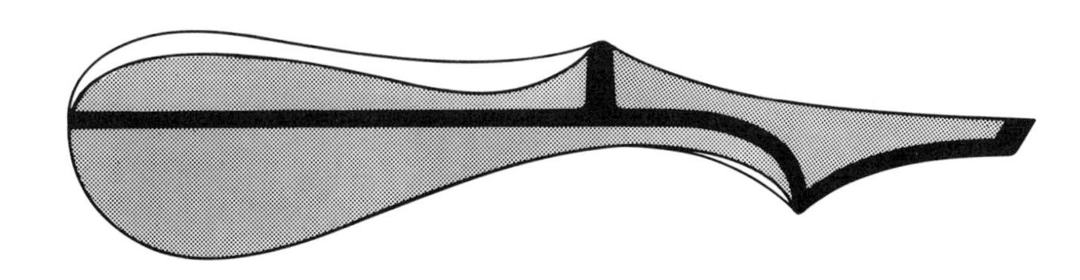

Rib structure

The Pacesetter III Electronic Cruise Control

An automotive control device which electronically governs the speed of a vehicle at a predetermined rate, the Pacesetter III is mounted on the end of the turn signal wand. The clean, simply shaped unit does not have an added-on appearance, rather it has been designed to look like factory-installed equipment. It fits all automatic transmission cars, vans, trucks, and recreational vehicles. To operate, the driver pulls out the main body and then rotates the knob to the desired speed. The speed setting may be altered when driving by simply turning the knob. A memory ring allows the driver to change the setting and return automatically to the originally set rate. This ring is located on the knob and floats freely until the desired speed is found. It is then pushed forward, sliding over detents which grab and hold it in place in relation to the knob. The ring has a raised portion which nestles under the indicator island on the mainbody. If the knob is turned to a different speed or accidentally disturbed, the operator can go back to the original setting by turning the knob until the ring fits under the indicator island again. This can be done by feel or at night without the driver having to take his or her eyes off the road. The unit is automatically disengaged when the driver brakes. This durable, temperature-resistant control device is 1 in. (2.5 cm) in diameter and 6 in. (15.2 cm) long with an indicator projection 5/16 in. (.8 cm) high. While competitive models require as much as 8 hours' installation time by a mechanic, the Pacesetter, retailing for $89.95, is the first after-market cruise control that can be installed by a do-it-yourselfer in about 1 hour. Energy efficient, the unit allows a 1- to 2- mph tolerance in speed setting that decreases the frequency of jetting gas into the carburetor, which results in increased gas saving.

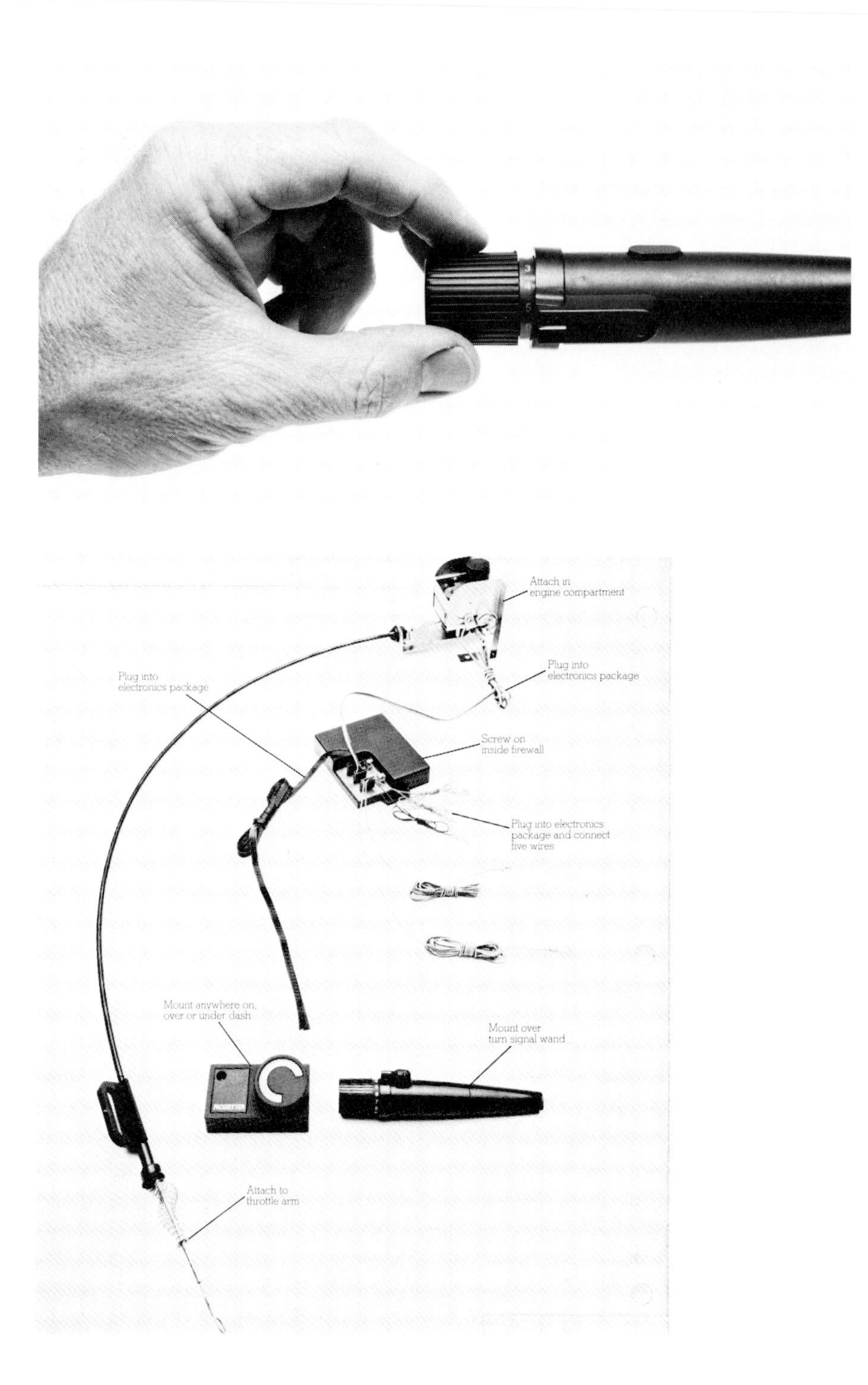

Materials and Fabrication: Main body parts are injection-molded ABS finished in black with a light texture; mounting clamp and collars are nylon with a black finish.

Manufacturer: Annuncionics Inc., Los Angeles, California.
Staff Design: James Smith, president; Al Berry, marketing; Max Wiesenberg, engineering.
Consultant Design: S.G. Hauser Associates, Inc.: Stephen G. Hauser, president; Daniel Ashcraft, associate designer; Ralph Bergo, vice president; Paul Greskovics, design draftsman.

Sparkomatic CB Equipment
Designed to fit under any dashboard, the CB mobile unit for receiving and transmitting features a distinctive instrument panel with a professional look. A larger unit can be installed in a stationary location. The panel with easy-to-operate controls offers a close arrangement of those controls used most often to provide convenient human factors. The under-dash unit measures 7 x 2¼ in. (17.7 x 5.1 cm) and is 8 in. (20.3 cm) in diameter. The base station measures 13 x 3¾ in. (33 x 9.5 cm), and its diameter is 8 in. (20.3 cm).

Materials and Fabrication: Back housing of under-dash unit is painted steel; front housing and knobs are injection-molded plastic finished in black and gray. Base station also has groove fold construction of walnut-grain wood rear cabinet.

Manufacturer: Sparkomatic Corp., Milford, Pennsylvania.
Staff Design: Richard Sabel, vice president.
Consultant Design: Ronald Emmerling Design, Inc.: Ronald Emmerling, president.

Sparkomatic Auto External Speaker

Focusing sound in many directions, this heavy-duty, yet flexible automobile accessory can be mounted in any location or position in a vehicle. Measuring 6 x 5 x 2¼ in. (15.2 x 12.7 x 5.7 cm), the unit, complete with tone purifier control for fine adjustment and sound clarity, swivels left to right and up or down with locking screws to prevent shifting from desired positions.

Materials and Fabrication: Injection-molded ABS plastic with a black matte finish and lithographed aluminum inlay.

Manufacturer: Sparkomatic Corp., Milford, Pennsylvania.
Staff Design: Richard Sabel, vice president.
Consultant Design: Ronald Emmerling Design, Inc.: Ronald Emmerling, president.

Arthur Fulmer Generation II Travel System

A new water- and dustproof travel trunk design for touring-type motorcycles provides large-capacity storage that does not interrupt airflow nor interfere with passenger comfort and safety. The system, retailing for $450, consists of a travel trunk, 20 x 15 x 10 in. (50.8 x 38.1 x 25.4 cm), which doubles as a backrest, and integrated sidebags designed to coordinate with motorcycle configuration and style, measuring 25½ x 15 x 10 in. (64.8 x 38.1 x 25.4 cm). Protected by a simple single-key locking mechanism, all components are portable and detachable, yet high-impact resistant.

Materials and Fabrication: Major material is approximately ⅛-in. (3.2-mm) twin sheet pressure-formed and trimmed ABS (Cycolac) with a smooth and glossy finish. The mounting tubes are chromed steel tube ¾ in. (1.9 cm) in diameter. Sidebags are black and leather-grained sewn vinyl fabric held in position by chrome snaps. Backrest is black and leather-grained sewn vinyl fabric bonded to urethane foam and held in position by chrome tube.

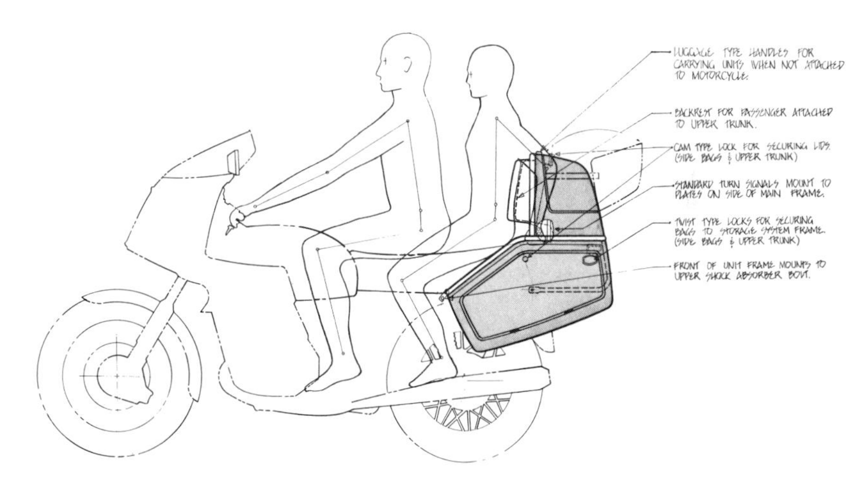

Manufacturer: Florida Safety Products, Miami, Florida.
Staff Design: Steven Molitoris, general manager; Kenneth Miller, vice president.
Consultant Design: Designworks: Charles Pelly, owner/design supervisor; Raymond Carter, senior designer.

The Eclipse Slide Mount Rack and Pannier System

This bicycle rack and pannier mounting system with superior strength-to-weight characteristics offers the first rigid rack that is completely adjustable. The pannier rack can accommodate various frame sizes and geometries without prying, bending, removal of brakes, or elimination of brake components. Weighing only 21 oz (595.4 g), the rack is rigid and sturdy. It derives its strength from a four-point attachment system and a truss-like rear strut configuration. The 8 in. (20.3 g) long extruded aluminum platform has a slide mount pannier system incorporated into it. An adjustable back stop allows the user to expand or contract the platform. The pannier mounting system without heavy complicated hardware, common to similar devices, is lighter and does not involve complicated hooks, springs, nuts, bolts, and rivets that can fail, fall off, or get lost. The complete system retails for $24.95.

Materials and Fabrication: Top platform is extruded aluminum that has been cut, punched, and deburred; struts are extruded aluminum formed with hand benders and in-house tooling. The platform has been tightly welded to the struts. The entire rack is heavily etched and then anodized with a satin finish.

Manufacturer: Eclipse, Inc., Ann Arbor, Michigan.
Staff Design: W. Shaun Jackson, president, designer; James C. Meyer, designer; Leslie Eric Bohm, designer.

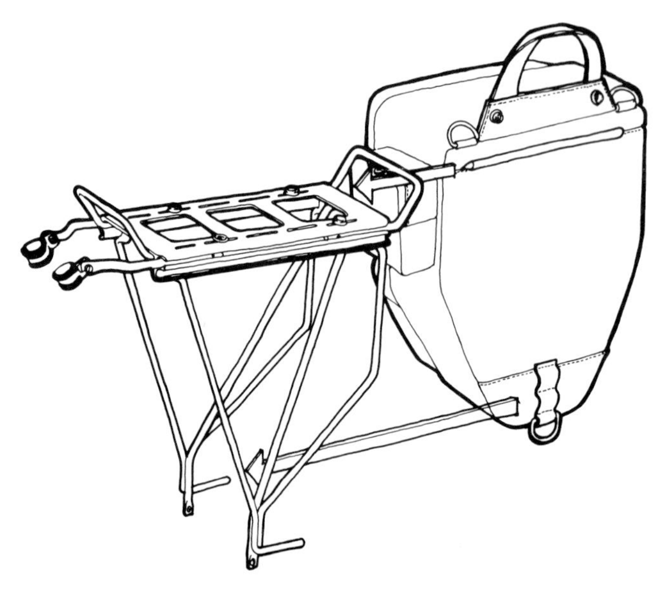

Radio Flyer Tricycle Model 312

Featuring plastic spokeless wheels to prevent youngsters' hands and feet from ever getting caught, this tricycle with nonskid tires considers user safety first. A patented safety frame provides wide-track stability, while eliminating axle or step so there is no "passenger riding" possible. Pedals are capped to avoid sharp metal protrusions. A securely mounted blow-molded seat with a high back has no raw edges or sharp part lines and is flexible and contour-shaped for comfort and support. The sturdy 13-lb (5.9-kg) model, retailing for $22, is produced for children from three to five years old. It is 30 x 20½ x 23½ in. (76.2 x 52.1 x 59.7 cm). The front wheel measures 12 x 1½ in. (30.5 x 3.81 cm); rear wheel is 7 x 1½ in. (17.8 x 3.8 cm).

Materials and Fabrication: Main frame is bent welded 1 in. (2.5 cm) square, 18 gauge steel tube to ⅞ in. (2.22 cm) round, 19 gauge steel tube with a baked enamel finish. Seat and wheels are blow-molded polypropylene with molded-in color. Tires are molded rubber.

Manufacturer: Radio Steel & Manufacturing Co., Chicago, Illinois.
Staff Design: Mario Pasin, president, product concept; Frederick Michelau, senior design engineer.
Consultant Design: Deschamps Mills Associates, Ltd.: Robert Louis Deschamps, president, design director; Robert J. Welch, account designer.

Largo 5 Meter Sailboat

Designed to fill an apparent void in the existing recreational boating market for a smaller but very complete, well-detailed sailboat, the Largo 5 Meter, priced at a moderately affordable $6,900, makes boat owning available to a greater number of consumers. According to the designers, no boat under 23 ft (7 m) offers as much interior cabin space or as much usable deck area as this 16 x 7 ft (4.9 x 2.1 m) sailboat. Careful detailing in the cabin interior allows space to sleep four adults in berths 6½ ft (2 m) long, with galley, portable toilet, and storage facilities for food and clothing. Four port lights, two of which can open, and a hatch window provide light and good ventilation for the cabin. The flush deck, with a nonskid surface, accommodates all sailing activities. The self-bailing cockpit, comfortably seating four adults, also provides floor storage and bilge pump. An optional camper top converts the cockpit to a second sleeping cabin in cool or wet weather. The high-lift keel makes trailering easy, even with a compact car. As a viable alternative to a second car, the boat can be stored in most garages when bow pulpit and lifelines are removed. Due to the 550 lb (249.5 kg) lead ballast, the 1,400-lb (650 kg) sailboat is self-righting even from the most extreme angles. Other safety features include: stable wide beam; foam flotation; and complete lifelines with bow and stern rails available. Life jackets and fire extinguisher are standard equipment. Inboard power motor with four-cycle control and a complete electrical and lighting system make the Largo a truly self-contained, reliable craft. Sophisticated sailing hardware like the midboom sheeting and roller traveler, providing better shape and control of the mainsail, characterizes the kind of quality equipment usually found only on large, expensive yachts. Attention to these fine details is unique in a boat of this size and price.

Materials and Fabrication: Hand-laid FRP laminate 3/16 in. (4.8 mm) thick with gel coat color (white with black stripe) on the exterior; teak and black anodized aluminum trim on the exterior and interior; 90 percent of all hardware is black anodized aluminum; bright hardware is polished stainless.

Manufacturer: Largo Sailboats, Inc., Aspen, Colorado.

Consultant Design: Simpkins Design Group: Terry J. Simpkins, engineering and marine design; Linda Simpkins, designer.

Pro-Tec PTH 3000 Hockey Helmet

In order to develop a structurally stronger helmet, this product was designed and styled for protection. The tough, lightweight shell is actually shaped like a head. While existing hockey helmets are largely structurally weak due to poorly placed ridges and holes and, in some cases, two-piece shells, the Pro-Tec features one-piece construction from a newly developed, lightweight, high-impact material. The only hockey helmet offering wrap-around ear protection, this product also provides a four-point chin strap anchored directly to the helmet to minimize slip or swivel. Cut high at the back with inner padding extended for ease of movement and safety, the Pro-Tec also features optimal cooling without reduced strength. Utilizing a two-stage foam padding system (one layer for shock attenuation, one for comfort), one size helmet will fit all. Because four different thicknesses of inner padding are provided, the user can easily interchange and intermix padding to achieve desired fit. Velcro fasteners make padding changes simple and fast. The permanently attached top padding is not involved in size changes. Designed from tested prototypes, the helmet was developed from anthropometric data supplied by Dr. Paul Belveder, material destruction tests, and data from the Canadian Standards Association. Available in six different colors with a smooth finish to accept paint, emblems, decals, and numbers, the helmet retails for $19.95 to $24.95. All popular face guards fasten easily to the product, which measures a standard 9.92 x 8.02 x 8.89 in. (25.2 x 20.4 x 22.6 cm) on the outside. It was developed for the widest range of users, from age 6 to 60 and amateurs to pros.

Materials and Fabrication: Shell is injection-molded Zytel-ST801 nylon with a gloss finish; liner is die-cut polyethylene foam laminated to polyurethane foam.

Manufacturer: Pro-Tec, Inc., Tukwila, Washington.
Staff Design: Dennis Burns, president.
Consultant Design: Frank Hosick/Industrial Design: Frank Hosick.

AMF VOIT Compound Archery Bow

For use in competition shooting and hunting, this easy-drawing archery bow, redesigned for increased accuracy and distance, is both sturdy and lightweight. While a regular bow requires 60 to 70 lb (27.2 to 31.8 kg) of pull to bring it to full draw, this bow works like a block and tackle. During the first half of the draw, it requires the same pull strength as a conventional bow, but when the pulley, with off-center axis, takes over, the strain lessens by as much as 50 percent. The bow, with a weight range from 45 to 60 lb (20.4 to 27.2 kg), can then be held at full draw long enough for the archer to hold it steady and take precise aim. The overall bow length is 48 in. (121.9 cm) with brace height, from center to back strings, 8¾ to 9¾ in. (22.2 to 24.8 cm). Models equipped with bow sight, arrow quiver, stabilizer (attached to the front of the bow), replaceable grip, and draw-string tension arms include: the Target at $300 light-finished with stainless steel or chrome accents; the Hunter at $275 with camouflage finish; and the basic Chaparral at $150.

Materials and Fabrication: Center section of the bow is a large magnesium die-casting, finished in baked enamel in a variety of colors. Arms are fiberglass plastic laminate with laminated wood centers, finished with a smooth polyester coating. Pulleys are aluminum stampings anodized black; bow string is Dacron Polyester stranded thread.

Manufacturer: AMF VOIT, Inc., Santa Ana, California.
Staff Design: Bruce Henderson, vice president, research and development; Rudy Holman, mechanical engineer; Eugene Jones, marketing and design coordinator.
Consultant Design: Keck-Craig Associates: Henry C. Keck, design supervisor; Roy K. Fujitaki, project engineer; Masao Morisaku, industrial designer.

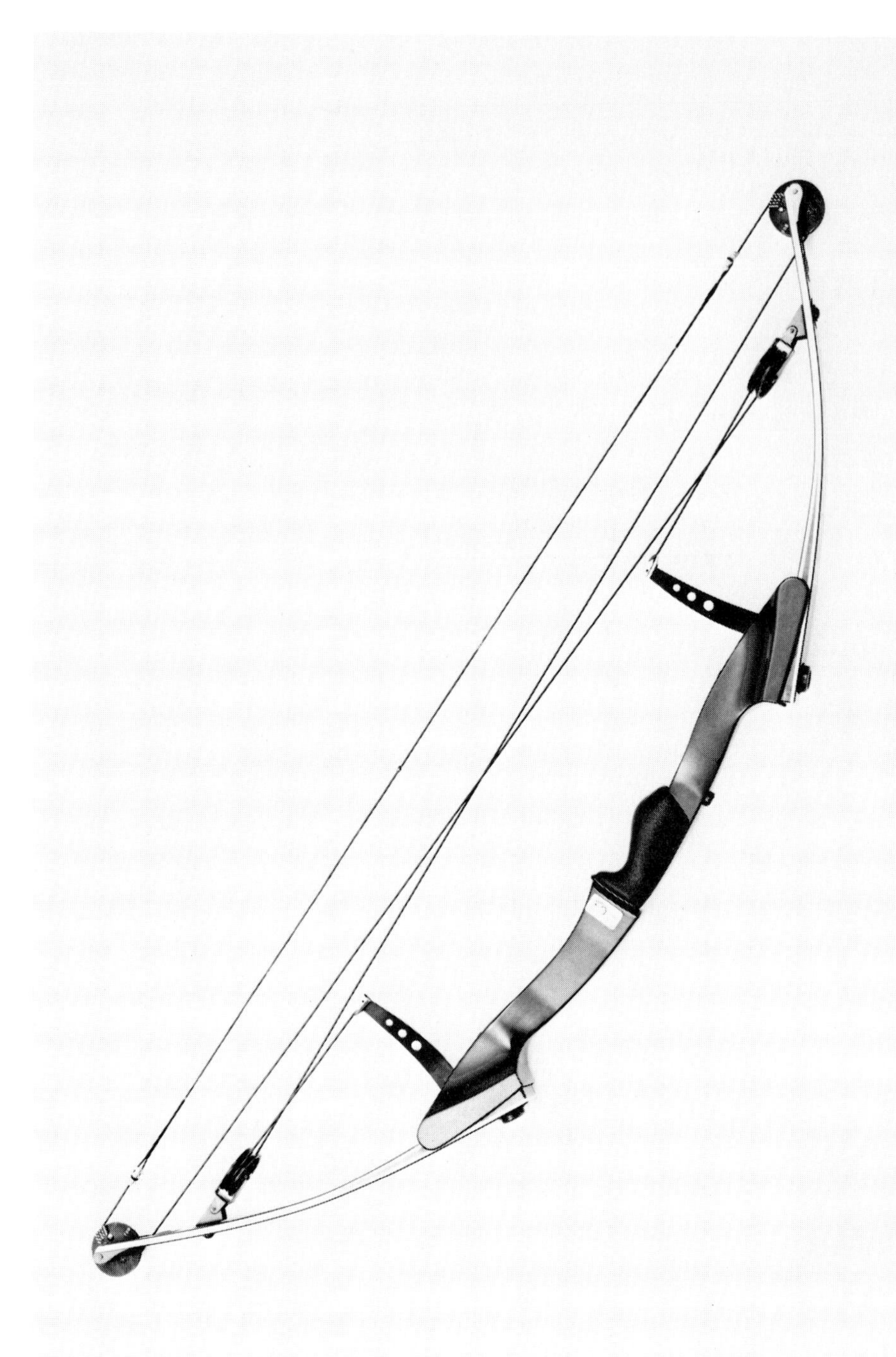

Night Lighter Quartz-Halogen Hand-Held Spotlight

This compact automotive accessory fits in glove compartments or under seats and features a very bright narrow beam. Retailing for $15 to $20, the 5 x 6 x 3 in. (12.7 x 15.2 x 7.6 cm) unit plugs into any standard dashboard cigarette lighter for emergency uses. An additional red lens and flasher can be snapped on when needed. The faceted case, with a cord storage compartment for the precoiled no-tangle cord, protects the lens and provides a handle. The case design eliminates all protrusions, providing an integrated hanging bracket and multiple-rest positions for the lens.

Materials and Fabrication: Case is two-part injection-molded ABS with a black leather-grained finish.

Client: Pathfinder Auto Lamp Co., Niles, Illinois.
Staff Design: Donald Shanklin, engineer.
Consultant Design: Designworks: Charles Pelly, owner, design supervisor; Raymond Carter, senior designer.

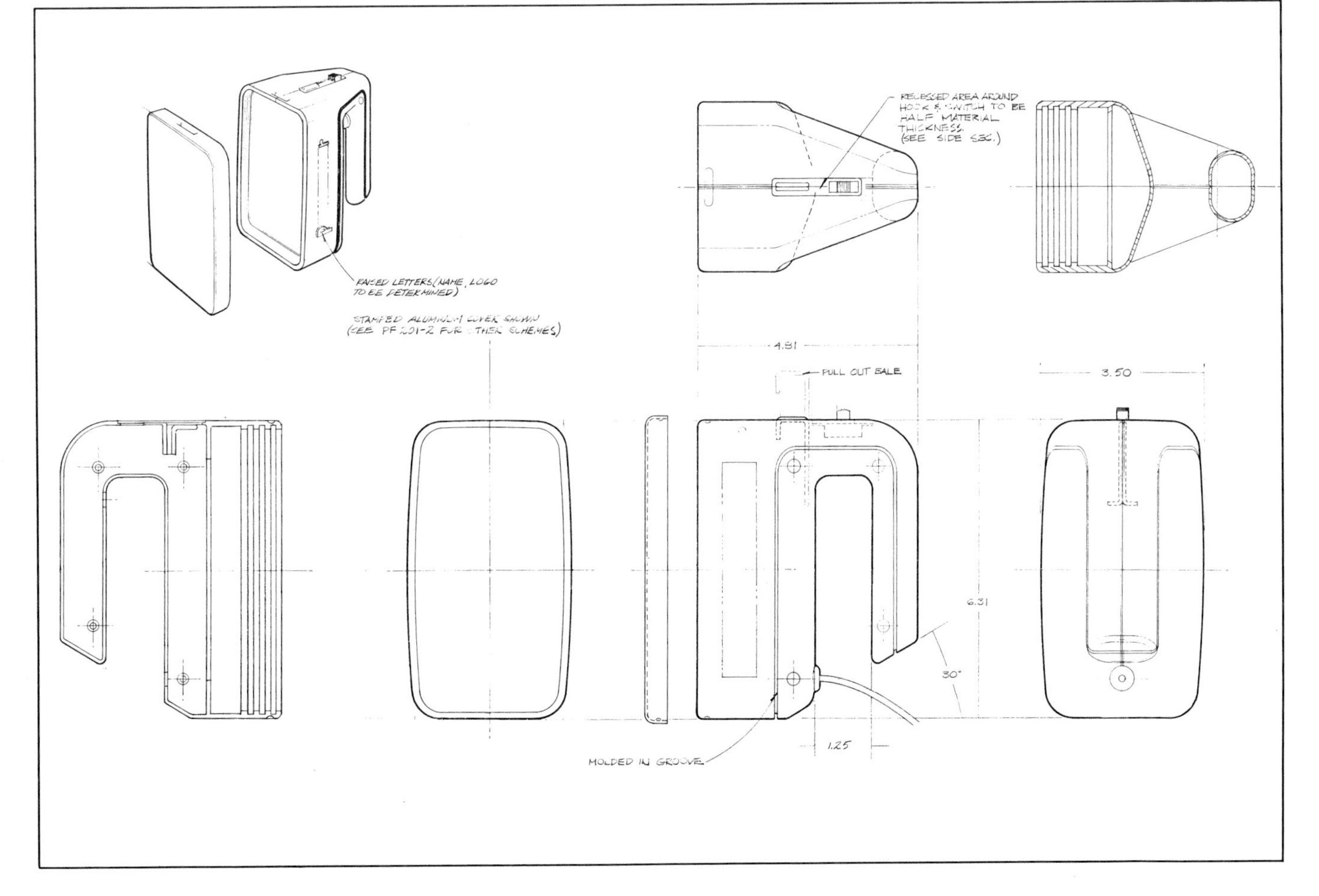

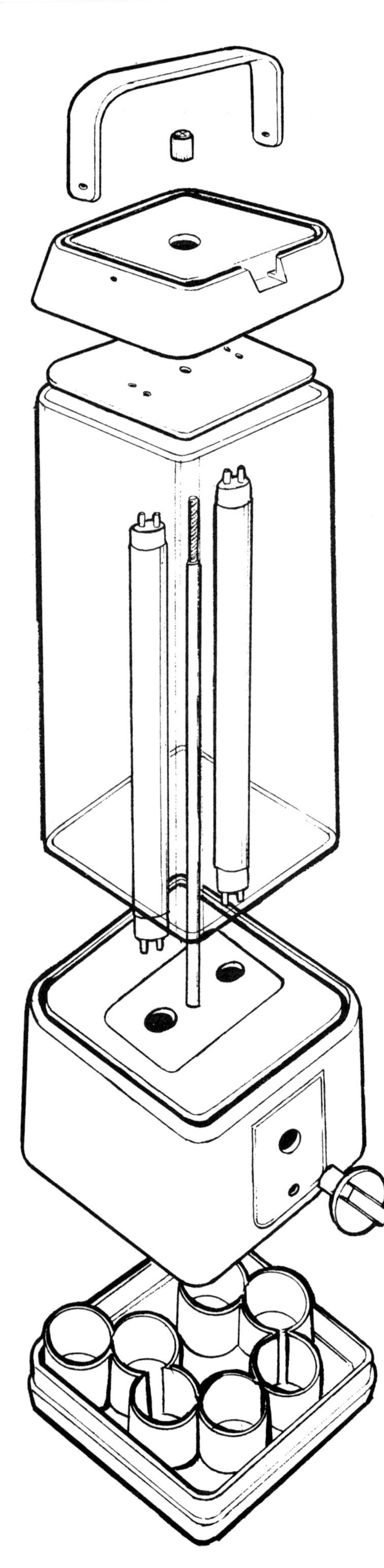

Q-Beam Outdoorsman Fluorescent Lantern

This compact, battery-powered fluorescent lantern with dimmer controls provides high-intensity portable lighting. For applications by sportsmen and campers or for home emergency lighting, the unit operates from eight standard D-sized flashlight batteries. It provides up to 58.5 hr of constant illumination. To recharge or operate without batteries, the lantern may be plugged into any 12-volt automobile cigarette lighter, with the universal adaptor and 6 ft (1.82 m) of cord provided. Switch control offers off/low/medium/high light intensity settings. Water- and shock-resistant, the unit weighs only 3 lb (1.4 kg) and is 13½ x 5½ in. (34.3 x 14 cm) square. An optically clear acrylic shield provides maximum protection for the two 9-in. (22.9 cm) fluorescent tubes, yet allows full 360-degree illumination. A tough plastic housing assures durability. Retractable handle makes for easy carrying, and hinges hang into a recess for compact storage. The unit, retailing between $30 and $40, operates in virtually any position.

Materials and Fabrication: The entire unit is scratch-resistant, satin finish, injection-molded ABS plastic, with the exception of the aluminum handle and assembly tie rod through the center of the product.

Manufacturer: The Brinkmann Corp., Dallas, Texas.
Consultant Design: Goldsmith Yamasaki Specht: Andrew L. Alger, product director, designer.

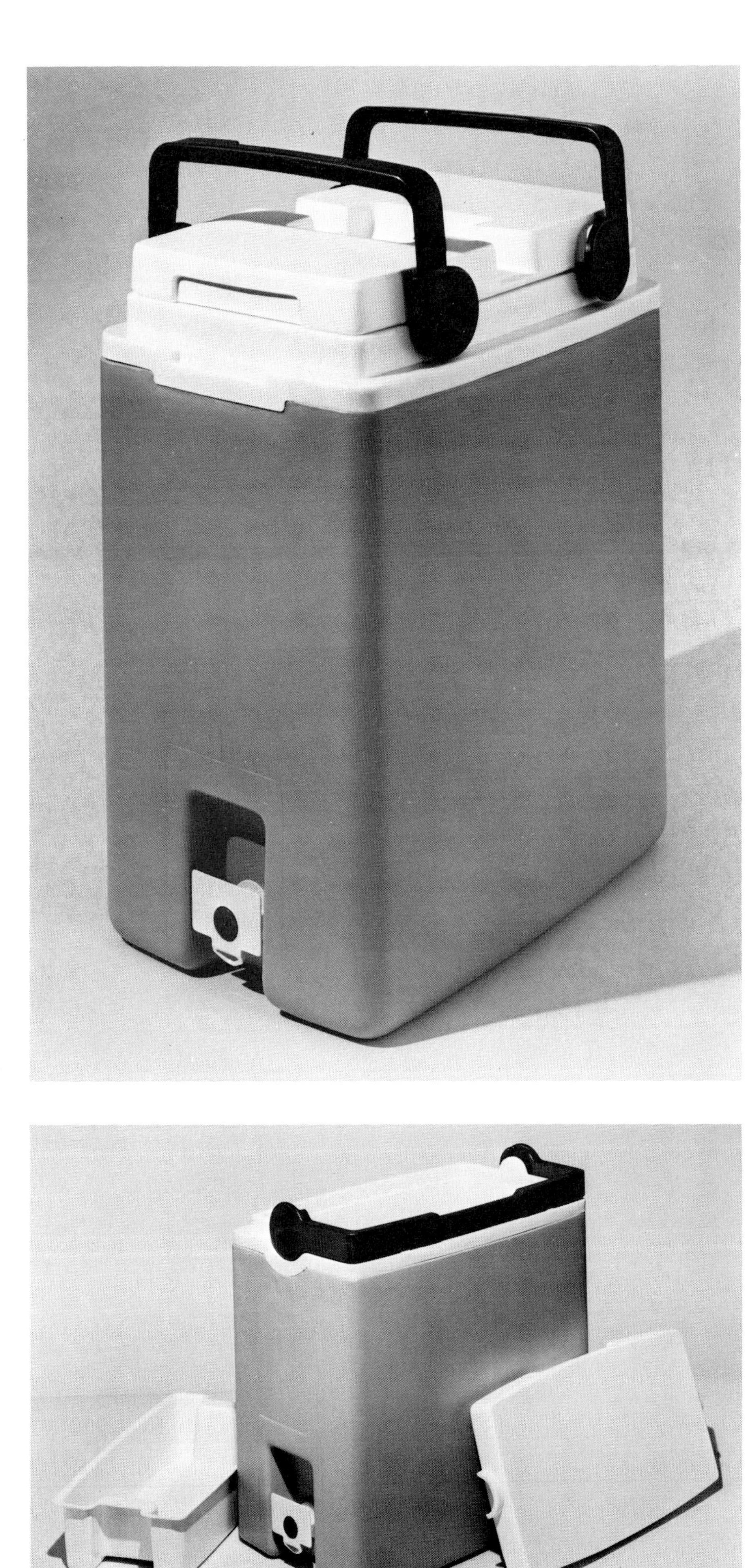

20-, 12-, and 8-Liter Jugler Thermoses

Wide-mouth, multipurpose insulated containers for transporting food or beverages function as jugs or as coolers with removable food trays. Recessed against breakage, fast-flow faucets with a wide finger area for convenient access dispense beverages from a stain-resistant, easy-to-clean liner. Recessed safety lock handles provide a sturdy grip and secure lid in two transporting and storage positions. Its rectangular shape, with no protruding parts, allows for easy packing and storing. Three impact-resistant sizes include: 20-l (5.3-gal) thermos, 18.1 x 14.9 x 10.8 in. (46 x 37.8 x 27.3 cm), retailing for $27.25; 12-l (3.1-gal) thermos, 14.4 x 14.3 x 8.5 in. (36.5 x 36.2 x 21.6 cm), retailing for $21.50; and 8-l (2.1-gal) thermos, 11.1 x 14.3 x 8.5 in. (28.3 x 36.2 x 21.6 cm), retailing for $15.75.

Materials and Fabrication: Lid and body are blow-molded/HDPE polyethylene; liner is injection-molded polyethylene with polyurethane insulation; handle is injection-molded polypropylene; faucet is injection-molded ABS; and tray is vacuum-formed/HDPS polystyrene. The body and handle are finished in textured blue or green with a white-textured lid. Faucet and liner are finished in high-gloss white.

Manufacturer: King-Seeley Thermos Co., Norwich, Connecticut.
Staff Design: Richard A. Tarozzi, industrial designer; Paul Morris, tooling engineer; Charles Formhals, project engineer.

GEI Pocket Pak Portable Water Purifier

In addition to removing bad tastes and unpleasant odors, this compact, lightweight water purifier eliminates harmful bacteria, amoebic cysts, microscopic worms, nematodes, radioactive fallout, asbestos, chlorine, and thousands of chemicals and particulate contaminants down to about 0.4 micrometers in diameter. The portable 9.2 oz (260 g) passport-size unit fits into a shirt pocket. Its 1.3 x 3 x 5.9 in. (3.3 x 7.6 x 15 cm) size is well suited for use by travelers, backpackers, bikers, boaters, campers, hunters, fishermen; for military and emergency needs; or for survival kits for aircraft, boats, homes, cars, and campers. Unlike bulkier previous products with similar objectives, the Pocket Pak, which retails for $29.95, does not require chemical injections or waiting time to poison or kill bacteria . Based on advanced technology, the proprietary microstraining filtration device purifies instantly without putting chemicals into the environment.

Materials and Fabrication: Anodized extruded aluminum chemically etched to a satin finish with double layers of clear anodizing treatment and injection-molded ABS plastic with a dark-blue, high-gloss, natural finish.

Client: General Ecology International Corp., Malvern, Pennsylvania.
Staff Design: Richard T. Williams, design engineer.
Consultant Design: Dixon & Parcels Associates, Inc.

TAG™ Modular Travel System

A system of three modular carry-on flight bags that clip and lock together in a variety of combinations, this product was designed as a kit whose parts may be mixed in many configurations adapting to different types of trips of either long or short duration. The vertical tapered shape of all component bags is contoured to fit the user's body, between the shoulder and hip, for safe and comfortable carrying. Cushioned shoulder straps adjust as padded handles, cross-body slings, or outboard grips. All pieces fit under airline seats or on overhead racks. The thin shell construction is both lightweight and durable, combining the dimensional stability of structured luggage without the weight, yet with the expandability of soft luggage. The system consists of a Day Pac, Week Pac, and Suit Pac, which may be used separately or locked together by means of military speed buckles. They are available in brown leather or tan or navy nylon canvas and feature stain-resistant red or blue linings. The Day Pac, an overnighter and personal carry-all, has a large, full-access interior, outer zipper compartment, and deep rear pocket. It measures 13 x 14 x 5 in. (33 x 35.6 x 12.7 cm) and weighs 2 lb, 5 oz (1.05 kg) when empty. The Week Pac, the basic travel module for a 7- to 10-day trip, organizes contents with shoe, shirt, and laundry pacs as standard accessories. Adjustable snap-up shelves permit redistribution of interior space to fit the user's specific needs; full access to clothing eliminates the necessity for unpacking; and two outside zipper compartments are provided for convenience. Measuring 13 x 22 x 6 in. (33 x 55.9 x 15.2 cm), the Week Pac weighs 3 lb (1.4 kg) empty. The Suit Pac for 3- to 5-day trips eliminates awkward garment bags. It includes a hangable suit form to carry clothes wrinkle-free. Interior divider shelves snap up when suit form is not used. Measuring 13 x 22 x 4 in. (33 x 55.9 x 10.2 cm), the Suit Pac weighs 2 lb, 9 oz (1.2 kg) empty.

Materials and Fabrication: Exterior material throughout is 11-oz (311.9-g) nylon with urethane coating for water repellency; lining and packing accessories are 2-oz (56.7-g) single-ply nylon taffeta with urethane coating; interior side lining panels are 1.7-oz (48.2-g) nylon ripstop with urethane coating; interior side stiffeners are sheet plastic; trim at wear points is 3.5-oz (99.2-g) cowhide; speed buckles are nylon. All fabrics are stack cut from rolls using paper patterns and are stitched with nylon thread; plastic sheet materials are die cut on a clicker press, heat formed, and inserted into stitched bags; leather is die cut and stitched into bags.

Manufacturer: Travel Accessories Group, Inc., Santa Barbara, California.
Staff Design: Arnold Saul Wasserman, conceptual/project director; Kenneth Gilliam, project assistant.

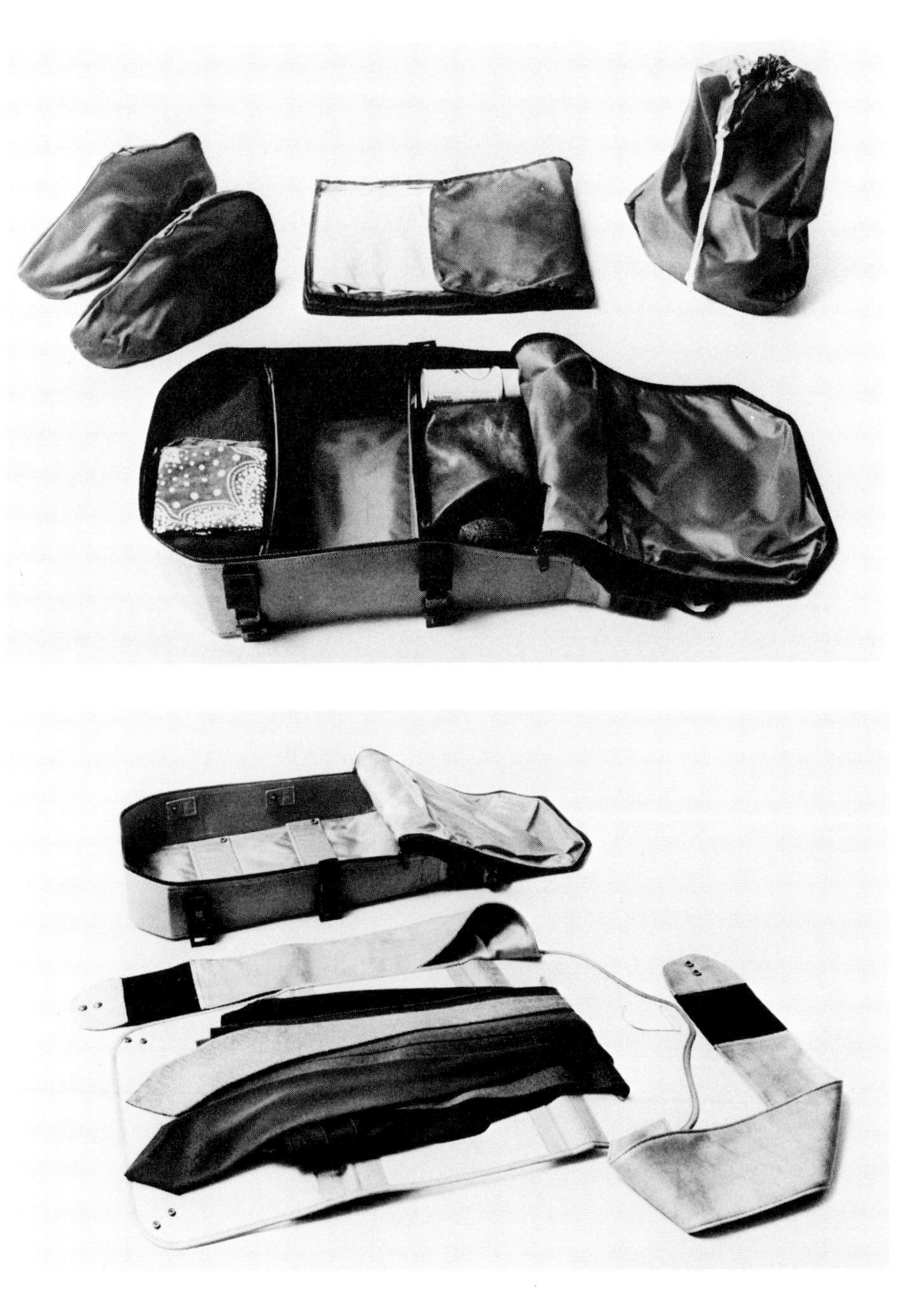

Polaroid SX-70 Telephoto/1.5 Lens

Offering a sharper image, brighter corners, and a larger aperture, the add-on 1.5 Telephoto adaptor, retailing for $67, significantly extends the capacity of the Polaroid SX-70 Land camera with the option of more than one focal length lens. Magnifying any scene photographed by 50 percent, the shock-resistant lens makes objects seem closer and corrects the perspective in portrait photography [with a minimum focusing distance of only 24 in. (61 cm)]. The lens, weighing 6 oz (170.1 g), is color-corrected and antireflection coated with styling coordinated to match the SX-70 camera and consistent with the Polaroid design image. The easy-to-operate mount design has a naturally secure grip to eliminate dropping and encourages rapid, accurate placement or removal of the lens with a simplified snap-into-place arrangement.

Materials and Fabrication: The mount and snap-on lens are injection-molded in one piece from polycarbonate (Lexan). The mount has a polished finish with texturing on the snap-on legs. The four optical elements are cemented together in doublet groups and attached to an aluminum spacer ring using silicone rubber. The glass lens elements are edged black with epoxy ink; lens elements are antireflection coated.

Manufacturer: Polaroid Corp., Cambridge, Massachusetts.
Staff Design: Robert Forsyth, designer, project engineer; John Zanardelli, principal engineer; John Sharp, senior engineer; Dr. James G. Baker, consulting optical designer.
Consultant Design: Henry Dreyfuss Associates: James M. Conner and James M. Ryan, industrial designers.

Falcon Print Positioner

Aimed specifically at the amateur photography market, the print positioner aids in finding the exact location on a matte board to mount photographic prints. To mount a picture, the user places a photograph in the upper-right-hand corner of the matte board. The positioner is then centered between the left edge of the photo and the left edge of the matte board. Once the center is found, the photo is aligned with the bottom horizontal of the board, so that its left side lies against the right edge of the centered positioner. The user then reads the large numeral on the positioner that appears opposite the top edge of the photograph. The photo is simply moved along the side of the positioner until its upper-left-hand corner meets the smaller number coinciding with the first numerical reading. At that point, the photograph is in the exact optically correct position for mounting. Once adhesive is applied, the picture may be set in place against the positioner. Retailing for $6.99, the product uses standard Greek propositions for determining top and bottom margins. The T-square-shaped aid is 1½ x 17 in. (3.8 x 43.2 cm). The top of the T is 10 in. (25.4 cm) long; overall thickness is ¼ in. (6.4 mm).

Materials and Fabrication: Injection-molded styrene with a typical .090-in. (2.3-mm) wall finished in tinted high gloss; graphics are in white, silk-screened with a solvent-activating ink.

Manufacturer: Falcon Safety Products Inc., Mountainside, New Jersey.
Staff Design: Steven Breslau, director of marketing.
Consultant Design: Innovations & Development, Inc.: M. Gary Grossman, vice president, account manager; Edward D. Levy, president, associate in design; Edward H. Meisner, vice president, associate in design.

Falcon Print Cutter
Improving upon the accuracy and eliminating the hazards of using a single-edged razor blade to cut photographic prints and matte boards, the Falcon Print Cutter offers a more reliable alternative. To operate this 2 x 16 x 5 in. (5.1 x 40.6 x 12.7 cm) unit, weighing approximately ½ lb (225 g), a single-edged razor blade is inserted in the holder. The holder is then shut, the whole arm of the cutter is lifted, and the sheet to be cut is placed in position. The holder is then pushed down, and after any further positioning, the user presses down on the lever and activates the blade. By releasing the lever, the blade retracts for safety. The unit retails for $19.95.

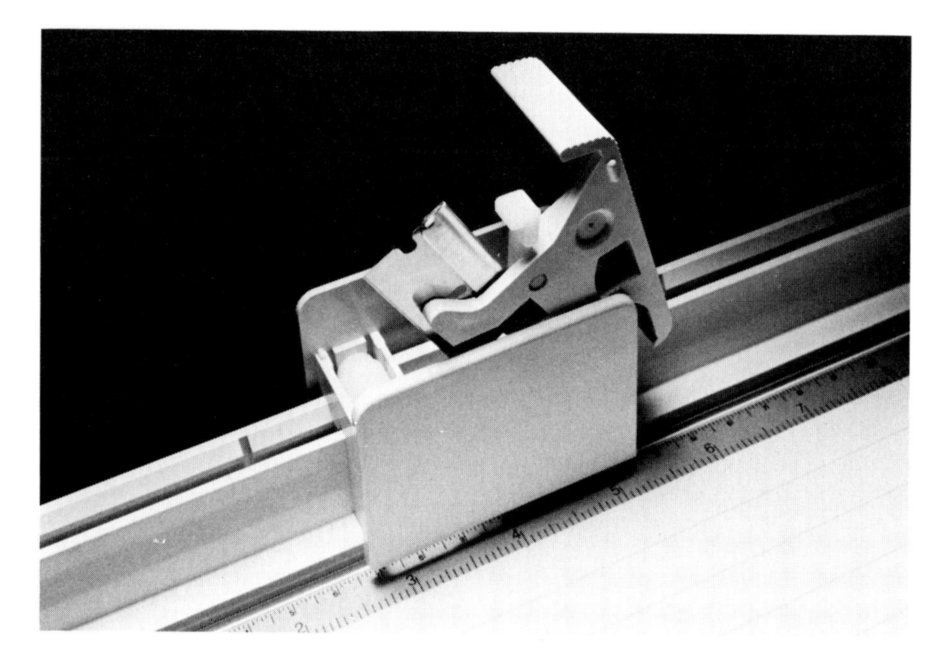

Materials and Fabrication: Cycolac ABS injection-molded in a family mold; feet are molded rubber; hinge pins are cold-headed steel; measurement scale is etched aluminum name plate; and blades are standard retail items. All parts are molded and then snapped together. Product is finished in high gloss with an EDM natural finish for the cutting surface.

Manufacturer: Falcon Safety Products, Inc., Mountainside, New Jersey.
Staff Design: Steven Breslau, director of marketing.
Consultant Design: Innovations & Development Inc.: M. Gary Grossman, vice president, project supervisor; Edward H. Meisner, vice president, design assistant; Edward D. Levy, president, design assistant.

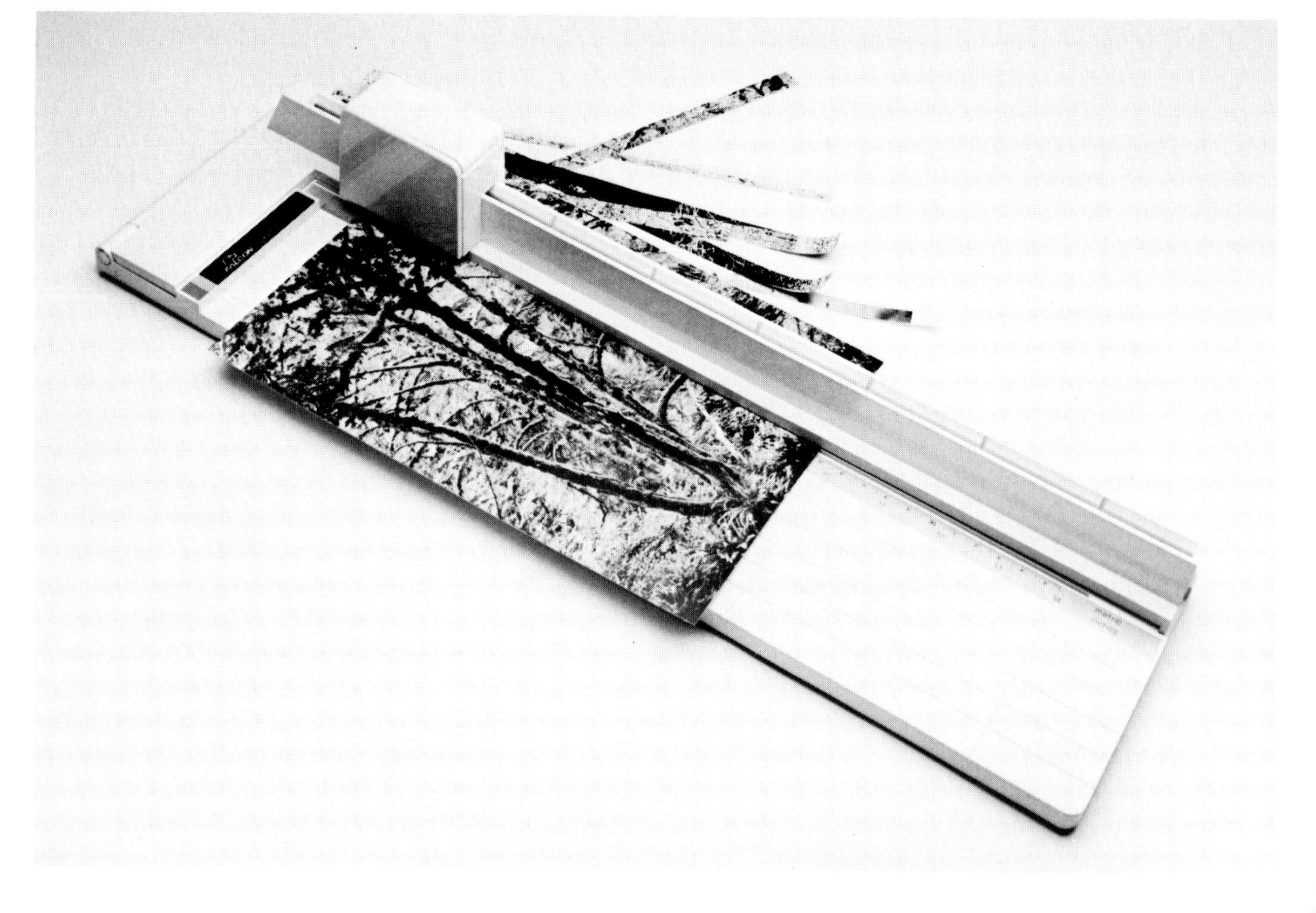

True Pointer Pencil Sharpener
This battery-powered sharpener provides a large-capacity slide-out tray for shavings. At 3½ in. (8.9 cm) high, with a 4-in. (10.2-cm) diameter, the unit includes a handy pencil storage compartment in the back.

Materials and Fabrication: Main unit is high-impact injection-molded styrene, finished in a variety of high-gloss colors. The tray is smoked acrylic.

Manufacturer: Shin Nissei Corp., New York, New York.
Consultant Design: Ronald Emmerling Design, Inc.: Ronald Emmerling, president.

Sentry Survivor Fire-Safe Deposit Box

Weighing less than 40 lb (18.1 kg), this fire-safe container used to protect important papers in the home is virtually portable. Measuring outside 13 1/16 x 8⅛ x 17¼ in. (33.2 x 20.6 x 43.8 cm) and inside 9⅜ x 4½ x 12¾ in. (23.8 x 11.4 x 32.4 cm), with a 537 cu in. (8,800 cm^3) capacity, the safe is easy to store. In addition to its small size, the unit meets industry fire-resistant standards. Developed from a nonconductive, nonmetallic material, it can withstand heat of 1700 °F (873°C) for up to one hour, with internal temperatures of less than 350°F (177°C). The 1¾-in. (4.4-cm) insulated walls have the fire-resistant quality of over 2 ft (61 cm) of solid concrete. Eliminating moisture problems that previously had been caused by the insulation, the safe protects its contents from rust and mildew. Other features include: easy-access slideout tray; key lock; double-locking bolt; and carrying handle. The unit, retailing for $49.95, carries an exclusive five-year replacement guarantee.

Materials and Fabrication: Outer shell, inner shell, and doors are injection-molded and bonded polystyrene, with a .100-in. (2.5-mm) wall; door handle is injection-molded polystyrene; lock housing cover is stamped steel; insulation is a formula of concrete and vermiculite poured in place in shells with a plug applied; handle is fabricated from plastic and sheet metal components. All parts are assembled with molded-in finish and color, except the lock plate which is painted. Graphics are vinyl labels.

Manufacturer: John D. Brush & Co., Inc., Rochester, New York.
Consultant Design: David O. Chase Design, Inc.: David O. Chase, president, design director; Dennis Coon, product designer.

Koss CM/1030 Loudspeaker
This solid wood veneer product for home high fidelity stereo music systems features a four bandpass speaker. One of three CM speakers introduced as a part of a complete product line, the 74 lb (33.6 kg) loudspeaker is crafted like fine furniture with rounded solid wood corners and a finished back. Solid brass recessed handles are not only decorative but a functionally important factor in an item of this size and bulk. Cabinet houses: a 10-in. (25.4-cm) parameter synthesized woofer; two 4½-in. (11.4-cm) parameter synthesized midrange drivers; a 1-in. (2.5-cm) acoustically loaded dome treble tweeter; and a 1-in. (2.5-cm) acoustically loaded dome tweeter. Retailing for $395, the unit measures 16½ x 14½ x 38⅞ in. (41.9 x 36.8 x 98.7 cm).

Materials and Fabrication: Tongue and groove genuine wood veneer with a completely sealed hand-rubbed finish.

Manufacturer: Koss Corp., Milwaukee, Wisconsin.
Staff Design: Joseph C. Besasie, director of industrial design; Jacob Turner, vice president, research and engineering; David Thomas, chief engineer.
Consultant Design: Dr. J. Robert Ashley, professor of electrical engineering, University of Colorado.

JCPenney Two-Motor Lightweight Vacuum Power Foot
To improve the cleaning properties of lightweight vacuums, this sturdy power foot was designed as part of a two-motor system. While one motor vacuums, the second rotates a beating brush to loosen dirt. With dual motors, efficiency increases by 20 percent. Part of a newly developed JCPenney vacuum cleaner, the power foot features a handy storage compartment for a spare replacement drive belt, located under the power head for emergency repair. The entire vacuum cleaner weighs 16 lb (7.3 kg) and measures 49 x 12 x 6 in. (124 x 30.5 x 15.2 cm). It retails for $60.

Materials and Fabrication: Injection-molded ABS.

Manufacturer: Bissell, Inc., Grand Rapids, Michigan.
Staff Design: Gordon Goodrich, product designer; David McDowell, engineer.
Client: JCPenney Co., Inc., New York, New York.
Staff Design: Cooper C. Woodring, product design manager; Frank Palazzolo, project manager; J.C. Hacker, product designer.

Norelco Gotcha Gun™ 1200 Hair Dryer Model HB1777

A compact 6.6 in. (16.8 cm) hand-held dryer with three heat settings and corresponding air velocities, the Norelco Gun conveniently converts to a free-standing unit for two-hand styling and drying. Integral to the design, a rotating folding handle placed in the intermediate D-dented position allows the unit to stand on any flat surface. Height with handle open is 7.7 in. (19.6 cm); 4.05 in. (10.3 cm) with handle closed. The lightweight, 14 oz (396.9 g) dryer is activated by a rotary switch located at the rear of the angled control panel. Together with the folding handle, the panel acts as a stand while allowing convenient manipulation of the switch. In use the balance is excellent, according to the designers. The off-white color that conveys lightness and quality was also selected so the product would appeal to both sexes. The high power, 1200-watt dryer, with a barrel measuring 2.5 in. (6.4 cm) in diameter, retails for $26.95.

Materials and Fabrication: The cabinet and handle are .090 in. (2.3 mm) injection-molded polycarbonate finished in a high-gloss, off-white color with silk-screened graphics in gloss PMS. Exhaust grill and intake grill/control panel are .040 in. (1 mm) blanked, pierced, and formed steel with an oxidized matte black finish. Switch control knob is .100 in. (2.5 mm) phenolic with finished texture in black and PMS graphics. The power supply cord is 6 ft (1.8 m) long.

Client: North American Philips Corp., New York, New York.
Staff Design: William J. Rakocy, manager, industrial design; Matt Tsuji, project industrial designer; Frederick Snyder, project engineer; Albert E. Simon, Jr., director of engineering.

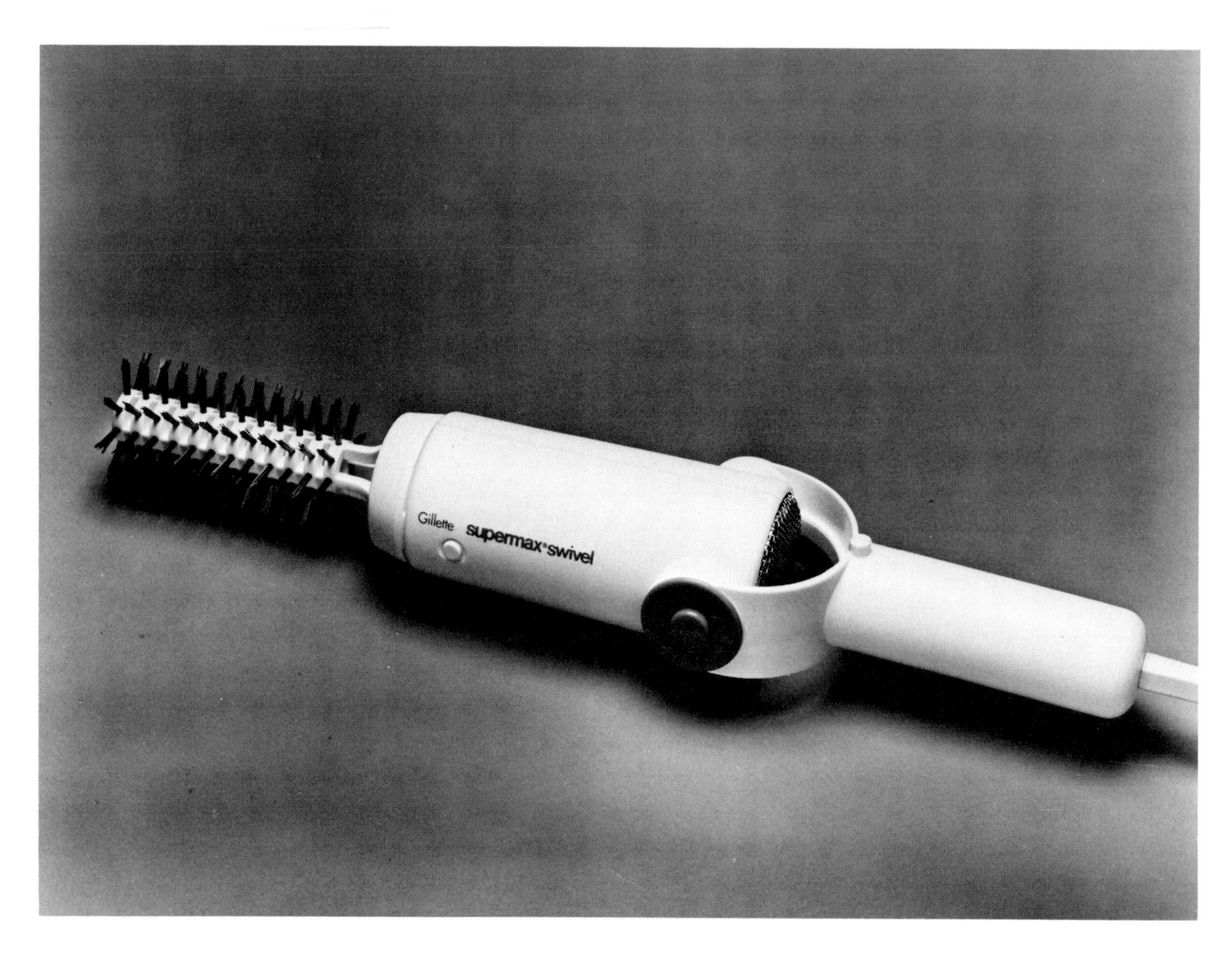

Gillette Supermax®
Swivel Hair Dryer

Evolved from the original Supermax hair dryer, the hand-held Supermax Swivel offers two products in one. The conventional blow dryer converts to a hair-styling wand when the brush attachment is added. By pushing a button, the unit swivels into a straight position and a brush can then be inserted in the end. The overall configuration of the dryer adapts comfortably to accommodate this dual purpose. It therefore fulfills the needs of all family members who may want different types of products. The dryer/styler, 9¾ in. (24.8 cm) long, retails for $25.99.

Materials and Fabrication: The case is polycarbonate finished in matte white with red swivel points. Plastic parts are injection-molded.

Client: Gillette Appliance Division, Boston, Massachusetts.
Consultant Design: Morison S. Cousins + Associates, Inc.

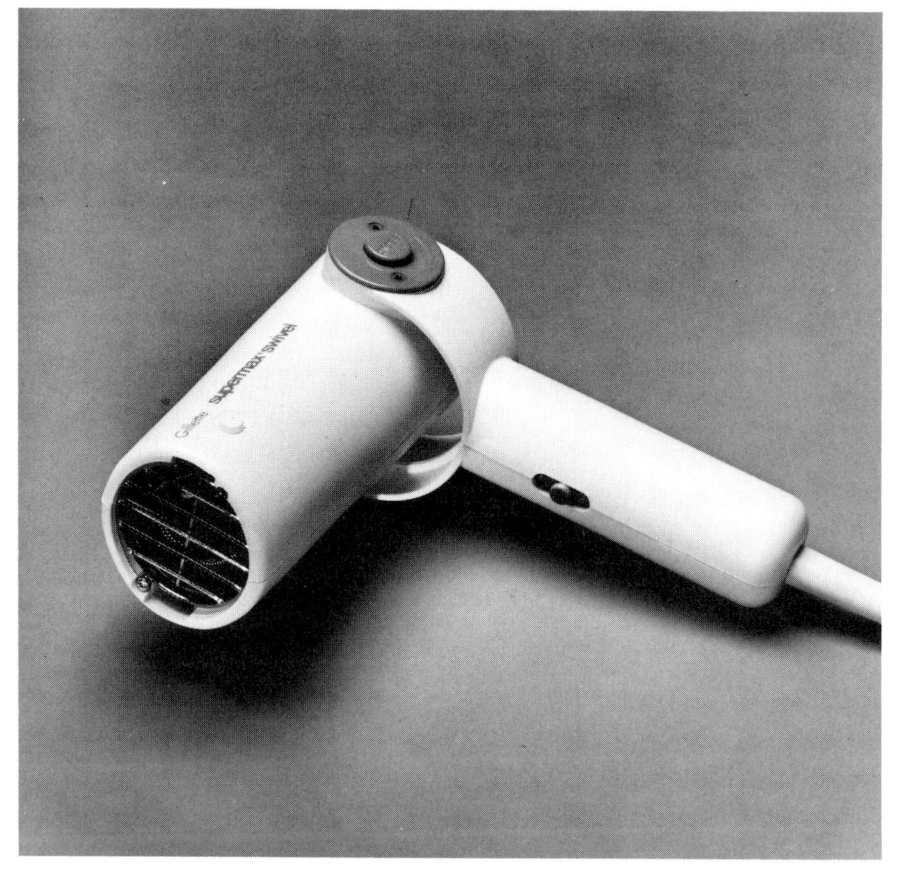

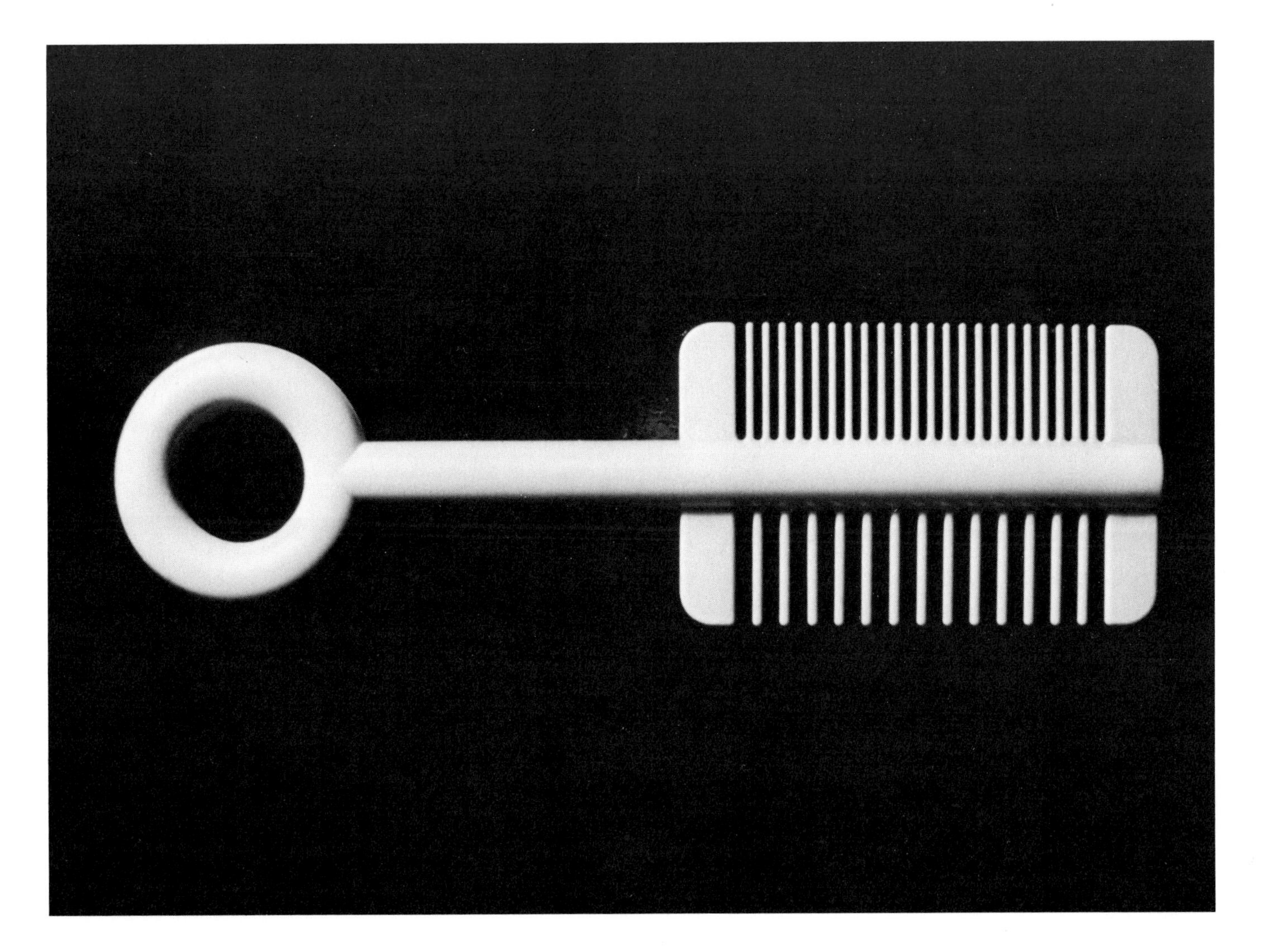

Accessory Comb for Gillette's Supermax Swivel Hair Dryer
Adding an element of fun and variety to the Gillette swivel hair dryer, this accessory comb was designed as a valuable marketing tool for a basic product, providing the consumer with an added incentive to purchase the hair dryer. The 8-in. (20.3-cm) comb features widely spaced teeth engineered to not break hairs in the process of detangling wet hair while blow-drying.

Materials and Fabrication: Comb is made of injection-molded plastic. The finish is a warm red color.

Manufacturer: The Gillette Co., Boston, Massachusetts.
Consultant Design: Morison S. Cousins + Associates, Inc.: Johann Schumacher, designer.

Rincon Soft Lens Disinfector Model SJL 100

An inexpensive "dry" heater for disinfecting soft contact lenses, this product is perfectly safe from electrical shock hazard. Because of its use in home bathrooms and its constant proximity to water, the unit is hermetically sealed. There are virtually no metal parts exposed and, though it may be submerged in water during operation, it will remain safe. It is the only heater available that the FDA (Food and Drug Administration) does not require to be grounded. "Dry" in this case means the container holding the lens (lenses are suspended in solution within the container) is itself in a dry heat bath or well. Two glass bottles hold the right and left lenses respectively in solution in adjoining wells. A white button activates the heat cycle. With a peak temperature of less than 90°C (194°F) and a flat heat curve, the disinfector maintains a temperature of at least 80°C (176°F) for 10 min. (The FDA has requested that each lens should be exposed to at least 80°C for a minimum of 10 min per disinfecting cycle.) Because clinical evidence cites lens damage if heat is in excess of 90°C, the unit maintains a constant and safe temperature. Heat is based on the melting of a temperature-specific paraffin which conducts heat from the heating element to the well in which the lens holders rest. Another safety feature is the heat indicator which turns from white to red in the viewing window, assuring the user that the unit is operational and that lenses are being successfully disinfected. This effect was achieved by placing a red wall ¼ in. (6.4 mm) behind the clear transparent viewing window and enclosing a layer of wax between the two surfaces. When the wax, white at room temperature, melts, it turns transparent and exposes the red wall. The disinfector weighs 1 lb (454 g); with the top lid in place, the unit measures 3¼ x 3½ in. (8.3 x 8.9 cm). The suggested retail price is between $29.95 and $39.95.

Materials and Fabrication: The housing is molded Lexan (polycarbonate) finished in high-gloss white and blue. After hand assembly of internal electrical components, the entire unit is sonically welded four times.

Manufacturer: Rincon Industries, Inc., Venice, California.
Staff Design: John G. Bowen, vice president, design/marketing; Lamont Seitz, electrical engineer.
Consultant Design: S.G. Hauser Associates, Inc.: Stephen G. Hauser, president, designer; Robert Bliven, associate designer, graphics; Sheldon Keith, associate designer, graphics.

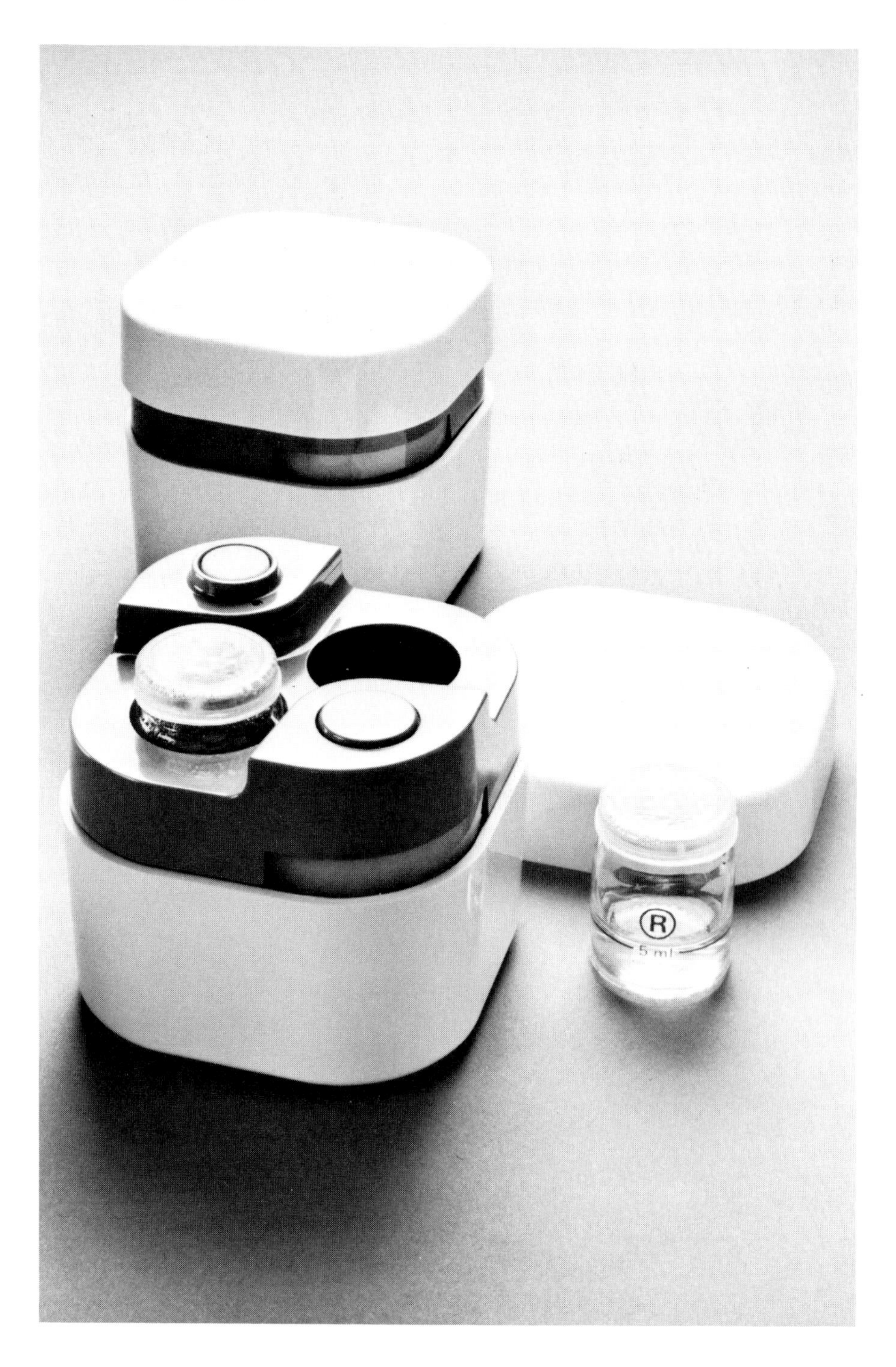

The La Costa Spa Shower Bar
An organized group of easy-to-reach shower products mounted on a wall rack was designed to solve the problem of bathroom clutter. The La Costa Spa, measuring 17½ x 5¼ x 1⅞ in. (44.5 x 14 x 4.8 cm), may be mounted on any shower wall with foam tape. The rack—which holds three bottles, each with a nonslip grip handle, containing 6 fluid oz (335 ml) of shower product, and a sponge—fits over square pegs in the mounted bar and locks into position. This easy-to-clean unit retails for the suggested price of $35.

Materials and Fabrication: Wall rack is injection-molded plastic finished in a dark beige color, engraved and hot stamped with a gold logo. Bottles are custom-mold PVC finished in a light beige color with gold hot-stamped lettering.

Client: La Costa Products International, Carlsbad, California.
Consultant Design: Design West: Dale D. Smith, senior industrial designer.

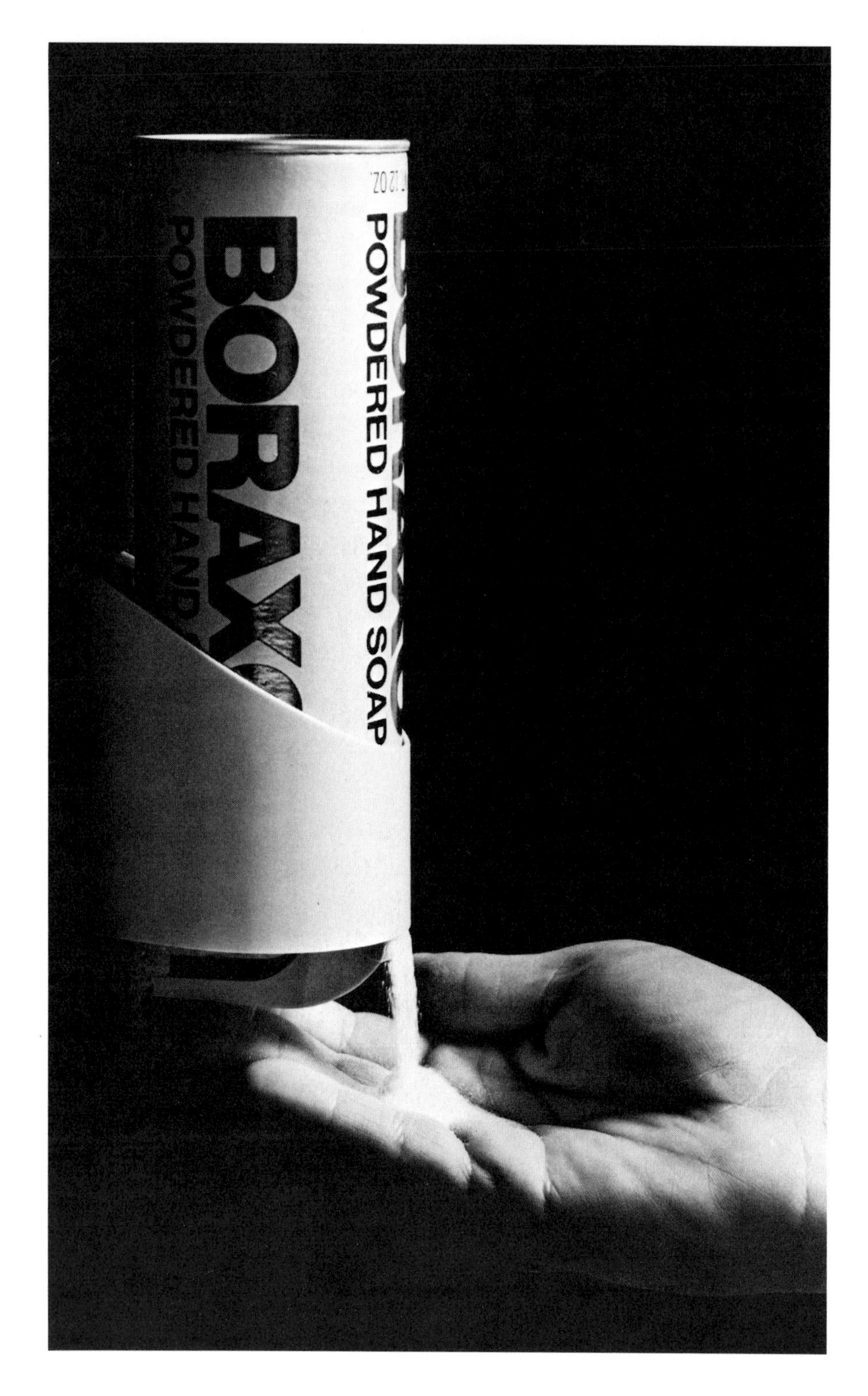

U.S. Borax Powdered Soap Dispenser

An inexpensive, reliable dispenser, this product was designed as part of a promotional campaign to ensure continued sales of Borax powdered soap after initial purchase of soap plus dispenser. Keeping assembly costs minimal because low-cost production was a primary objective, the lever merely pops into the main housing and the wall bracket locks in position. The assembled unit is then simply dropped into a box with the soap cannister in place for shipment. A cannister of soap with dispenser retails for about $0.61. The dispenser can be mounted on any surface with screws or with the double-faced adhesive tape provided. Several working prototypes were tested to ensure a dependable working unit. Human factors considerations include: position of user's hands in relation to the dispenser; ease of operation; and dispensing level. The unit weighs 2 oz (56.7 g). The height from tip to tip is 4⅝ in. (11.8 g); width is 3 in. (7.6 cm).

Materials and Fabrication: Main body and wall-mounting bracket are injection-molded from high-impact styrene finished in off-white; the dispensing level is injection-molded acetal finished in gray.

Manufacturer: U.S. Borax, Los Angeles, California.
Staff Design: Michael Pascal, coordinator.
Consultant Design: S.G. Hauser Associates, Inc.: Stephen G. Hauser, president, designer; Sheldon Keith, associate designer; Paul Greskovics, design draftsman.

Airwick "Stick Ups"
A small-room air freshener composed of two halves and a "blotter-paper" odor counteractant carrier can be hidden from sight without reducing its effectiveness. Completely automated in assembly, the air freshener screws tightly shut for shipment and is easily unscrewed again when in use (like the lid of a jar), exposing an opening that allows the chemicals to enter the air. This opening extends the height of the container from ⅞ in. (2.2 cm) when closed to 1⅛ in. (2.9 cm) when fully opened. 3M double-stick tape allows the small, 2¾-in. (7-cm) diameter unit to be placed under tables, against walls, and in other inconspicuous locations.

Materials and Fabrication: Injection-molded 0.080-in. (2.1-mm) wall polypropylene with a matte textured finish in off-white, black, or brown.

Manufacturer: Airwick Industries, Inc., Carlstadt, New Jersey.
Staff Design: Wes Buckner, vice president, marketing; Donald Fischer, vice president, research and development; Lawrence Graf, vice president, operations.
Consultant Design: Robert Hain Associates, Inc.: Frederick B. Hadtke, vice president, industrial design; Peter F. Connolly, vice president, industrial design.

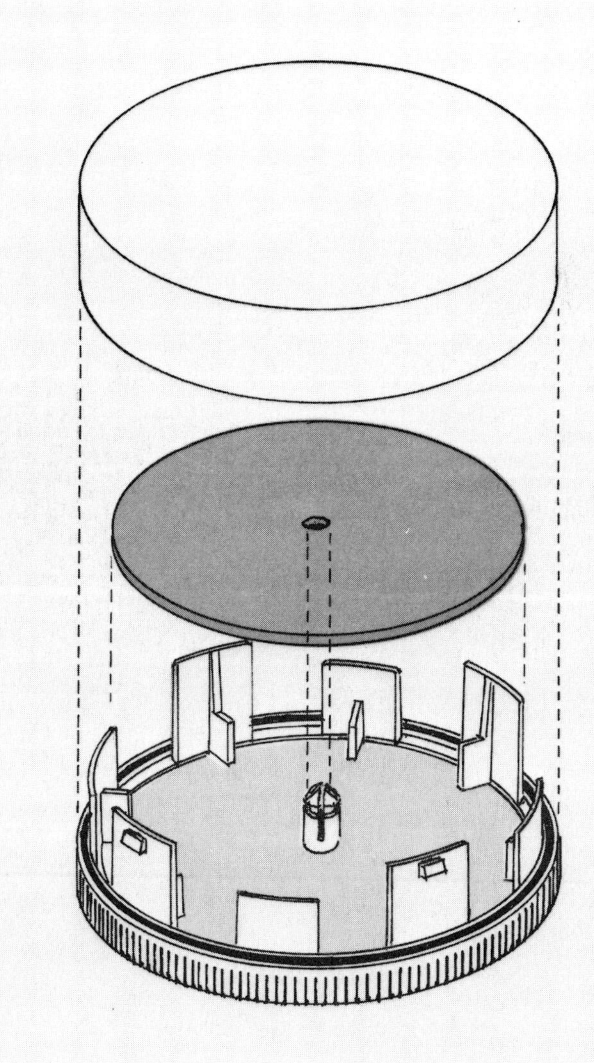

Norelco HB1115 Food Processor
Taking the place of at least five conventional kitchen gadgets and doing the job with ease, this multi-purpose counter-top appliance chops, grates, mixes, shreds, whips, slices, kneads, blends, and purees in a matter of seconds. The user simply feeds food through the funnel, moving it down with the food pusher provided so that the food makes contact with the appropriate attachment. The processed food collects in a bowl with an eight-cup capacity. When chopping meat or kneading dough, for example, the food is placed in the bowl first, with the proper attachments, and then processed. The four attachments include: stainless steel chopping blade, plastic mixing blade, and stainless steel slicing/grating disks. In addition the processor comes equipped with a food pusher, which doubles as a one-cup measure, and a plastic spatula for food removal. All parts that come in contact with food are dishwasher safe. Unlike competitive units, which feature round bowls sitting atop rectangular bases, this product is totally rounded, taking less counter space. The processor measures 14¼ x 8¼ (36.2 x 21 cm), with a 9¼ in. (23.5 cm) diameter. Wherever possible sharp corners have been eliminated for safety and cleaning purposes, with a conscious effort made to integrate the form of the bowl to the form of the base. A simple-to-operate slide switch for on/off/pulse action is located on the machine's left. Users can operate the food pusher with the right hand while the left hand controls the switch. The special pulse action provides instant control for split-second precision in processing. The unit also features a safety lock lid assembly and sturdy base to prevent shifting; direct drive motor provides quiet, dependable operation. The 550-watt processor retails for $109.98.

Materials and Fabrication: Cabinet, bowl, and bowl cover are .120-in. (3.1-mm) injection-molded polycarbonate; base and rear panel are .100-in. (2.5-mm) injection-molded polycarbonate; food pusher is .080-in. (20.3-mm) injection-molded polycarbonate; mixing attachment is .140-in. (3.6-mm) injection-molded polycarbonate; slicing disc is .020-in. (.5-mm) stamped and drawn stainless steel; blade is stamped, ground, and spot-welded cutlery grade stainless steel. Cabinet base and mixing attachment are all finished in polished off-white; rear panel has a textured black finish; bowl and bowl cover are finished in a polished transparent bronze tint.

Manufacturer: North American Philips Corp., Consumer Products Divisions, New York, New York.
Staff Design: William J. Rakocy, manager, industrial design; Masao Tsuji, project designer; Frederick Snyder, project engineer; Albert E. Simon, Jr., director of engineering.

JCPenney Slow Cook Broiler Oven

Designed for broiling, baking, roasting, and slow-cooking efficiency, this energy- and space-saving countertop appliance measures a compact 10½ x 21½ x 14½ in. (26.7 x 54.6 x 36.8 cm). The small, self-cleaning, insulated oven reduces wasted heat and cooking time. Retailing for $69.99, the product also holds foods at proper serving temperature and defrosts frozen food. Uncomplicated, clearly marked controls aid in ease of use and have earned a best-buy recommendation from *Consumer Report* magazine.

Materials and Fabrication: Stamped and injection-molded cold-rolled steel chrome plated phenolic with a chrome and black phenolic finish.

Manufacturer: McGraw-Edison Co., Portable Appliance and Tool Group, Columbia, Missouri.
Client: JCPenney Co., New York, New York.
Staff Design: Michael Boehm, senior product designer, JCPenney; Harold W. Rice, manager of design, McGraw-Edison.

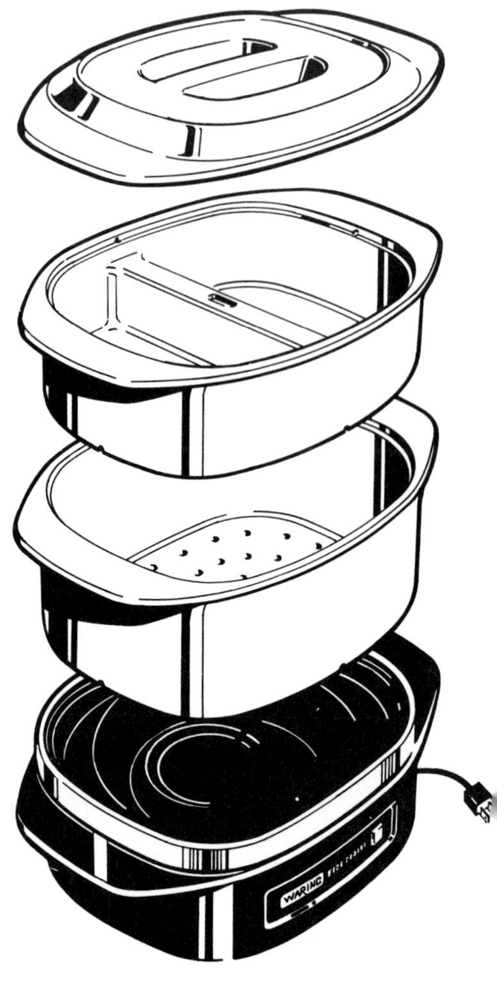

Waring Steam Chef™
Designed to cook whole meals at once, this pressureless steam cooker will prepare most foods in less than 30 minutes. Unlike boiling, baking, and frying, steam cooking retains essential vitamins and other nutrients, uses no additional fats or oils, and provides naturally low-calorie meals. To operate, the user pours water, wine, or beer into the bottom heating section and places meat, fish, or poultry in the lower, larger steaming vessel with a perforated bottom. A choice of two sidedishes in the divided upper vessel is possible. The final step is simply to stack the meal and steam it. As a safety feature, the product will automatically shut off if more liquid is needed. All vessels double as serving dishes. The lid, used as a cover while cooking, inverts to become a drip/serve tray for the large perforated steaming vessel. This perforated bowl may also be used independently with the lid for cooking. All vessels are easy-cleaning, heat-resistant Melamine. Additional bowls are also available. Using only 750 watts, one-sixteenth of the wattage of an electric oven and two range burners, the product is fuel-efficient. In addition, the stackable Steam Chef™ occupies little counterspace. Measuring 10½ x 11⅝ x 8½ in. (26.7 x 29.5 x 21.6 cm), the product weighs 26.2 lb (11.9 kg). Suggested retail price is $55.

Materials and Fabrication: Steaming vessels are .100 in. (2.5 mm) congression-molded Melamine finished in off-white; heating vessel is .100 in. (2.5 mm) congression-molded phenolic finished in dark brown; heating vessel top is .100 in. (2.5 mm) cast aluminum with "Rock Bottom" coating applied to exposed cast piece finished in black with brushed rim.

Manufacturer: OEM, Winona, Minnesota.
Client: Waring Products Division, Dynamics Corp. of America, New Hartford, Connecticut.
Staff Design: Earl McCleerey, project supervisor, engineer.
Consultant Design: Herbst/LaZar Design, Inc.: Randall Bell, partner, project leader, designer.

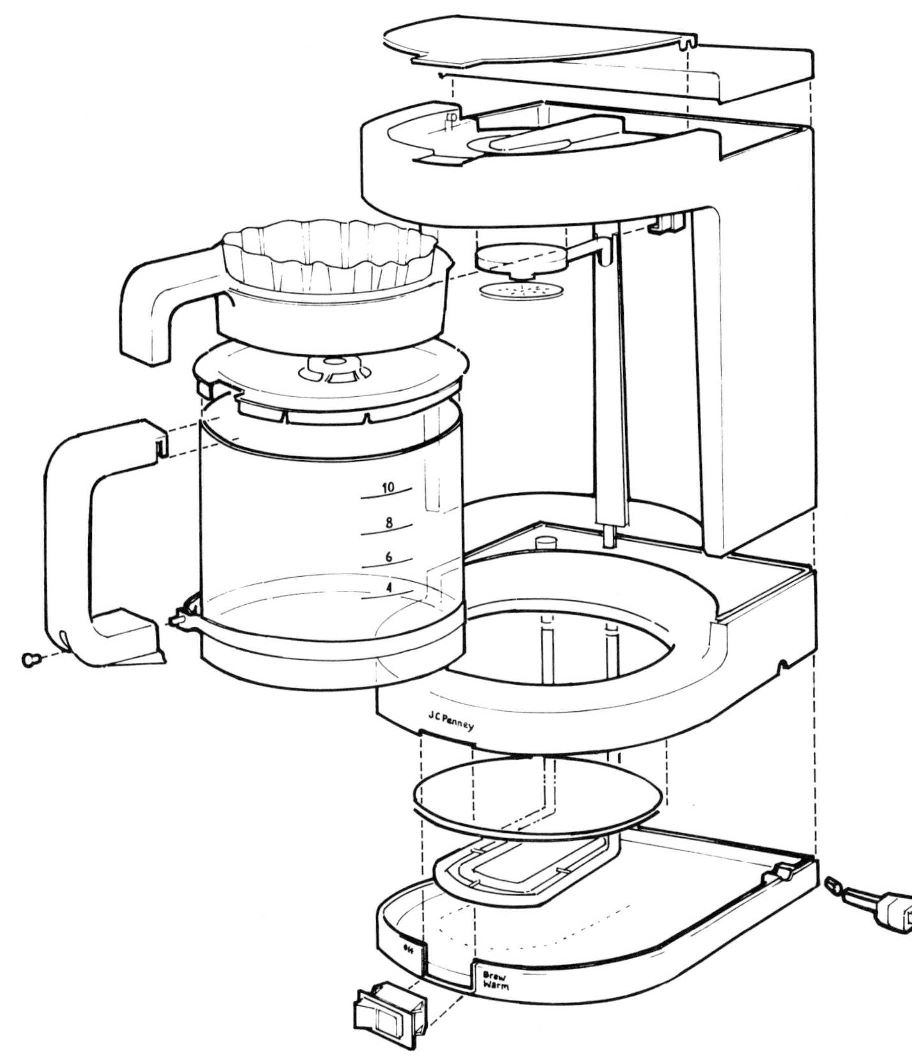

JCPenney Drip Coffeemaker
Eliminating the need for filter-papers, the JCPenney drip coffeemaker with a permanent plastic filter can brew up to 10 cups of coffee in less than 10 minutes. The unit, which can also be used with paper filters, keeps coffee at the "perfect" serving temperature with an automatic thermostat. Its compact, low-profile design allows the user to fill the unit with water without having to move it from under kitchen cabinets or similar limited-space storage placements in the kitchen. Its flat back that fits snugly against any wall also boosts space efficiency. One lighted warm/brew, on/off switch and a carafe lid that won't fall off aid in ease of use. With a 4- to 10-cup capacity, the unit is 7¼ x 10¼ x 11½ in. (18.4 x 26 x 29.2 cm). Other features include: a shower-head type of water dispenser which distributes water evenly, wetting all the coffee and eliminating the need for mechanical levers on the "coffee saver"; short cord line for safety; and removable coffee basket. The 1000-watt appliance retails for $24.99.

Materials and Fabrication: Injection-molded ABS; transfer-molded phenolic, painted to match body color; drawn and stamped aluminum; molded glass; silkscreened logo and switch instructions; tooled in instructions in lid and technical data on bottom.

Manufacturer: Munnekata Co., Japan.
Client: JCPenney Co., New York, New York.
Staff Design: Michael Boehm, senior product designer; J. Christopher Hacker, product designer; Joan Grieb, product designer; Marion Costa, detailer.

Norelco Super Juicer™
Model HB1110

Operating on four flashlight batteries, the cordless, portable, dishwasher-safe citrus juicer can be used anywhere and will provide approximately 16-qt (15.1 l) of juice before batteries need changing. To activate the motor, the user removes the cover and presses fruit halves down on the reamer; lift fruit and the unit stops. Safe to operate and clean, the switch is engaged only during momentary use. When the reamer is removed, the juice may be poured or stored in a lower container with a 1-pt (0.5-l) capacity. All fibers and pulp are strained automatically. By compacting the gear train and relocating the batteries, the center of gravity has been lowered to stabilize the unit and prevent tipping. Nonskid rubber feet also steady the product, discouraging movement while in use. All corners have been radiused for easy cleaning. Other convenient features include a storage lid cover to eliminate preliminary rinsing of a dusty container and integrated handle for compact storage. Retailing for $14.95, the unit is 6 in. (15.2 cm) high and 6 in. (15.2 cm) in diameter and weighs 2½ lb (1.13 kg).

Materials and Fabrication: Cover and container are .100 in. (2.5 mm) thickness RN-103 polyethylene teraphthalate finished in a clear bronze tint; the reamer is .100 in. (2.5 mm) thickness Sho-allomar FA-410 polypropylene finished in bright yellow; cabinet and base are off-white .100 in. (2.5 mm) thickness medium-impact styrene. All major components are injection-molded.

Manufacturer: North American Philips Corp., Consumer Products Division, New York, New York.

Staff Design: William J. Rakocy, manager, industrial design; Ronald Muller, project industrial designer; Frederick Snyder, project engineer; Albert J. Simon, Jr., director of engineering; Masao Tsuji, industrial designer.

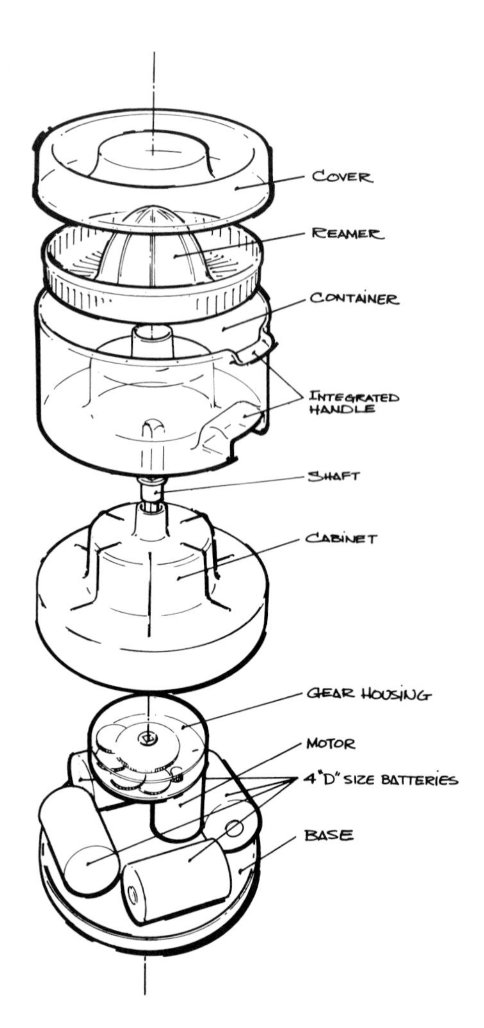

Copco Cast Aluminum Cookware
Copco stove-top cast aluminum cookware, featuring even heat distribution, offers a lightweight alternative to cast iron cookware. All pieces come with ground bottoms for perfect contact on countertop burners, discouraging the scorching or sticking usually associated with uneven heat distribution. The line includes: an 11-in. (27.9-cm) grill pan retailing for $33; a 10-in. (25.4-cm) skillet at $33; 10-in. (25.4-cm) skillet cover for $17; an 8½-in. (21.6-cm) omelet pan at $20; a 12-in. (30.5-cm) chicken fryer with cover, retailing at $60; and a 7½-in. (19.1-cm) crepe pan for $19. Each item is hand polished to provide a beautiful surface that's easy to clean. Teakwood handles are designed for balance.

Materials and Fabrication: The line is made of die-cast aluminum with a hand-polished surface.

Manufacturer: Copco, New York, New York.
Consultant Design: Michael Lax, designer.

Corning Ware® Grab-It® Bowl
Fabricated from a glass ceramic material, this versatile ramekin for cooking or reheating food may be used on range tops and in broilers, ovens, or microwave ovens. The 15-oz (425.3-g) bowl then goes directly to the table for individual service. In addition it is safe for all methods of cooling. Its size and shape, with integral handle, meet the functional requirements of cooking and the esthetic requirement for table service. A set of two retail for $7.99.

Materials and Fabrication: Pressed Corning Ware® glass ceramic finished in white.

Manufacturer: Corning Glass Works, Consumer Products Division, Corning, New York.
Staff Design: Richard W. Greger, project coordinator.
Consultant Design: Davin Stowell, designer.

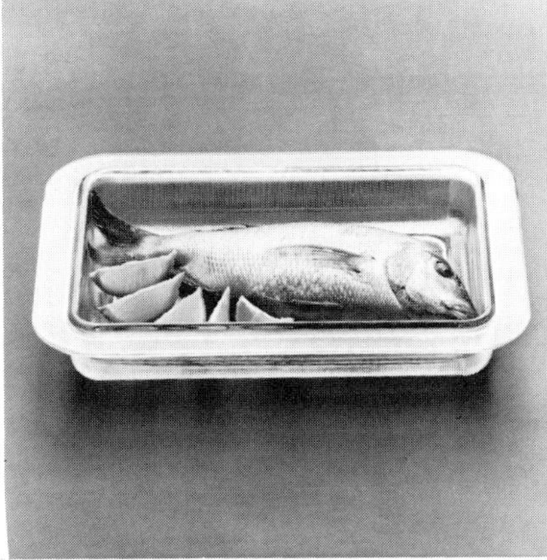

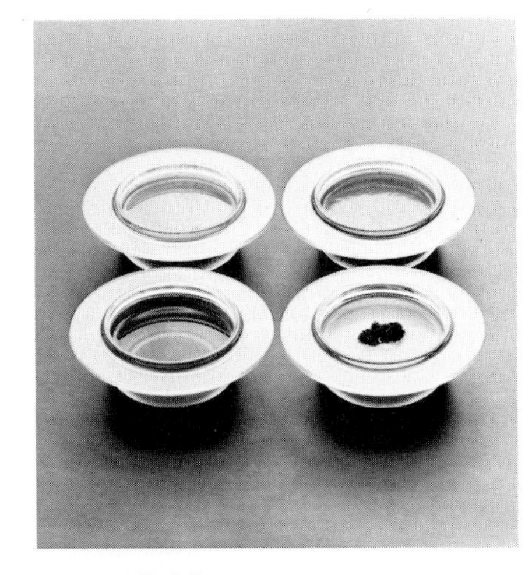

Heller Designs Bakeware
8-in. Square Cake Baking Dish
1-qt Casserole with Au Gratin Cover
2-qt Casserole with Au Gratin Cover
9-oz Custard Ramekin
#509 Pie Plate

Dual-purpose, ovenproof glass bakeware was designed to also function as attractive serving dishes. A convenient border rim completely surrounds each product, providing a handle for easy grasping. These well-designed alternatives to Pyrex include: a 10 x 10⅛ x 2 1/16 in. (25.4 x 25.7 x 5.2 cm) baking dish retailing for $8.95; 9-oz (0.3-l) custard ramekin (set of four), measuring 6⅜ in. (16.2 cm) in diameter and 2 in. (5.1 cm) high for $11.95; 1-qt (0.9-l) casserole, 8 in. (20.3 cm) in diameter and 4 13/16 in. (12.2 cm) high at $9.95; 2-qt (1.9-l) casserole, 9½ in. (24.1 cm) in diameter and 5½ in. (14 cm) high at $12.95; and pie plate, 11½ in. (29.2 cm) in diameter and 1⅝ in. (4.1 cm) high at $6.95.

Materials and Fabrication: Automatic pressed Borosilicate ovenproof glass.

Manufacturer: Heller Designs, Inc., Mamaroneck, New York.
Consultant Design: Lella Vignelli and Massimo Vignelli, designers.

Contract and Residential

Nelson Workspaces
Steelcase 400 Series Designs in Wood
Steelcase 454 Series Office Seating
Vertebra Seating System
Robin Modular Soft Seating
Floating Seating by Harvey Probber
Sico Floating Fold Wall Table
Shelf Life Unlimited
Attache and Credenza Light Dimmers
Versaplex Light Dimming System
Air Plastics Salt and Pepper Shakers
Becker Model Q1 Time Instruments

The jurors touched many bases in the course of the judging. The impact of the inflationary spiral in economics on design is important here. Consideration of ergonomics continues as an expected requirement in design. And, as in Consumer Products, the endorsement situation of nondesigners is a concern. The number of submissions in the category was 49, up from 37 last year. Of these, 12 were accepted, compared with 8 in 1976.

Members of the jury panel were Randall Peter Buhk, Olga Gueft, and Noel Mayo.

Randall Peter Buhk
As industrial design project manager for Steelcase in Grand Rapids, Michigan, Peter Buhk has total responsibility for coordinating projects and is involved in all phases of engineering and project planning and to a lesser extent marketing and sales. His position involves human factors research, analysis, and project supervision of the design and development of a new product from concept to manufacture. A full member of the Industrial Designers Society of America, he is also presently a member of the Kendall School of Design advisory committee. A University of Illinois graduate with a BFA in industrial design, Buhk has received numerous awards, including honorable mention for a mobile home design in the Reynolds Metal National Creative Design Award contest; the Design in Michigan award for the 430 Seating Series; the Institute of Business Designers Silver Award for the 454 Seating Series; and the selection of the 421 Seating Series for the 1976 Design Review in the Contract and Residential category. Before beginning work as a senior industrial designer at Steelcase in 1967, Buhk worked with Lawrence H. Wilson Associates in Franklin Park, Illinois, for two years and with Good Design Associates in South Bend, Indiana, for a year.

Olga Gueft
Editorial director of *Contract Interiors* since 1973 when *Interiors* magazine split into separate contract and residential publications, Olga Gueft has won, both personally and for the magazine, 20 Neal Editorial and Industrial Marketing awards for excellence since she became an editor with the magazine. A participant in the design scene during three decades of exciting and rapid development, Gueft received the first and only Joint Press Award for her contribution to the profession from the Association of Interior Designers (AID) and the National Society of Interior Designers (NSID), prior to their consolidation into the American Society of Interior Designers. A Hunter College graduate, Gueft also studied design, art education, and textile arts at City College of New York and New York University. Joining the staff of *Progressive Architecture* in 1943, Gueft became managing editor of *Interiors* in 1945 and editor in 1953. Currently an ASID press member, she lectures frequently on the interiors industry and its role in the design world.

Noel Mayo
As chairman of the industrial design department at Philadelphia College of Art (PCA), Noel Mayo is dedicated to the task of turning out design professionals, as opposed to students who become professionals at someone else's expense. For the past nine years he has also owned and operated his own firm, Noel Mayo Associates in Philadelphia, which does work in commercial interiors on a custom basis. While currently president of the Greater Philadelphia Community Development Corporation and a member of the Philadelphia Design Group, he was invited this year to participate in a workshop on the built environment sponsored by public television's WNET 13 to aid in the development of a pilot series that would make design understandable to the general public. Mayo holds a BS degree in industrial design from the Philadelphia College of Art, where he graduated in 1960. He was the recipient of the third Alcoa Adventures in Design grant for promising young design-

ers and the Alumni Award from PCA.

Comments from the jury panelists on the submissions in this category follow.

Moderator: What are your feelings about the quality of what you have seen today? What trends do you see emerging in the area of contract and residential furnishings, and where do you think it is headed?

Mayo: I'm not sure I see any trends at all emerging out of the things we just went through. I think the design problems are still the same. The biggest problems that we face as designers, generally, is to recognize this inability to communicate our ideas to management so that we can have a major kind of influence on the future. One thing that's really going to change the marketplace, I believe, is economics—the idea that you don't have to keep making 400 clock radios under one brandname to compete successfully in the marketplace. Economics won't justify that much longer. And that's going to change, hopefully, the quality of design.

Buhk: I didn't see any real trends in any of the entries, either. I didn't see anything that was knocked out that I hadn't seen knocked out before or attempted before. I'm still somewhat appalled with designers who design seating that wasn't meant to be sat in, and I'll never change my feeling about that. I think something you sit in isn't really a seat unless it is sittable.

Moderator: What are the trends in this whole area—whether or not they're represented in what you saw here?

Buhk: I think, as an architect told me last year, the buzz word is "ergonomics." I think that's a trend. I think a requirement of office chairs is that they be comfortable. At Steelcase we get involved in the seating project right from the word "go"—how we're going to make it a comfortable thing. Comfort is a very subjective quality to a certain extent, yet it's pretty well defined by a lot of people who are doing human factors and anthropometric research. So I think this is a definite trend, but it isn't going to change very quickly. And I think industry is going to eventually address itself to chair-related problems, the desk or work surface problem. You can knock your head off trying to hit all the human factors, and yet if you get a chair at

Left to right: Noel Mayo, Randall Peter Buhk, and Olga Gueft.

the right height for a fifth percentile female and put her at a 30-inch desk, she'll bump her chin on that desk top. So the problem isn't in the chair, it's really in relationship to the work surface.

Gueft: You've already covered the basic points—the effect of the economy and the effect of ergonomics. We're at a period following some extreme sophistication and the economic boom. We have had a very highly developed industry with many new ideas brought sharply about partially by the economy, but also by the fact that so much has been rapidly developed. And now suddenly, we have had to cut down. Yet one of the oddities of bad times, hard times, speaking economically, is that even while the cost of things rises, the willingness of the few people with money to pay for quality remains constant or even continues to rise. So there are all kinds of anomalies and contradictions that are occurring simultaneously. For example, I don't remember what the Finule Chieftain chair cost when it first appeared on the market in 1955, but it was very blandly presented in *The New York Times* recently at an astronomical price.

Mayo: If you have an understanding of economics, then it doesn't matter what you pay for that chair. We're locked into an inflationary spiral, and that's a very good investment because it's only going to go up. People will buy a Rolls Royce or a Finule chair or a $4,000 desk because they simply see it as a better place to spend than putting it in the bank.

Moderator: Do you think it is the designers who are making the products expensive?

Mayo: I think they contribute to it.

Buhk: There are a lot of people who call themselves designers that I don't really classify as industrial designers. They are capable, they communicate well with sketches and renderings, they have a basic knowledge of materials and how to handle them. But when it comes to delivering the goods, they don't seem to care one iota about who the eventual user is or what he can afford. And I think that's very important. For instance, it's very easy to design a $9,500 desk. But try to design one that functions for $150. That's design, when you have limitations that seem like they're insurmountable, when there is a challenge of doing something within the means. It doesn't mean that someone should never do anything for rich people. But it seems like you should be able to find something as gorgeous as the Olafson stereo equipment, for instance, at Sears Roebuck.

Moderator: In this area of furnishings, do you see any trend in terms of more purely functional, simple, elementary kinds of design, such as those being marketed in places like Workbench or Conrans?

Mayo: I think that's a result of economics, as well. As we try to continue to reduce the cost, we have to simplify the design. The economics are beginning to support good design—indirectly, unfortunately. I think many of the people whose work we reviewed have been sincerely concerned about this, but never could influence the marketplace directly.

Moderator: How do you feel about the designer's responsibility to give the people what they need?

Buhk: A designer has a responsibility to people as users, mostly. Perhaps he's the only one in an organization who has thought all the way through the life of a developing product until it goes out the door. The marketing people are concerned with selling the product. The advertising people are concerned with advertising it. The engineering people are concerned with structural aspects. Manufacturers are concerned with manufacturing it, inventorying it, and all that, while the designer has to be responsible to the end-user. Unfortunately, most of the time, not enough information is given to the designer as to the characteristics of the end-user of the product.

Moderator: Most designers would not argue that the designer has a responsibility to provide what the user needs in terms of function and human factors. But esthetics is not as tangible—it's certainly a subjective matter. Does the designer have a responsibility to fulfill his own esthetic or to do something which will presumably satisfy a certain segment of the population, or all of it?

Buhk: In my business you can't separate esthetics from function, manufacturability and the human factors elements in a design. Many times esthetics follow those other, necessary elements to create a total design product.

Moderator: But why is there such a divergence in the esthetics?

Mayo: The critical issue is that esthetics tends to relate to art. Art to me is an emotional decision. It's based on a person's feelings at that moment being expressed about whatever it is. What I'm trying to get people to understand, and move away from, is that good design relates to rational thinking and decisions. If you cannot verbalize those decisions about the design, you're probably wrong. When you say you can't figure out why this thing is kind of idiotic in its esthetics, it's because it is not rational. Good design has to be rational. But what we do is mix up the esthetic kind of intuitive approach to good design as if it contradicted the rational approach to good design.

Moderator: Do they, in fact, conflict with each other? Or do they go hand in hand?

Mayo: I think they can run parallel, perhaps, but in two different areas completely. I think that if you begin to make rational decisions about any kind of form/function relationship, the more rational the relationships are, the clearer and better the design is going to be. The moment the relationships become dominated by emotions—let's put a 40° angle on this based on an intuition or some other arbitrary decision—it's going to be wrong. There's no function to that, there's no reason to it.

Moderator: Aren't there places where, in fact, there are no real functional considerations?

Mayo: I don't think so.

Buhk: I don't think there's a thing that exists without some functional consideration, if it is nothing more than pleasing to the eye.

Moderator: So the visual resolutions are quite limited?

Mayo: They're very rational and limited in terms of the input you have versus the outgrowths. Obviously, you can get 4,000 different chairs that people can sit on, but those are based on the inputs. You can design a chair that will support a back and all that. But the inputs are completely different. This one is upholstered, the other one uses a metal material, and so on. So you get a variety of designs, but that's based on the inputs and the rational decisions of how one uses them.

Moderator: What do you have to say about manufacturers and other business people who are bringing in personalities, like Pierre Cardin, to promote a broad range of designed products?

Buhk: I feel sorry for them because they're going after one man's name and selling it to death. It's an endorsement situation and not a good design situation. And besides, a designer who is good with clothes or perfume isn't necessarily good designing automobile interiors, or stainless steel dinnerware, or anything else for that matter.

Moderator: Is there any way that designers can counteract that or capitalize on it themselves?

Mayo: Designers do not understand what their real skills are. Good designers have skills in analyzing the problem and addressing themselves to the simplest kinds of solutions. But most of them are good designers by intuition only. They haven't learned to verbalize it and market it rationally.

Buhk: When our firm gets bombarded with outside designers coming in with furniture, which we encourage, some of them arrive with the least-thought-out designs you could possibly imagine. They're only selling their name and an esthetic.

Moderator: Isn't there some advantage to that, in terms of pushing technology further through research and development?

Buhk: No. Because you're only going to push technology so far. If a company hasn't got the capital to change its technological base, you're in trouble. I learned a long time ago that you can only push technology so far. It's only ready to move a certain amount. There are all kinds of neat processes for manufacturing out there. When they become practical, large manufacturers get into them, but when they're still in their postbirth stage, most manufacturers are going to stay away from them. When a design comes in the door, it's not going to be strong enough to change technology unless it's a massive system, rather than an individual product. The designers who designed radios did not push transistor technology. Transistor technology pushed them. The designers did not push for a quartz clock. The quartz clock said, "Hey, we can do something." An industrial designer is not the best engineer, he's not the best materials and processes man, he is not the best human factors man. He is not the best communicator there is through rendering or art work, and he is not, perhaps, the best esthetic type. What he has to do is tie it all together.

Mayo: It's the synergy idea. And that's the strength of most industrial designers—the ability to look at all those components and bring forth a better thing, a better solution.

Moderator: Is the task lighting approach simply a buzz word, a marketing concept, or is it a practical improvement in the way we're lighting offices?

Gueft: It is practical. It's very real.

Buhk: The thing which disturbs me is that there are a few power groups in the lighting industry which have a tendency to push for their particular thing—sodium vapor lights, for example, which distort color very badly. If one industry can railroad something like that through, then I think we're in real trouble if we allow it to happen.

Mayo: The whole task lighting system is not the result of good lighting. It's the fact that the rental of floor space is going up, and it's terribly expensive to move. It's one way to cut economically.

Buhk: If you start getting into ambient lighting and task lighting, which is supposed to be more economical? When people start placing table lamps—you can call them task lamps or whatever you like—in different areas of an environment to get illumination, then where is the economy of design starting to go? All it is accomplishing is building up another system with a subsystem, rather than the old-fashioned way.

Moderator: Where is the whole office landscape approach going at this stage?

Buhk: The first thing that anybody saw publicly was the Herman Miller total approach to the office within an office with a roof over it, and George Nelson's umbrella for the privacy routine. I think you're going to see more and more of that. What's happening is we're running into an industry that's trying to develop its own office capsule to go inside a building's skeleton as a sort of solution. I think the open office is not all that it was cut out to be or ever has been. A lot of the investigations people are doing now, gathering research material on the effects of office landscaping over an extended period of time, has somewhat disappointing results. People aren't so gung-ho for office landscaping anymore. It works great when you've got a large amount of space, but that's not economical. It doesn't solve the economic reasons for being there.

Mayo: I read an article that absolutely stunned me. It had to do with the idea that a human being is a computer, and in the next 30 years we will be able to duplicate the brain in the approximate size of a suitcase. With that kind of information transfer, I think the office is going to go right home. You're going to wind up almost never leaving your own private environment.

Buhk: That's the long-range office of the future. Things will become so computerized that businesses will just have several terminals. A guy could work out of his house.

Mayo: They're already taking them home right now. I think in less than 30 years it will be uneconomical to buy a separate space to put people in for eight hours a day when you already pay rent in your own home and can stay there and communicate. We'll pay for the communication systems. I think that's something that the furniture industry really ought to start looking into.

Nelson Workspaces
This office furniture system was developed so that its components could be adapted to the needs of both privacy and openness. The basic core of the system is a desk which can be raised or lowered to suit user preferences. The addition of standard L-shaped panels to the desk provides shelving and privacy screens. Acoustical panels 75 in. (190.5 cm) high in a modular format are also available for conference and executive spaces. The system also features L-shaped bumper bases for the various components, with deep horizontal corrugations and inserts for levelers at three positions on each side. According to the designers, the Nelson Workspaces strike a viable balance between flexibility and "emotional factors" in office systems, (such as faultily designed details which snag on clothing). Work surfaces range in size from 36 x 75 x 1¼ in. (91.4 x 190.5 x 3.2 cm) to 20 x 60 x 1¼ in. (50.8 x 152.4 x 3.2 cm). Unit drawers may be stacked in any configuration required to a height of 24 in. (61 cm). A wide variety of shelf and panel sizes is available, as are a number of office accessories. Baked enamel finishes are available in white,

warm gray, chocolate brown, dark green, green, dark red, red, blue, and yellow.

Materials and Fabrication: The L-shaped bumper base is made of molded high-density polyethylene. Work surfaces are steel core with a high-pressure plastic laminate writing surface and soft vinyl edging. Shelves and drawers are of steel construction, while the accessory panels are made of tubular steel and wood frames, fiberglass core, and fabric covering.

Manufacturer: Storwall International, Toronto, Canada.
Design: Designer initiated this product. George Nelson & Co., New York, New York: George Nelson, designer; Daniel Lewis, collaborating designer; David Schowalter, contributing designer.

Steelcase 400 Series Designs in Wood

This series consists of a full line of medium-priced general and executive office desks, credenzas, and wing units that can be arranged into a variety of conventional work stations. The line features a hidden wiring feature which enables a three-finger amphenol to be fed down the inside of the desk panel by simply removing the panel top cap. This cap is then replaced to conceal all but the ½-in. (1.3-cm) opening for the cord. The structure basically combines the strength and durability of a concealed steel inner frame with the tactile quality of a solid exterior; thus, a "soft edge, all-wood" look is created. The line also has a central lock feature, located in the unit's top, that controls all drawers with one key. All work surfaces are 29½ in. (74.9 cm) from top to floor and all machine height surfaces are 26 in. (66 cm) from top to floor. Knee clearance on all units is 25 in. (63.5 cm). According to the manufacturer, the new line is successful in minimizing labor and finishing operations while retaining the rich qualities of costlier, softly detailed desk lines.

Materials and Fabrication: Steel components are formed and welded by conventional methods and painted with a high abrasion-resistant acrylic-baked finish. Wood panels are fabricated by cold-pressing veneers to the particleboard core. All exposed wood exterior surfaces, machined with conventional woodworking machinery, are finished with a synthetic super-catalyzed oil finish. A six-step process is used to obtain the light oak, dark oak, and walnut veneer finishes offered.

Manufacturer: Steelcase, Inc., Grand Rapids, Michigan.
Staff Design: James Breidenbach, industrial designer; Jack Hockenberry, director, new product research and design.

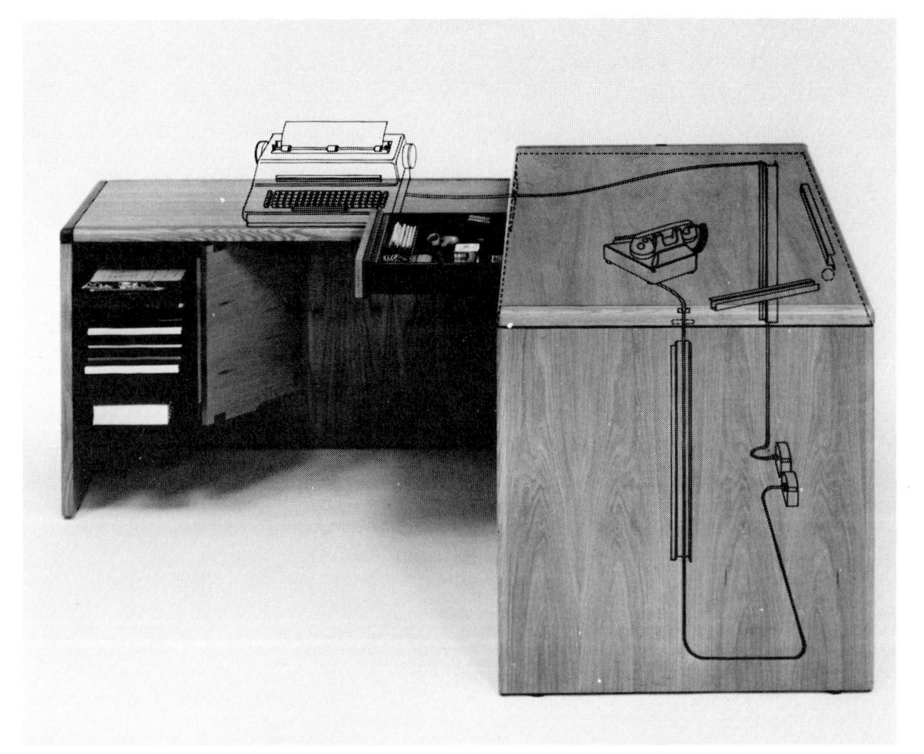

Steelcase 454 Series Office Seating

The 454 is a general purpose chair which, according to the manufacturer, can accommodate adults ranging in size from the 5th through 95th percentiles, minimize most factors that cause discomfort in long-term sitting, and still maintain the economic advantages of double shell technology. Much of the research that went into this design was developed by Dr. Clara Ridder at the University of Arkansas, who studied the relationship between proper posture and contoured shapes. The chair's overall dimensions are 33 in. (83.3 cm) to 35 7/16 in. (90 cm) high, 24⅝ in. (62.6 cm) wide, and 24⅛ in. deep (61.3 cm).

Materials and Fabrication: The basic construction of this seating series consists of an outer trim shell attached to an inner structural assembly. The outer shell is injection-molded polypropylene with its perimeter so formed as to be its own bumper. The inner structural element consists of a structural steel frame assembly with suspended, contoured seat and back panels. All other elements—the outer shell, arms, chair control, seat, and back panels—are attached to this structural frame. The foam cushioning is urethane. The various models include: arm or armless, swivel/tilt, swivel or fixed base, and casters or glides. Upholstery is available in a variety of Steelcase SCM fabrics, vinyl, leather, and COM.

Manufacturer: Steelcase Inc., Grand Rapids, Michigan.
Staff Design: R. Peter Buhk, industrial designer.

Vertebra Seating System
Extensive cardiovascular and orthopedic research played an important role in the design of this new seating system, which provides healthful support for any seated body posture. The system was designed to fulfill the seated person's functional, psychological, behavioral, esthetic, and comfort needs. The manufacturer worked out a group of simple mechanisms which automatically change the chair's configuration without manipulation of controls or levers. These mechanisms are hidden beneath neoprene bellows, which also serve as armrest padding on certain models. A five-blade base with rounded edges was adopted for the system. Several models are offered: executive, managerial, operational, institutional, and tandem seating, each with its appropriate operational characteristics. Chair dimensions range from 37⅜ x 22½ in. (94.9 x 57.2 cm) for the executive to 28⅜ x 19⅛ in. (72.1 x 48.6 cm) for the operational chairs. Ergonomic tests were performed by the Instituto Rizzolli of Bologna, Italy, and the structural tests were based on Business and Institutional Furniture Manufacturers Association (BIFMA) standards.

Materials and Fabrication: The outer and inner shells are made of injection-molded polypropylene for strength. The pedestal bases are made of die-cast aluminum. The upholstery is polyester stretch fabric over polyfoam. Movable mechanisms are made of tubular steel and injection-molded polyurethane and nylon. Most parts are black; fabrics are available in 10 colors.

Manufacturer: Krueger, Green Bay, Wisconsin.

Staff Design: Richard J. Resch, executive vice president; Thomas H. Tolleson, director of design.
Consultant Design: The Center for Design Research & Development: Emilio Ambasz and Giancarlo Piretti, designers.

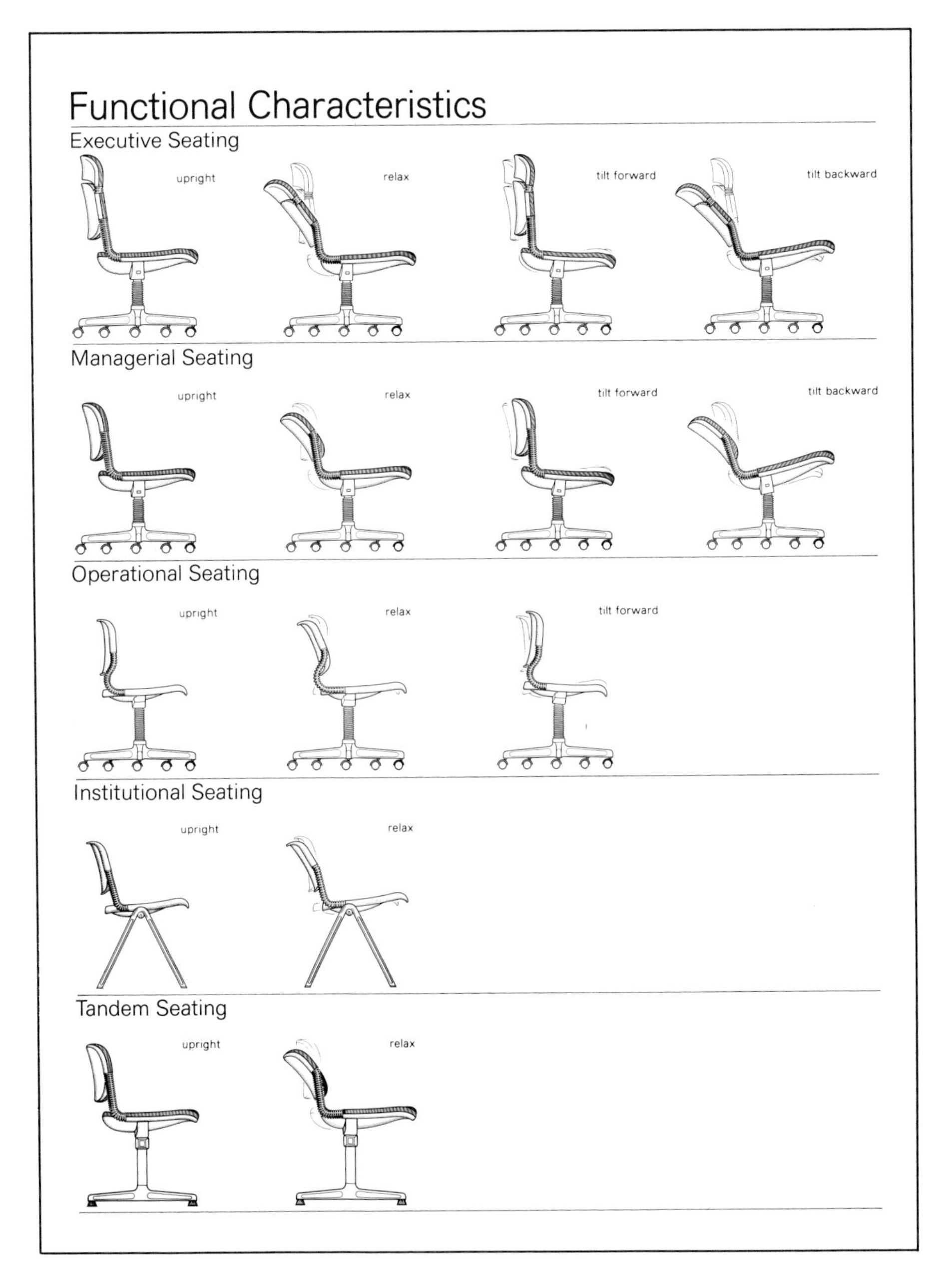

Robin Modular Soft Seating
The aim of this project was the development of a comfortable, easily manufactured, moderately priced lounge seating group. Design for the seating support frame, purposely kept simple and non-labor-intensive to lower costs, contains a minimum of standard modular steel tubes for ease of assembly and shipment. Research using numerous prototype pieces allowed the investigation of materials, sources of supply, and fabrication techniques. The frame accepts interchangeable and reversible cushions for the seat and back and the armrests are removable and can be used both right and left. Upholstery for the unit is zipper closed and can be easily removed for cleaning. Robin is available in one- to four-seat versions that are convertible to other sizes with stock manufacturer's parts. Overall depth of the unit is 31 in. (78.7 cm). Overall width of the single seat unit is 37 in. (94 cm); 62 in. (157.5 cm) for the two-seat unit; 87 in. (221 cm) for the three-seat unit; and 112 in. (284.5 cm) for the four-seat version.

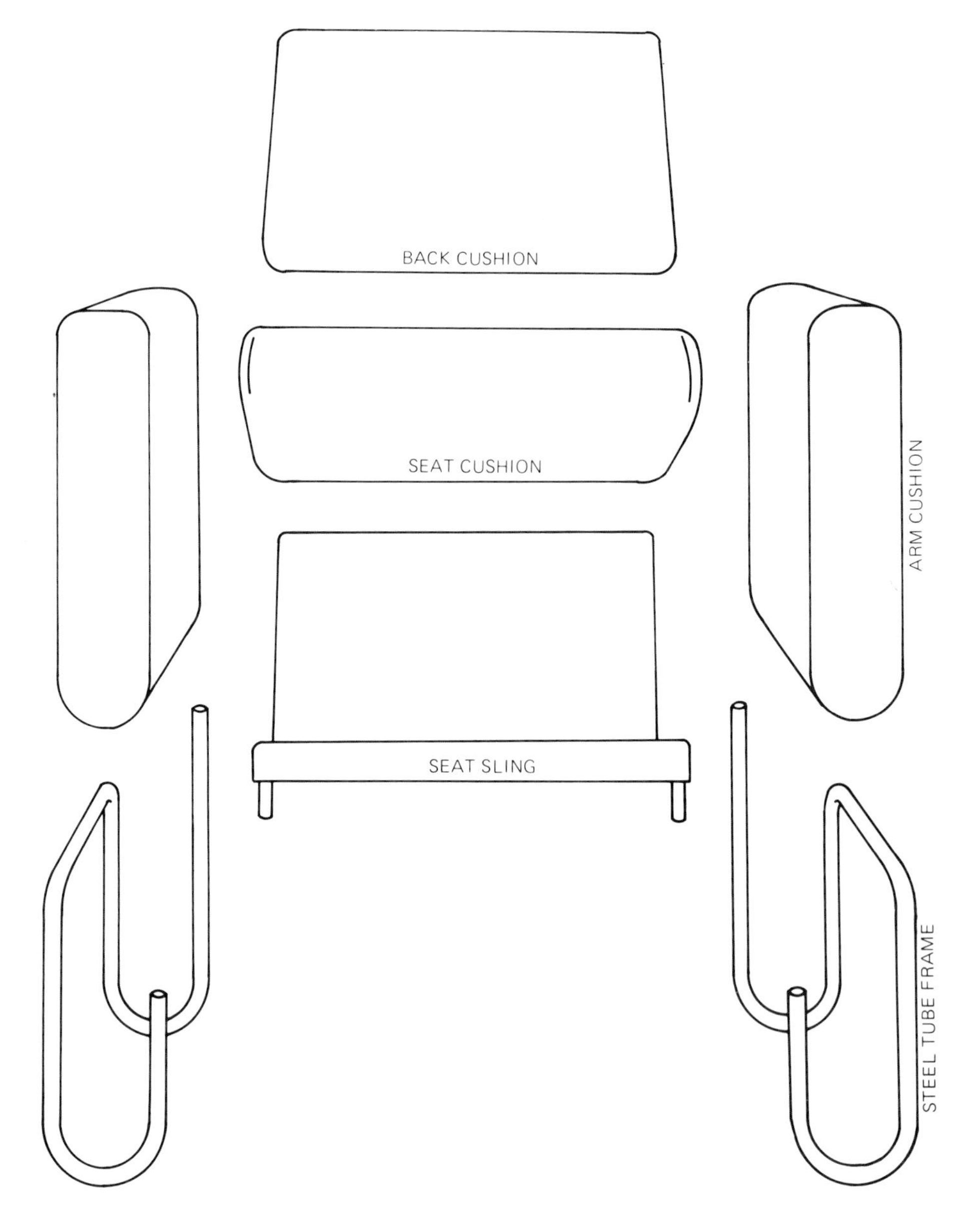

Materials and Fabrication: Side support frames are made of 1 in. (2.5 cm) O.D. 12 gauge furniture grade welded steel tubing with mirror-polished chrome finish and steel screw joinery. Seat and back cushions consist of dual density polyurethane foam with dacron wrap. Upholstery covers are available in fabric, vinyl, or leather.

Manufacturer: JG Furniture, Quakertown, Pennsylvania.
Staff Design: David Woods, design director.

Floating Seating by Harvey Probber

The concept behind this project was to design lightly scaled seating for contract applications. Durability and minimal maintenance were prime criteria in the planning. As a result, this new line of lounge seating has little ground-level structure to block cleaning apparatus and contains no loose parts which can be taken away. It is also constructed from a minimum amount of material, in contrast with most competitors' products. The use of in-house prototypes and evaluations by factory employees were important in planning comfort considerations. The seat "floats" above two steel rails that support, but do not restrict, the flexing of the seating surface. Upholstery is fastened to the plastic shell by means of staples. Side support panels are made of plywood when covered with fabric or oak butcher block when exposed. Jurors had mixed feelings about the comfort of this seating, but the all-around soundness of the solution was enough to win acceptance.

Materials and Fabrication: The seating shell is made of vacuum-formed styrene injected with urethane foam. The unit's structure consists of bent and welded steel tubing, while the table elements are fiberglass with metal clip fasteners. The backrest, also molded, contains a fully sprung frame encapsulated within the foam. Dimensions of the unit are 28 in. (71.1 cm) wide, 28½ in. (72.4 cm) deep, 18 in. (45.7 cm) high to seat; 32 in. (81.3 cm) high to top of backrest.

Manufacturer: Harvey Probber Inc., Fall River, Massachusetts.
Staff Design: Harvey Probber, president; Charles Keane, director of product development.

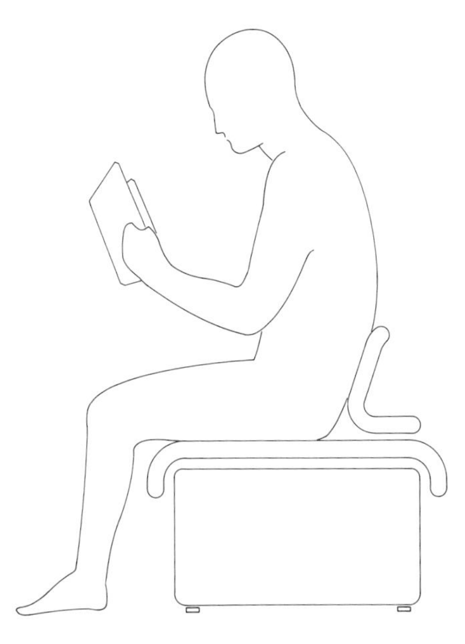

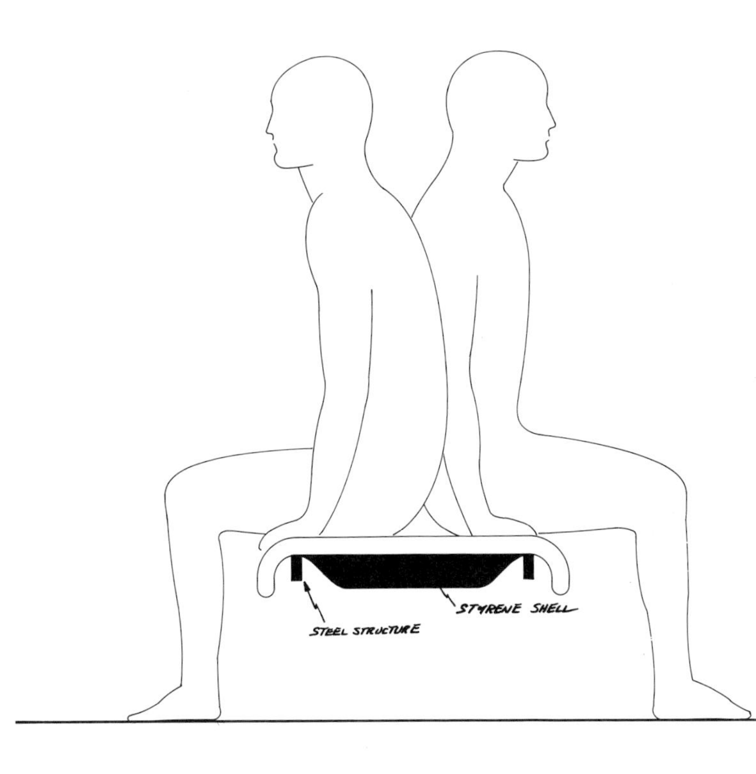

Sico Floating Fold Wall Table

This wall-mounted folding table was developed from the manufacturer's standard inventory items to meet the needs of a study done of efficiency apartments. The table can be used for dining or utility purposes and then be returned to the wall by releasing two lock pins. Less than 10 lb (4.6 kg) of force are required for this operation, enabling the widest number of consumers to use it conveniently. The specially developed steel hinge minimizes interference with usable space (so important in the limited spaces in which many are forced to live) without sacrificing sturdiness. The top measures 30 x 48 in. (76.2 x 121.9 cm), dining room enough for five people. The unit may be installed at any height above 25 in. (63.5 cm), with the recommended installation height 29 in. (75 cm). Shipping weight is 77 lb (36 kg), the majority of which is carried by the wall or is above the center of gravity.

Materials and Fabrication: The unit is largely made of 1 in. (2.5 cm) by 16 gauge square steel tubing which is welded, punched, and connected in places with standard fasteners. The top is ¾ in. (1.9 cm) riveted particleboard with laminated plastic top and edges. Six colors are available: butcher block, Wexford Irish linen, walnut, glazed oak, harvest leather, and frosty white in durable melamine finish. Other surface materials are also available upon request.

Manufacturer: Sico, Inc., Minneapolis, Minnesota.
Staff Design: Richard Bue, vice president, engineering; Casey Carlson, designer; Kermit Wilson, president/owner.

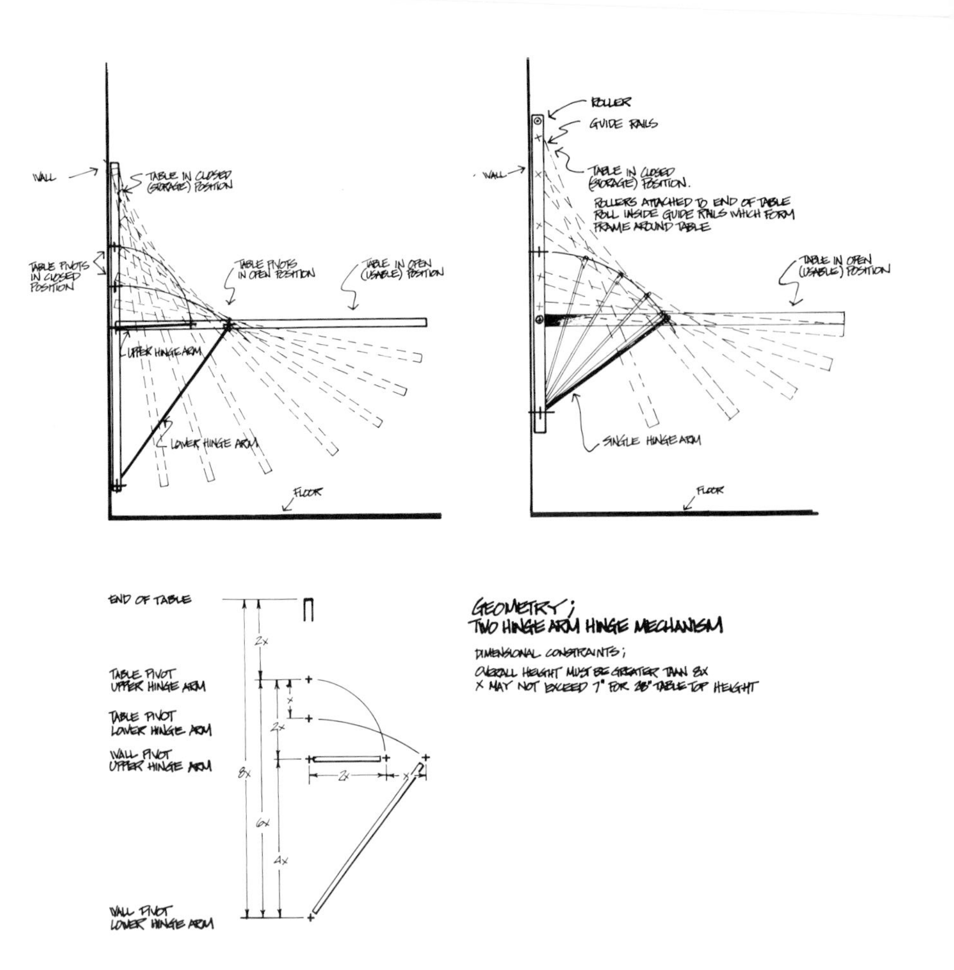

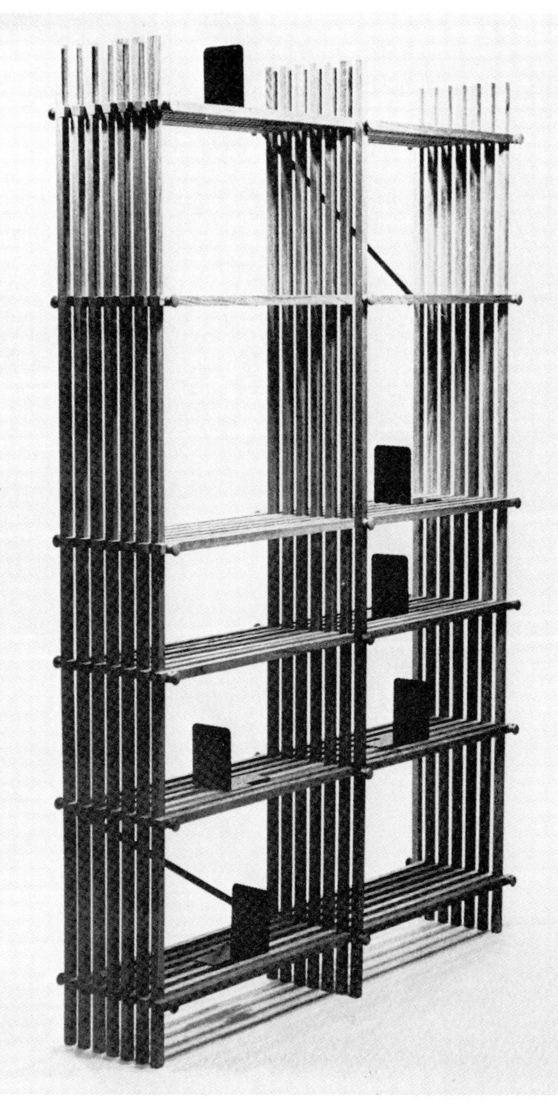

Shelf Life Unlimited

These comparatively light-weight shelf units made with only five basic parts were developed for ease of transportation and economic use of materials. They are shipped in parts and can be stored or consumer assembled. Steel rods running through slat-like wooden members constitute the structure of the unit. The rod ends are hidden under solid knobs, also of wood. The design functions in both a free-standing format and against a wall, finds ready application for a number of household situations, and disassembles for moving or flat storage. In consideration of the merits of this design, the general neatness of its packaging system outweighed the jurors' doubts about its stability.

Materials and Fabrication: Wood members are oiled oak ¾ sq in. (1.9 cm^2) to counteract warpage. Metal braces and optional bookstops are black enameled steel. Four sizes are available: 76½ x 74 in. (194.3 x 188 cm), 76½ x 50 in. (194.3 x 127 cm), 45 x 74 in. (114.3 x 188 cm), and 45 x 50 in. (114.3 x 127 cm); and in two depths, 13 in. (33 cm) and 18 in. (45.7 cm).

Manufacturer: Ray Wilkes & Co., Grand Haven, Michigan.
Staff Design: Ray Wilkes, president, designer.

Attache and Credenza Light Dimmers

Developed to be the first linear dimmers on the market, these compact units—3 x 1½ x ⅞ in. (7.6 x 3.8 x 2.2 cm)—work on a table top or on a lamp cord itself. The credenza can dim up to 300 watts of incandescent light for table and floor lamps that are as far as 4 ft (121.9 cm) away from outlets. The lamp is plugged into the dimmer plug, which is then plugged into the outlet. Also having a capacity of 300 watts incandescent, the Attache is connected to the lamp cord by a molded connector clamp for permanent electrical contact. Both dimmers are operated by a sliding button that can be used by child or adult and feature a positive (audible) off. The dimmers were tested by Underwriter's Laboratory, which approved them.

Materials and Fabrication: The units are made of injection-molded ABS and are available in eggshell white with dark brown buttons or in brown with white buttons.

Manufacturer: Lutron Electronics, Coopersburg, Pennsylvania.
Consultant Design: Noel Mayo Associates, Inc.: Noel Mayo, president, designer.

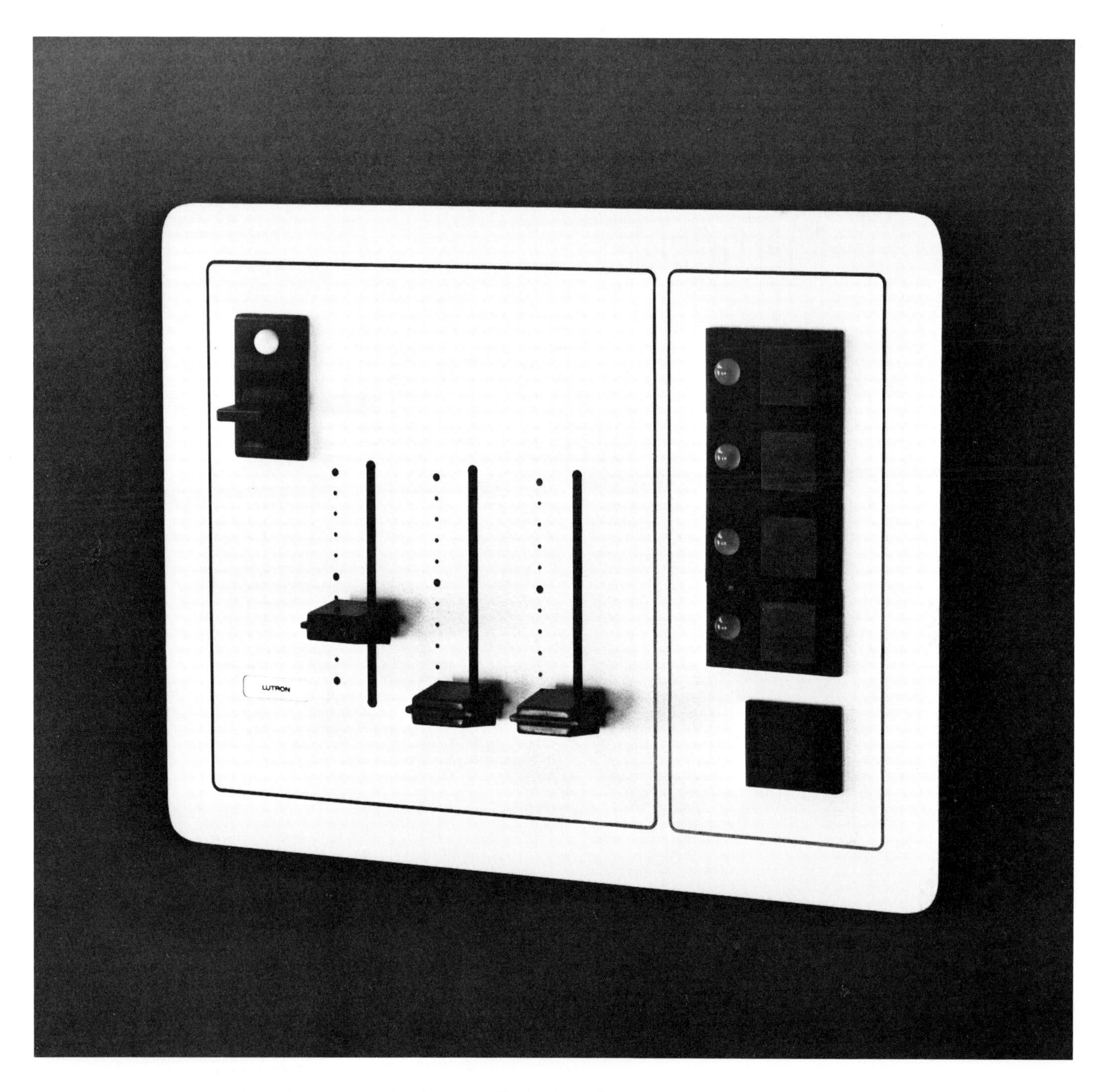

Versaplex Light Dimming System
According to the manufacturer, this electronic system aims for improved, more esthetically pleasing appearance at reasonable cost. It is intended for use in upper-level offices, theaters, and restaurants. The device is capable of dimming up to four light systems in a given area, including both fluorescent and incandescent fixtures. Control can be automatic or manual. A built-in automatic system dims light down to predetermined levels; LEDs indicate which system is in operation. Faceplates for this custom-designed item are available in almost unlimited configurations, depending on need. The faceplate measures 6¾ x 5 in. (17.2 x 12.7 cm). The system was tested and approved by Underwriter's Laboratory.

Materials and Fabrication: The faceplate is ⅛ in. (3.2 mm) brushed aluminum and is produced on an automatic milling machine. The company logo is lithographed onto a clear, anodized finish.

Manufacturer: Lutron Electronics, Inc., Coopersburg, Pennsylvania.
Consultant Design: Noel Mayo Associates, Inc.: Noel Mayo, president, designer.

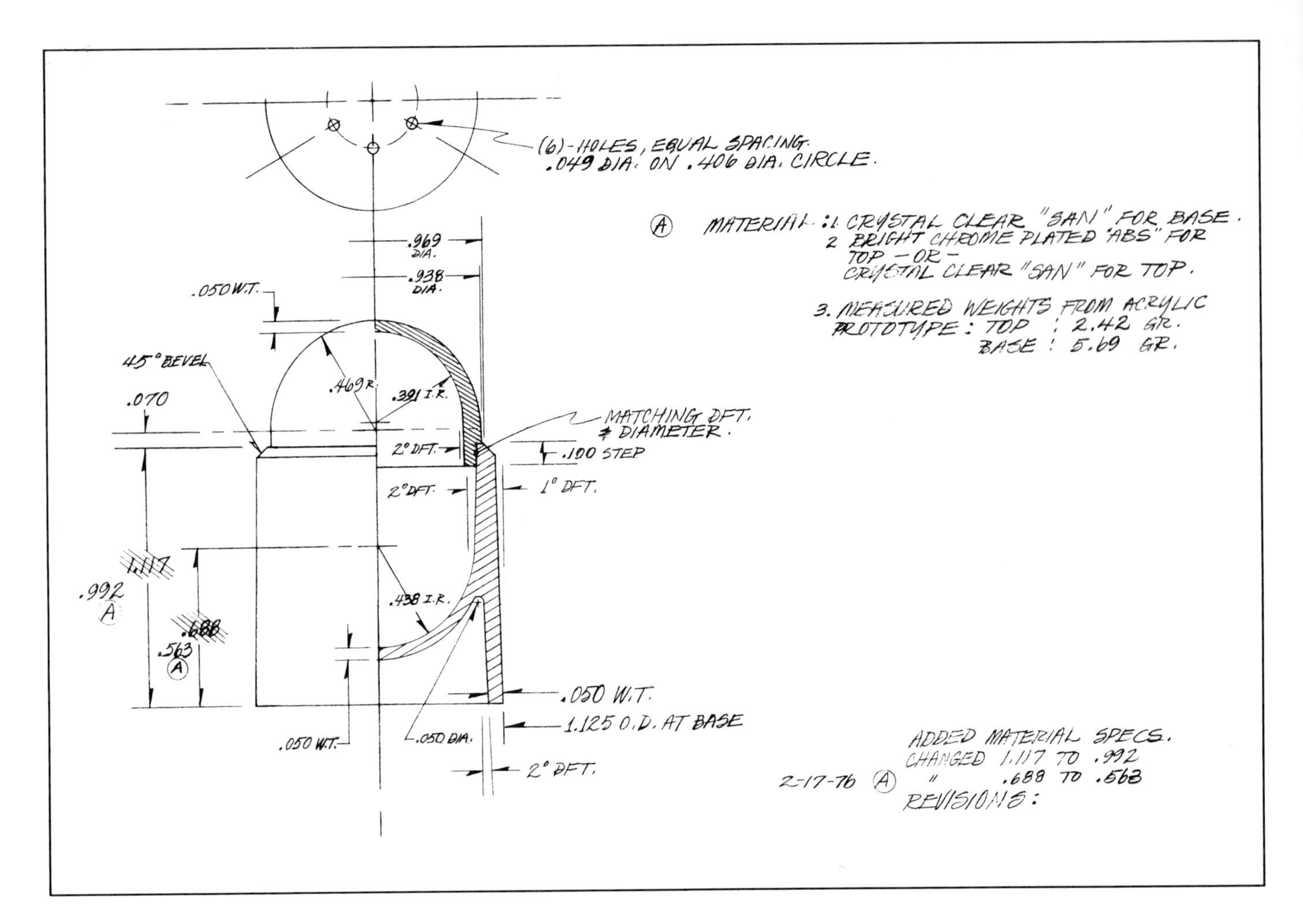

Air Plastics Salt and Pepper Shakers

Developed to provide an up-to-date, contemporary shaker for the airlines, these items are refillable and washable with commercial equipment. A crystal-clear body lends these products a clean appearance. The inside surface of the base is hemispherical to speed drying the product after washing. The top and bottom are interchangeable and are fastened by a matched draft friction fit. The capacity range for these shakers is from .15 cu in. (2.5 cm³) to .60 cu in. (9.8 cm³).

Materials and Fabrication: Top and bottom of this item are made of clear SAN plastic, injection-molded in an eight-cavity mold. The top and bottom each measure .050 in. (1.3 mm) Nom, and the top weighs 2.4 gr while the bottom weighs 5.7 gr.

Manufacturer: Air Plastics, Inc., Olathe, Kansas.
Staff Design: James T. Yoder, president.
Consultant Design: R.E. Bourke Associates, Inc.: Robert W. Johnson, vice president.

Becker Model Q1
Time Instruments

One of a line of five clocks developed to serve a wide range of users, this timepiece was designed to incorporate the features of silent performance, convenient size, an illuminated dial, and a high level of accuracy. The quartz crystal movement of this item was designed to be as small as possible and to operate for a minimum of one year on a 1.5-volt penlight battery. Seconds are separated into individual so-called stepping-action motions. The clock measures 2¾ x 2 7/16 x 1 11/32 in. (7 x 6.2 x 3.4 cm).

Materials and Fabrication: This clock is made of injection-molded ABS, chosen for its durability and good form retention. The body has a sprayed silver finish with integral colored controls.

Client: Becker Time Instruments, Westport, Connecticut.
Manufacturer: Tokyo Clock Mfg. Co., Tokyo, Japan.
Consultant Design: Richard J. DeMartino & Associates: Richard J. Martino, owner/designer, overall design & development; Michael Zambelli, designer, graphics.

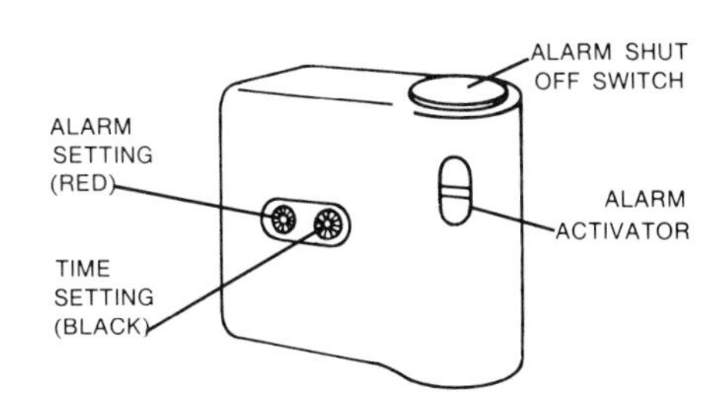

Equipment and Instrumentation

Hewlett-Packard Model 18053A Line Clip
Genave Ecom 4 Business Band Hand-Held Portable Transceiver
Atex Editing Terminal
IBM 5211 Printer
IBM 5922 Document Reader
Niranium Supersonic Grinder
Theta Dilatronic™ II, High Temperature Automatic Recording Dilatometer
Abbott ADC 500 Slide Spinner
Imed 960 Volumetric Infusion Pump
Detecto Series 7000 Digital Scale
Synerview Computed Tomography System

In this category there were 138 total submissions, an increase of almost 50 percent over last year's 95. However, only 11 were selected by the panel. According to Richard C. Schneider, "Ninety percent of the work submitted turned out not to be up to some kind of standard."

Members of the jury panel were James Barnes, Jr., Robert P. Gersin, James LaDue, Richard C. Schneider, and David Tompkins.

Left to right: David Tompkins and James Barnes, Jr.

James Barnes, Jr.
James Barnes is an industrial designer in a group called Advanced Engineering Industrial Design, a part of the Medical Systems Division at General Electric Company in Milwaukee, Wisconsin. With a strong emphasis on human factors, Barnes' work with GE has taken him into "nuclear, R&F, RADs, and dental" areas of industrial design. Having progressed rather rapidly in the three years he's been with the company, Barnes recently received a position as a project leader. After graduation in 1973 as an industrial designer from Pratt Institute in Brooklyn, Barnes free-lanced for about a year until he landed a job working primarily on graphics at Lightolier. Working in a team at GE, he was recently involved with the development of an interior room environment which included graphics design and strong physical human factors input. One of a group of six industrial designers, Barnes has been engaged in fast-paced, advanced industrial designs such as a mobile data camera unit weighing about 25 pounds.

Robert P. Gersin
As a principal for the past 19 years in his own New York consulting office, Robert P. Gersin Associates, Robert Gersin's work has ranged from product design to interiors, packaging, exhibitions, and specialized architecture, such as world fairs, retail facilities, and shopping centers. The firm's work also has included computers and telemetry equipment. "Telephones & Telephones," a system of retail stores that sell telephones and related services, is a much publicized recent design effort for AT&T and the Bell System. In terms of product design work, Gersin's firm may be asked to develop a product from its conceptual stage to the marketplace. Currently Gersin Associates is involved with word processing equipment, some consumer products, and product design work with a lot of electromechanical aspects to it. Gersin is an active member of the American Institute of Graphic Artists (AIGA) and on the Advisory Board for *Industrial Design* magazine. His work has won numerous awards and appeared in several publications. Gersin is an industrial design graduate of the Cranbrook Academy of Art. Before starting his own firm, he was a designer with the Office of Naval Research during the Korean War. As a member of a unique development group called the Special Devices Center, Gersin was principally involved with creating training aids and devices for the government.

James LaDue
James LaDue is manager of industrial design for IBM's Systems Products Division and the Design Center at Poughkeepsie, New York, where he has been involved for the

past couple years in the development of a series of five large-scale processors. LaDue's career with IBM has spanned more than 25 years. In 1951, a year after graduating from Syracuse University and after teaching as an instructor in the industrial design department there, LaDue joined IBM to work as an industrial designer on some of the first large-scale data processing systems. In 1960, two years after becoming manager of the department in IBM Poughkeepsie, he moved to Europe as manager of industrial design for IBM World Trade Corporation's five labs. During LaDue's eight years abroad, he hired and trained European industrial designers as well as doing project work, first in Holland and then in Germany and France. IBM's other two labs are in England and Sweden. In 1968 LaDue came back to the U.S. to manage IBM's Kingston, New York, Product Development Lab, a design center involved with all facets of design that a major site requires, such as interiors, products, graphics, and exhibits. In 1970, prior to LaDue's present position, he moved to the manager of design's Poughkeepsie staff, where he worked on interdivisional design planning.

Richard C. Schneider
Richard C. Schneider is manager of industrial design for Digital Equipment Corporation, a product design group in Maynard, Massachusetts. Until 1973, when Schneider joined the 15-year-old company, Digital had always had one or two industrial designers on its staff. The company now has 20 people in its design department, including 15 industrial designers and a couple of graphics and mechanical designers. Schneider is involved with new product development as well as modification of old designs, advanced development, and some package graphics. Before coming to Digital, Schneider spent several years on his own and worked for seven years as a consultant with Peter Yarmouth Associates.

David Tompkins
David Tompkins is a recent immigrant to Boulder, Colorado, where, as a partner in Design Center, he is in the process of building his own firm after 17 years of working in two older, prominent design consulting offices. An interesting area with many comparatively small, high-technology companies, Boulder is part of the projected high-density area of entrepreneurial inventors extending along the east slope of the Rockies. Since the expansion and decentralization of many large corporations has been encouraged by vastly improved communication and transport medium, new centers of business and industry, such as Boulder and the southwest generally, are being developed; the beautiful weather and spectacular scenery make for a better life style than that which older urban centers can now offer. A part of this national migration, Tompkins and his partner left Columbus, Ohio, where they had been working for Richardson-Smith. Tompkins joined Richardson-Smith in 1963, at a time when the outfit was comprised of four people; there are now over six times that many on staff. For the last eight years of his stay, Tompkins was director of product design activity, including design of such nonconsumer items as fork-lift trucks, mining equipment, road graders, and metal equipment. Tompkins

Left to right: Robert P. Gersin, Richard C. Schneider, and James LaDue.

also worked for about two years for the Teague office after graduating from Pratt in 1961. His design office is currently working in areas of medical equipment, computer peripheral products, and specialized environments, such as an infant environmental chamber. One recent environmentally oriented project that Tompkins has been involved with is a self-contained water recycling system for residential homes that eliminates the need for a municipal water supply and a sewage system at the same time.

The jury had the following comments to make on the submissions in this category.

Moderator: How do you feel about the state of design in equipment and instrumentation as we have reviewed it here?

LaDue: I think in judging the quality of design, the profession, and what we expect of it, we just have to hang on to our principles for dear life. Of all the products we reviewed, we selected only a small percentage. And the reason why is because, in most cases, the forms do not resolve well. Resolve is almost a musical term. When chord structures end up the way they do, gracefully, they come around again and are beautiful all the way. This is what design is when it's very good and solves the problems too. It's easy to make something that solves the problems, but doesn't look good. And it's just as easy to make something look good, but which doesn't solve the problems. We need finesse. The profession is asking for a lot when it wants status and it can't even resolve a decent design beyond anything more than 5 percent.

Moderator: Do you think that the level of performance is lower than in most professions?

LaDue: I think maybe not. I hear a lot of complaining about the medical profession and the legal profession, and architects, too.

Schneider: I was reading a dialog about the quality of films being made today, in which someone said that 90 percent of the movies coming out of Hollywood are junk. And the rejoinder was, 90 percent of everything is junk. We saw that demonstrated today. Ninety percent of the work submitted to this review turned out not to be up to some kind of standard.

Barnes: I don't agree with you. I think what we probably missed a lot of is the hands-on situation, the human factor, and just the lack of information that we had to make judgments with. I think there was so much missing, as far as the amount of information that we had or the amount of products that are out there, that we still can't say, "These are the best designs in the country." I don't think we made that statement today. Based on the amount of information that we had to pass judgment on, I think we made pretty good decisions. I think we made a statement that this is the best of what we had to deal with.

Tompkins: Getting back to the status of the output of the profession, feel we're moving into an area in the industrial and business equipment field that's a kind of fine tuning. A lot of the stuff that was submitted is good, professional quality work. Some of it is repeating a pattern that has been established by the company and is now being elaborated on. I've seen it in lift truck design. When we started doing stuff in the late fifties, you couldn't lose. Everything was so terrible, there was nowhere to go but up. But in most of these areas now, it appears as if the industrial designer is approaching the point of being a well-integrated part of the development cycle. They do good work. They contribute their end of it. When we review the submitted work, many times we're looking for the somewhat innovative approach. I wouldn't want to see it pushed to that point of novelty for its own sake.

Gersin: It has been. This is the problem with it. I think the industrial design profession is dancing on eggs because it isn't properly grounded. There are so many aspects to practicing this profession well. It has to do with everything from a materials understanding to an understanding of anthropometrics, to a sense of esthetics, to an understanding of marketing, to an understanding of personal relationships, to understanding environmental relationships. All those things are very, very difficult to manipulate for either one individual or for one firm or for a group of people. In addition to that, you've got a political game to play, whether you're in a corporation or whether you're outside. You're playing with power. And the power is money and authority. What's more, this damn profession was founded on a lot of frail egos and a lot of insecurity. And it's never outgrown that. It gets its jollies from a kind of vicarious power by telling somebody what to do and having them take your advice. A lot of the people practicing this profession, in my opinion, are responding to that need for ego gratification, and it colors a hell of a lot of other stuff they do. That's why there's so much junk. What it comes right down to is the profession doesn't have a sufficient number of well-founded fundamentals. For a few years people are running around with buzz words that have to do with marketing, and after another few years they're running around with anthropometrics. Next they talk about engineering, and for another few years it will become something else—materials or whatever. We need to get our feet on the ground and say, "This is what our function is. We're a valuable contributor to the economy as well as to humanity, if we choose to be." We have to own up to our mistakes and police ourselves, in a sense, by talking honestly instead of patting each other on the back and being afraid to say, "You made a big mistake. Don't do it again."

Moderator: How do you feel about licensing?

Gersin: Unfortunately, as giantism grows, so does mediocrity. So you say, I'd rather that schools train people well, that we talk to each other and create an environment with a certain amount of stimulus so that we don't need licensing as a means of admitting people to a certain level of confidence. However, if you talk to lawyers, architects, and doctors and become aware of what goes on in various states and agencies, you realize that licensing brings you to the nadir of bureaucratic entanglement. I don't think the profession would profit from this.

Moderator: Do you think that the design profession will grow in numbers?

Gersin: My personal opinion is no. As a population of people calling themselves designers, yes, but as a profession of skilled or qualified or well-trained people, I don't really think so. What's going to happen is like what's happening to architects. They're losing their power because they have failed to adapt to a changing environment. Now it's the contractor who calls the shots. Before, the client paid the money and got pushed around by heroic figures in architecture. That's no longer the case. Now it's the giant construction firm that's in charge. The architects are on staff, like designers or lawyers are, or anybody else for that matter. So the age of heroism is probably behind us. It's not ahead of us, in my opinion.

LaDue: There are going to be more people calling themselves industrial designers, and there will be more corporations with so-called industrial staffs. But the number of really good industrial designers is probably not going to grow at that same rate.

Barnes: What's going to make a good industrial designer of the future?

Gersin: That's a long conversation, but one thing that will bring it about is a decent educational system. Design schools were fairly undisciplined places to begin with, and the student revolt of the sixties knocked everything out from under them. Nobody had the guts to stand up and say to the students, "Sit down, shut up, and do something." So basically, the schools have to come together, and I don't think that can happen without the aid of better practicising professionals. Educators have a really tough time because they are trapped inside. I think that the professionals are not terribly responsible in terms of relating to the schools and helping them do better. It's a medieval profession in many respects. I don't know who is pulling it together. The IDSA [Industrial Designers Society of America] doesn't seem to be. And I don't think the profession is going to get any better as a group until somebody does really make it mature—not wait for it, but force it to mature.

LaDue: I think there's a lot more design going on now than there was 25 years ago. When I first started working then, nobody but IBM was working in industrial design in the computer business. There's broader coverage now. Maybe the sophistication hasn't developed, but the coverage has. And in a few isolated cases, like our 10 percent here, the sophistication is there. Some of the work that we have judged here I would have been happy to have been able to accomplish myself. But some of it I would have been very happy to see coming out of industries 20 years ago. So our standards as judges are increasing and we're never satisfied. Our level of dissatisfaction has to keep climbing.

Tompkins: In a lecture series that Nelson gave, he talked about evolutionary design in terms of a time frame. For instance, the evolution of the bow has a long history to it. You make it one way and somebody else comes up with a little better design, and so on, until it becomes thousands of years of repeating that one basic concept. We have hit a cycle now where technology changes so fast you can never get a chance to do it again, except within short decades of time. We're seeing a refinement stage now where, for instance, computers are moving from freestanding big cabinets to smaller cabinets, incorporations on desktops.

Moderator: Do you think that the design of computer housing has reached a plateau?

LaDue: I think it's sort of peaked out. We've noticed for quite a long time that nobody was really doing very much at all. They were just boxing them in, and IBM was the only one trying to keep them clean and make them even good looking.

Schneider: The idea of furniture, or the term "furniture," is interesting in relation to computers because computers are becoming more like pieces of furniture, in the sense that they are not boxes that sit there. They are boxes at which someone sits and works and interacts. As computers become smaller, it becomes possible to integrate them with a desk or workstation. Yet, if you look at the furniture industry and the computer industry, there is a difference in outlook. Computers don't look totally at home in that office environment where the furniture was designed to exist. I know we're working at bridging that gap.

Hewlett-Packard Model 18053A Line Clip

The line clip's design provides a fast way to make electrical contact with an insulated pair of twisted wires, e.g., telephone wires. Sold as an accessory to Hewlett-Packard's model 4961A Pair Identifier Field Unit, the line clip's wedge-shaped nose spreads the pair of wires, separating and then piercing each wire. After the wires are pierced, the field unit is activated to identify the wires. The waterproof line clip has an integral start switch and built-in tensil coil cord. Spare pin pads are included in depressions in the handles. Tests were conducted with prototypes to determine ease of usage. The panel decided that though the line clip could be labeled as a "nondesign," it deserved selection as a straight engineering solution that is mechanically clever. Thirty percent glass-filled nylon was chosen for its good rigidity and stability outdoors at temperatures ranging from −40°F (−40°C) to +158°F (70°C).

Materials and Fabrication: The line clip is made of LNP glass-filled nylon, 1½ oz (42.5 g). The clip is injection-molded with one half red and the other black.

Manufacturer: Hewlett-Packard, Delcon Division, Mountain View, California.
Staff Design: Peter Guckenheimer, product design manager.

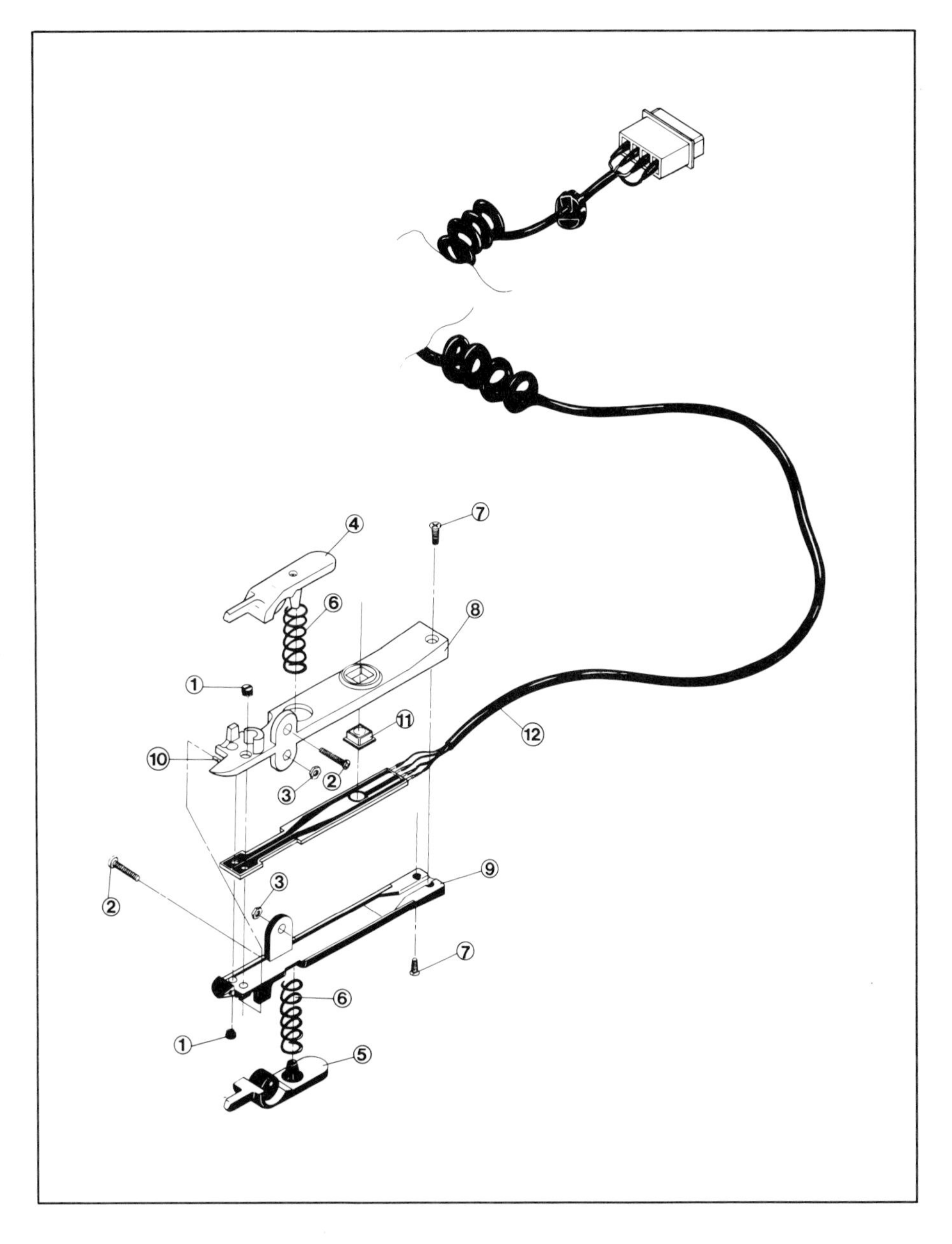

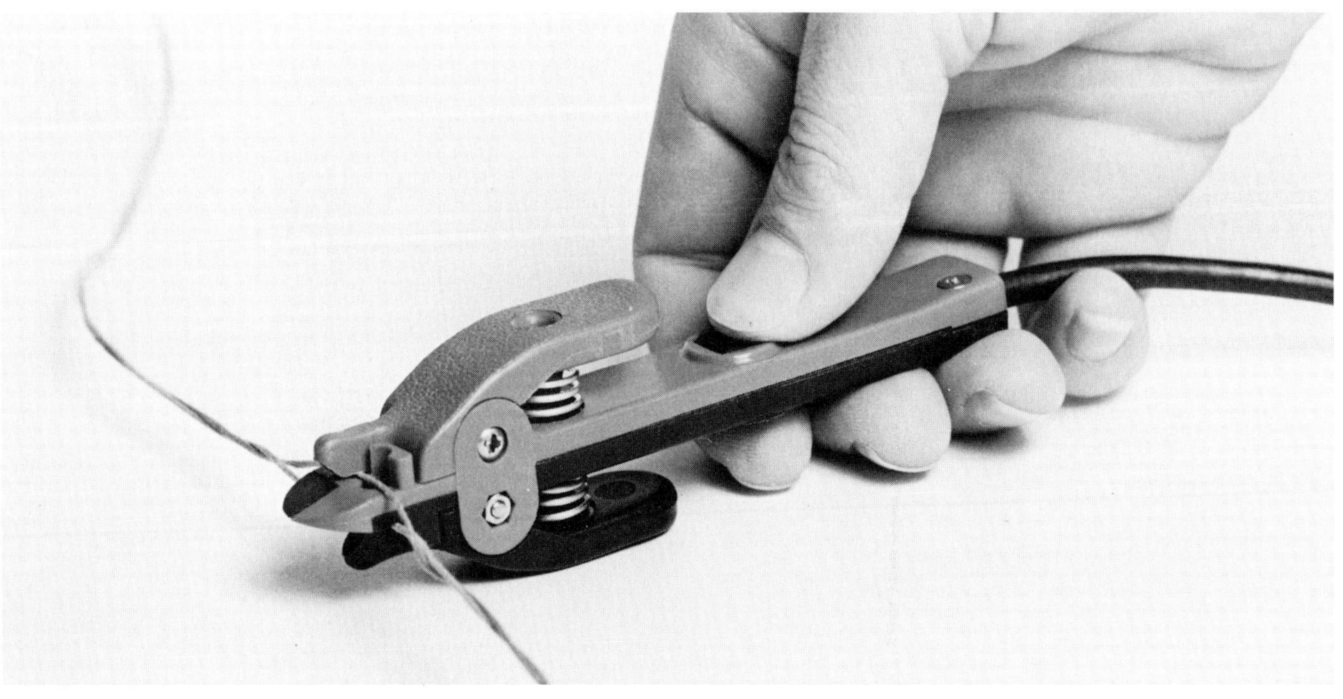

Genave Ecom 4
Business Band Hand-Held
Portable Transceiver

The Ecom 4 was developed as a lower-cost companion to an existing business band portable in Genave's line. While the approximate cost of the existing unit's case is $20, the injection-molded case of the Ecom 4 costs about $2. Ecom 4 is an FM business band portable radio used for business communications—not a CB unit—that includes a battery-powered, four-channel transmitter, receiver with an integral speaker, and microphone. It is used by placing the larger speaker grill next to the ear and talking into the smaller microphone grill located in the lower half of the case. Weighing 1 lb (453.6 g) and measuring 7 x 2⅞ x 1⅛ in. (17.8 x 7.3 x 2.9 cm), the unit can be operated from a shirt pocket. Lower in cost than its predecessor, this redesign, with its controls and microphone arranged for easy one-hand use, has simplifed finishes with less parts and less variety of materials. Recessed controls cannot be accidentally brushed. ABS was selected for its moldability and impact performance. Several study models were constructed during the design process in order to lay out circuit components and controls and to ensure good one-hand control access.

Materials and Fabrication: Case is injection-molded Cycolac ABS with a .10-in. (.254-mm) wall thickness. The overlay, glued into place on the control panel, is polycarbonate sheet. The case is dark brown and ivory. The overlay is screened dark brown with white graphics. Case graphics are orange and white hot stamp.

Manufacturer: General Aviation Electronics, Indianapolis, Indiana.
Staff Design: Claude Henderson, president; Lowell Atkinson, chief engineer; Edward Abner, senior mechanical engineer.
Consultant Design: Industrial Design Associates: Sergey Gary Podwalny, associate.

Atex Editing Terminal

This display terminal, including the keyboard enclosure and the monitor base and enclosure, was designed for use in editing books, magazines, newspapers, classified advertising, and similar types of work. The jury panel thought the design was refreshing, full of character, and identity. Available either in a standard gray or with a custom finish, the enclosures for both the monitor and keyboard are made from injection-molded Noryl structural foam. The monitor base, which allows the screen to be tilted from front to back within a 30° arc, is sandcast and machined. The keyboard measures 19 x 11½ x 5¼ in. (48.3 x 29.2 x 13.3 cm). The monitor is 13¼ x 15 x 15½ in. (33.7 x 38.1 x 39.4 cm).

Materials and Fabrication: Monitor and keyboard cases are injection-molded of Noryl structural foam. Monitor base is sandcast and machined.

Manufacturer: Atex, Inc., Bedford, Massachusetts.
Staff Design: Richard Ying, executive vice president.
Consultant Design: George Nelson & Co.: Daniel J. Lewis, designer.

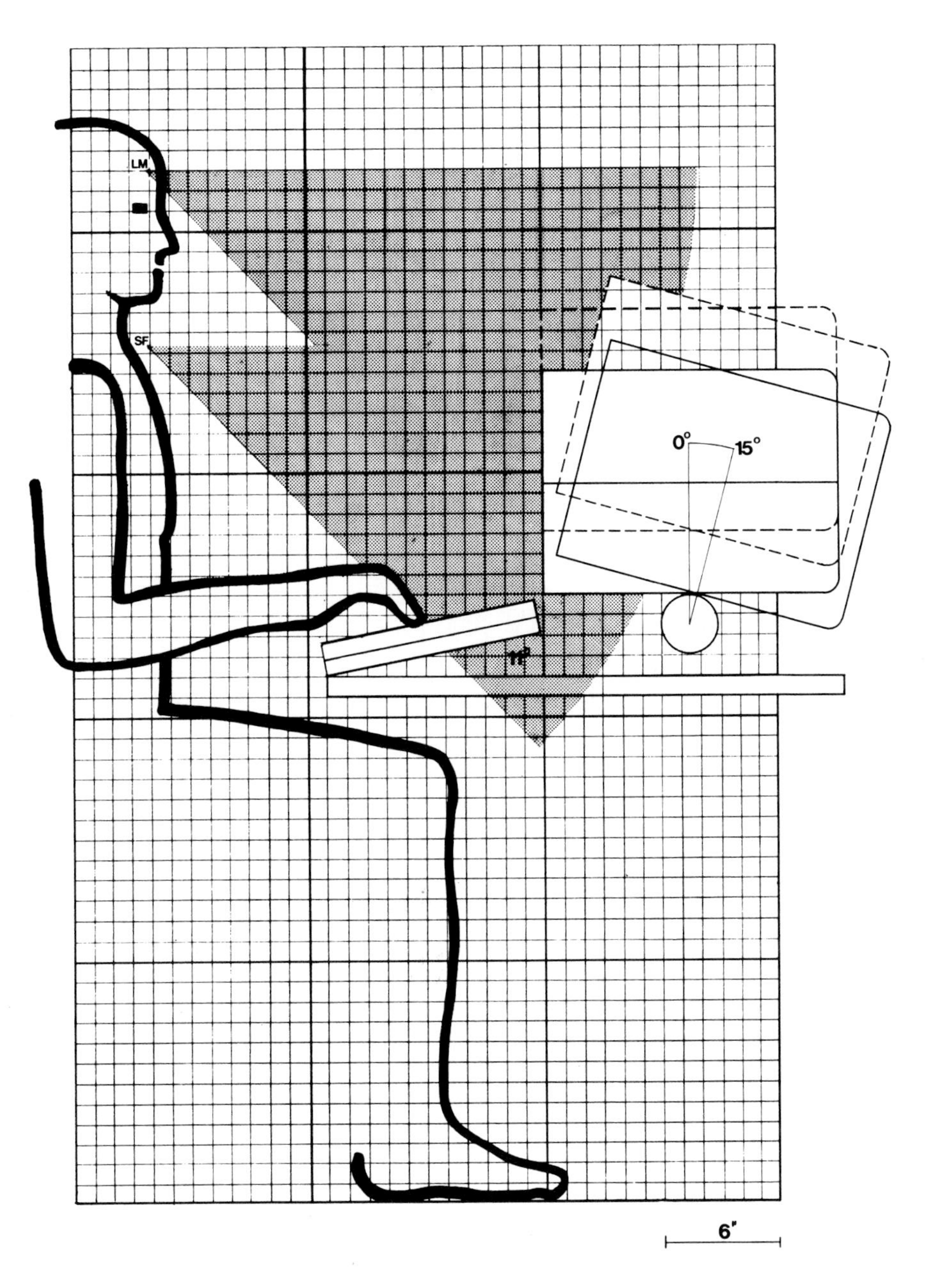

Atex Editing Terminal

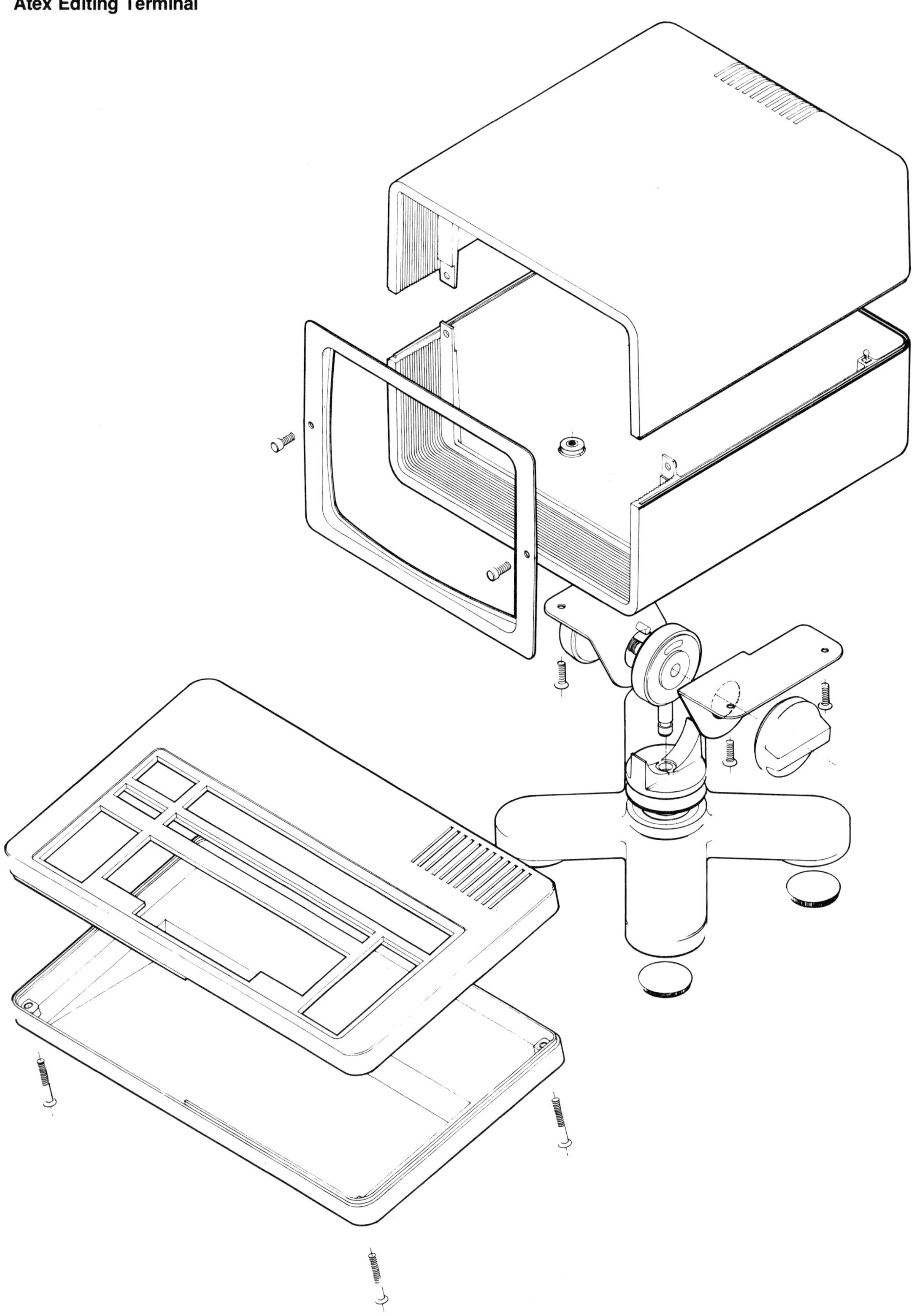

IBM 5211 Printer
The 5211 Printer was developed by IBM to satisfy refined customer needs involving cost performance, interchangeable type fonts, and improvement of the machine's impact on the office environment. All components, paper forms supply, and stacking for the 5211 were designed to be contained within the printer covers. The printer forms path and indicator lights were designed to be visible for both direct and remote operator interaction. The designer proposed that switches utilize a touch-sensitive panel which extends the hardware life of the printer and lowers maintenance costs. Through the designer's input, the printer's acoustics were also improved. Prior to its entrance on the market, IBM tested the printer at its Product Assurance facilities and by personnel use of installed systems. The printer measures 39.4 x 38 x 29.5 in. (100 x 96.5 x 75 cm), with the top cover surface's control panel back 10.2 in. (26 cm) from the machine's front edge. All external covers are painted with a textured epoxy. Front, top, and rear covers are pearl white, with optional coloring for end covers. The only design aspect mentioned by the panel as being unacceptable in their opinion was the choice of casters. The jurors found them to be ugly!

Materials and Fabrication: Window covers are 23-943G polycarbonate. The control panel housing is molded 23-943B polycarbonate. Sheet metal covers of .047 gauge steel are folded and welded. The control panel is molded, and the top cover window is formed.

Manufacturer: IBM Corp., Endicott, New York.
Staff Design: Loring C. Bixler, industrial designer.

IBM 5922 Document Reader
For use in banks and similar institutions, this document reader is a neat, new addition to IBM's 3600 finance system. There is a definite European air to its styling, which comes close to the look of a clean-lined consumer product. During each transaction a bank employee places the check, or bills of exchange, upside down on the feedtable, allowing the document to be transported to the read station where digits and special symbols printed in magnetic ink can register. Then the document is processed out underneath the feedtable. Since the reader can be located on the employee's counter, flexibility of placement contributes to the machine's operation. A human factors study was undertaken in order to define the relationship between user's convenience and either horizontal or vertical document paths, as well as the relationship to both left- and right-handed users. Size limitations were stringently set by IBM. The finished product measures 7.9 x 15.8 x 8.3 in. (20 x 40 x 21 cm) including legs. The three-part cloud white cover is molded out of PVC. The cover snaps together and is further held in position by hooks molded into the cover. According to the designer, this was done to prevent extensive drafts on the part and to provide various undercuts needed to assemble the product. The main chassis of the product, supporting most of the components, is the black, z-shaped vertical wall, made of gravity-die-cast aluminum. This part combines all the operator interfaces, giving the product its character. In contrast to the black and white colors, the document feedtable is made of grinded stainless steel, visually marking the area for document placement and affording easy transportation as well.

Materials and Fabrication: Back and cover are injection-molded PVC. These parts are snapped together and painted as one piece. The black, finely textured z-shaped part is made of gravity-die-cast aluminum and grinded stainless steel is used for the feedtable. Lights are LEDs.

Manufacturer: IBM Laboratory, Lidingö, Sweden.
Staff Design: Jan van Hoek, industrial designer, IBM Laboratory, Uithoorn, The Netherlands.

Niranium Supersonic Grinder
High-speed grinding machines are designed for use in dental laboratories by skilled workers. The machine's function is to grind and shape alloy castings of impressions taken for dentures. Workers usually operate the machine for a full eight-hour day. Therefore the designers' concern was to develop a precision instrument with ease of operation that could replace a machine which, in their opinion, was not just ugly and outdated, but also poorly engineered and designed. Relying on already-existing anthropometric data developed by Henry Dreyfuss Associates, the designers created a large, padded, open area for the worker's hand to rest on beneath the lever-activated automatic spindle, as well as repositioned and adjusted the safety glass shield and twin incandescent light source and improved dust exhaust. Ease of assembly and servicing of parts, especially belt replacement, were also main areas of concern. In the designers' own words, "The combination of sand castings and sheet metal gave us the best structure to support the motor and high-speed spindle with excellent appearance, for a low-quantity production run of from 100 to 500 units per year." Having seen before-and-after photos, the panel agreed that the grinder's redesign has created a clean, well-related set of complex forms. Measuring 9½ x 12 x 15½ in. (24.1 x 30.5 x 39.4 cm), the grinder is coated in a medium-textured, semigloss armorhide paint, available in such colors as "tangerine," "pumpernickel," or "gorgeous gray."

Materials and Fabrication: Base, spindle support and lock, belt guard are sand-casted aluminum with a 7/32-in. (5.6-mm) wall. Motor cover and light housing is of # 20 .036 CRS. Aluminum rod, ⅜ in. (9.6 mm) diameter, is used to support the light and 3/16-in. (4.8-mm) tempered safety glass.

Manufacturer: Niranium Corp., Long Island City, New York.
Staff Design: Douglass Mann, designer.
Consultant Design: Carl Yurdin Industrial Design, Inc.: Carl Yurdin, design, engineering; Arthur Eisenkramer, engineering.

Before.

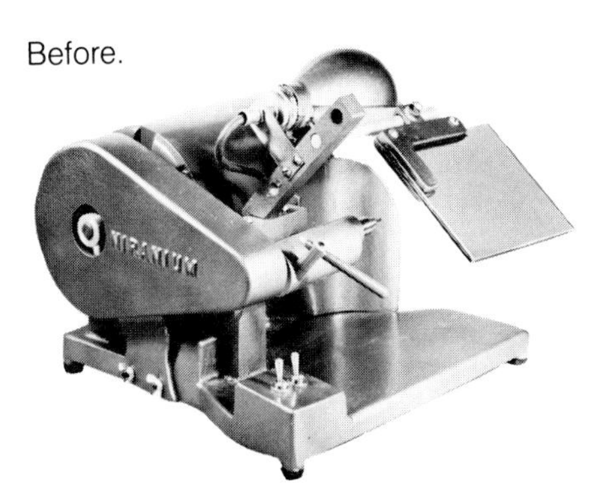

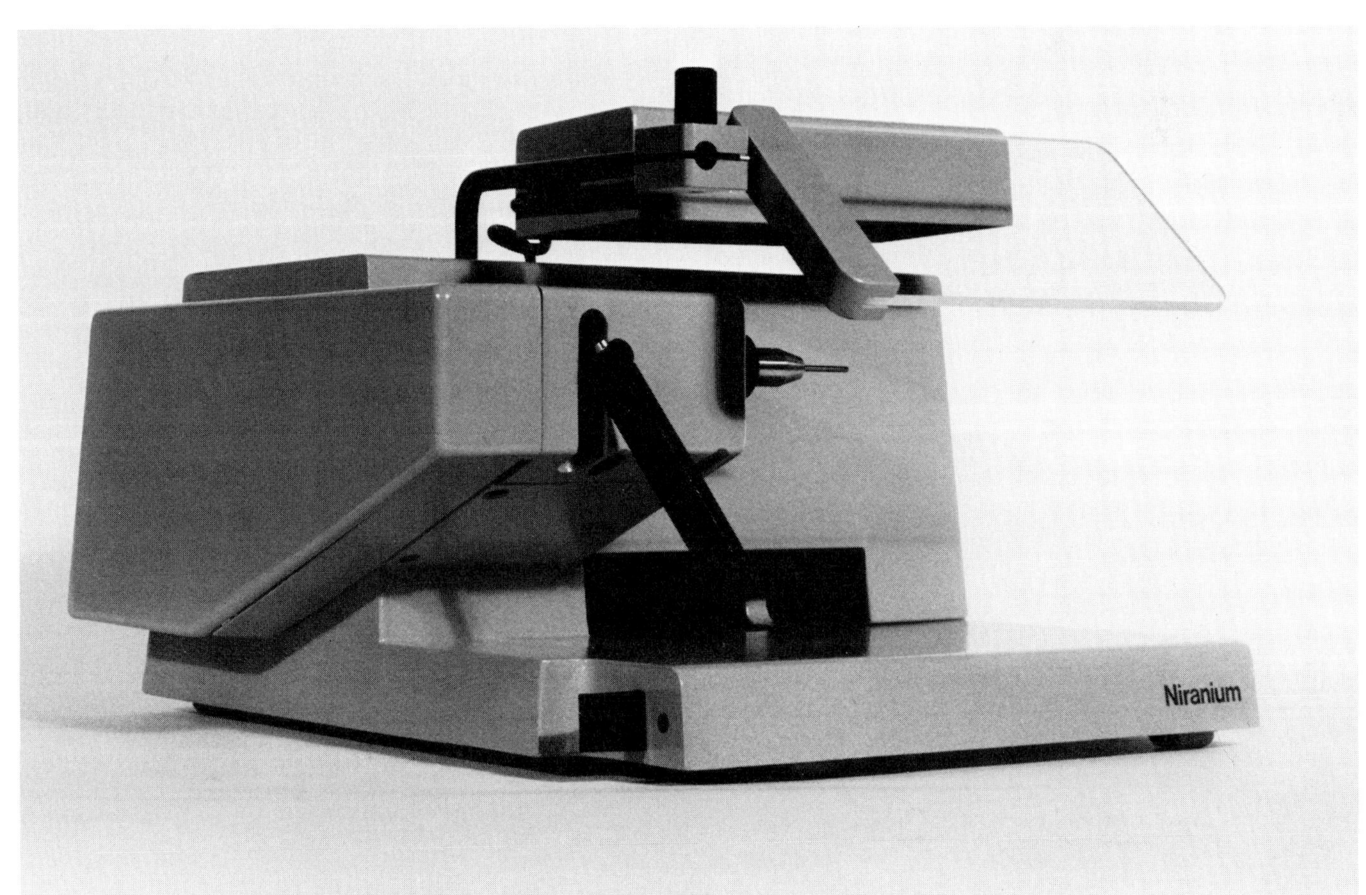

Theta Dilatronic™ II, High Temperature Automatic Recording Dilatometer

Used by scientists and technicians, the design parameters surrounding this precision measuring device were the improvement of its form and function and, therefore, the credibility of the instrument as a whole. The instrument is used for determining the coefficient of linear thermal expansion and for detecting phase transitions in material for analytic purposes. Though impressed with its clean appearance, especially compared with its predecessor, some of the jurors were a bit concerned with the demands placed by the housing's design on the sand-casting process that was used. The question was raised: Can you really get the close, precision fits necessary? One suggestion was to put in some offsets to successfully accomplish what was wanted, without trying to create smooth forms all over. The designer however, stated that he felt his choice of materials and processes were best suited to the possibility for good form on a very low production run of 50 units a year. The dilatometer's dimensions are 40 x 12 x 10 (101.6 x 30.5 x 25.4 cm).

Materials and Fabrication: Base, furnace slide, and measuring head slide and cover are sand-cast aluminum, with ¼ in. (6.4 mm) walls. Measuring head support is machined aluminum. Furnace cover is # 18.049 CRS. The instrument is coated with armorhide textured paint in light biege with black and orange graphics.

Manufacturer: Theta Industries, Inc., Port Washington, New York.
Staff Design: G. Clusener, A. Richter, engineering.
Consultant Design: Carl Yurdin Industrial Design, Inc.; Carl Yurdin, designer.

Before.

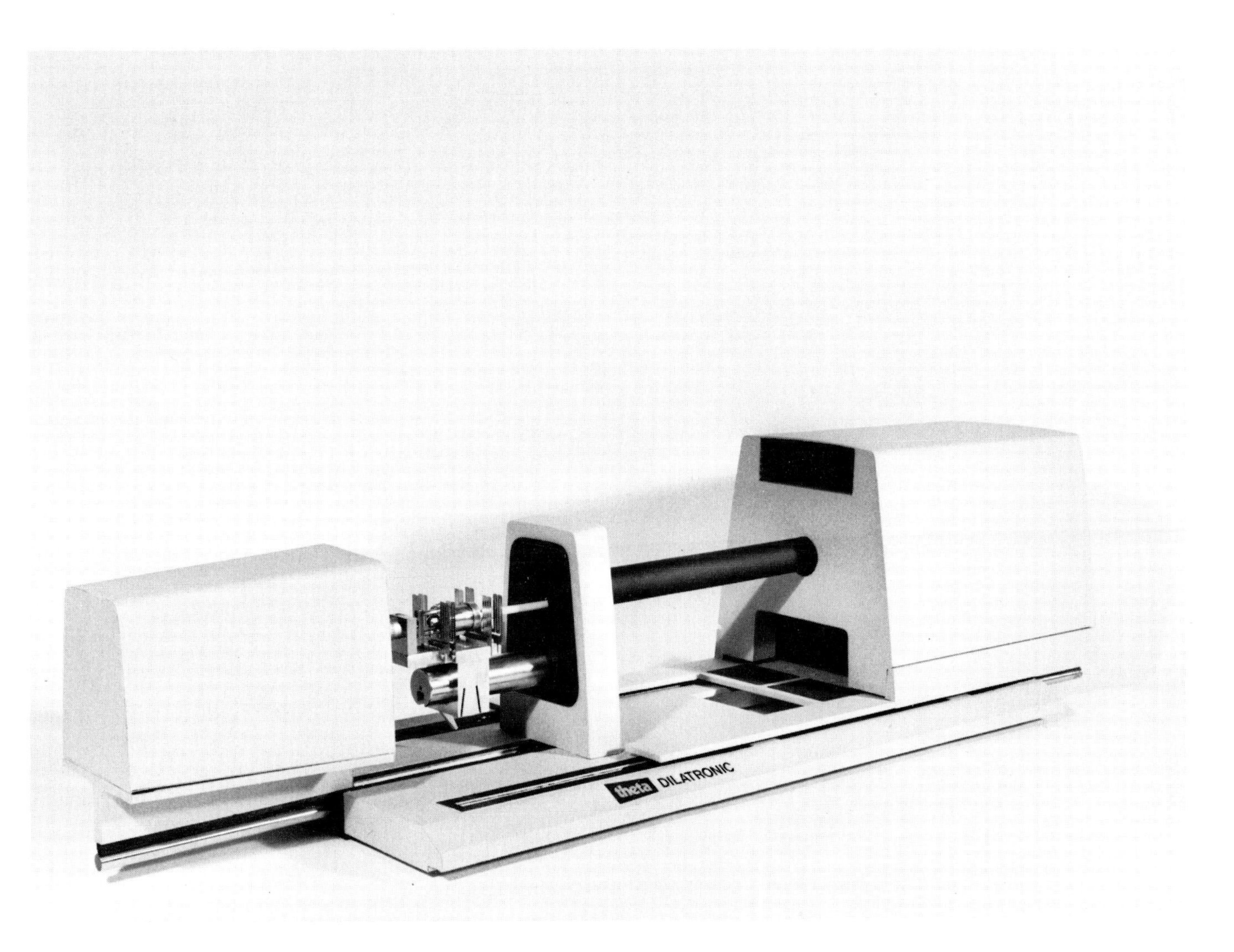
theta DILATRONIC

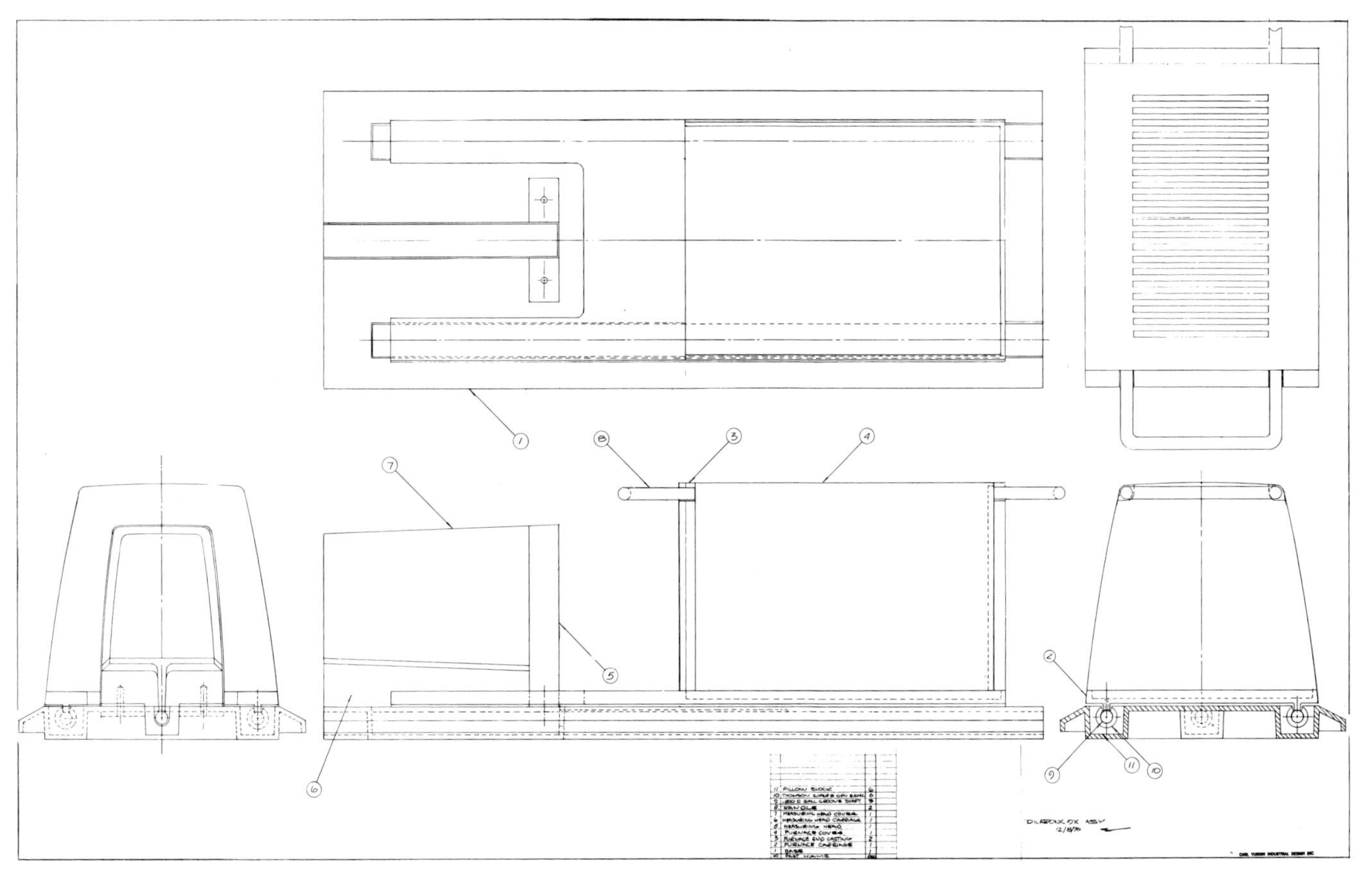
1
2
3
4
5
6
7
8
9
10
11
11 PILLOW BLOCK 6
8 HANDLE 2
7 MEASURING HEAD COVER 1
6 MEASURING HEAD CARRIAGE 1
5 MEASURING HEAD 1
4 FURNACE COVER 1
3 FURNACE END CASTING 2
2 FURNACE CARRIAGE 1
1 BASE 1
PART NAME

AUTOMATIC
SPIN TIME
ADC 500

Abbott ADC 500 Slide Spinner
Used in medical laboratories, the ADC 500 Slide Spinner produces a single layer of cells with a uniform distribution on a microscope slide. The unit supports Abbott's Differential Classifier ADC 500, and as such it was developed to provide a total system for handling blood. From the standpoint of fabrication and maintenance, the Spinner's main advantage is that all internal components are mounted to a single, main chassis. The chassis is also the outer housing. The unit has good accessibility to its components and may be operated with the base removed. Advantages to the operator include ease of operation and cleaning, access to controls and filter, plus pertinent built-in safety features. The designers were responsible for analyzing all components in order to arrive at the best functional arrangement, a form which would reflect a logical, economical manufacturing procedure while offering a visually provocative exterior. The result is a main chassis, the visible portion of the main housing, of sand-cast aluminum. This material was chosen by the designers because it could provide most internal detailing, mounting bosses, and an easily cleaned spin chamber and filter compartment all from one structural part. The bottom side is made of a sheet metal pan which can be easily removed for access to the entire underside. Control panel and filter cover are also sand-cast aluminum, repeating the main housing's form. The hinged slide chamber cover is a two-piece assembly of sand-cast aluminum so designed as to obtain its circular form, minimize air turbulence, protect optical components, and provide a rugged hinge. The visually striking raised disc on the slide chamber's cover is a direct result of lowering the surface height around the spin chamber. The black anodized handle is machined from aluminum bar stock. The unit's other colors are a dark and a light gray. Extensive research and in-house testing were done by the manufacturer during the product's development.

Materials and Fabrication: Dimensions are 8¼ x 11¾ x 14⅞ in. (21 x 30 x 37.8 cm). The main housing, hinged cover, control panel, and filter cover are all sand-cast aluminum. Bottom pan is brake-formed sheet metal. Sand-cast parts are painted light gray with Sherwin Williams Polane T, a polyurethane paint. Painted a dark gray, the base is also Polane T. Handle is black anodized.

Manufacturer: Abbott Diagnostics Division, Dallas, Texas.
Staff Design: Jay Clifton, program manager, Abbott; Stephen Brown, director of engineering, and Robert Herr, mechanical design engineer, Bowmar Instrument Corp., Ft. Wayne, Indiana.
Consultant Design: S.G. Hauser Associates, Inc.; Stephen G. Hauser, president; Sheldon Keith, associate designer.

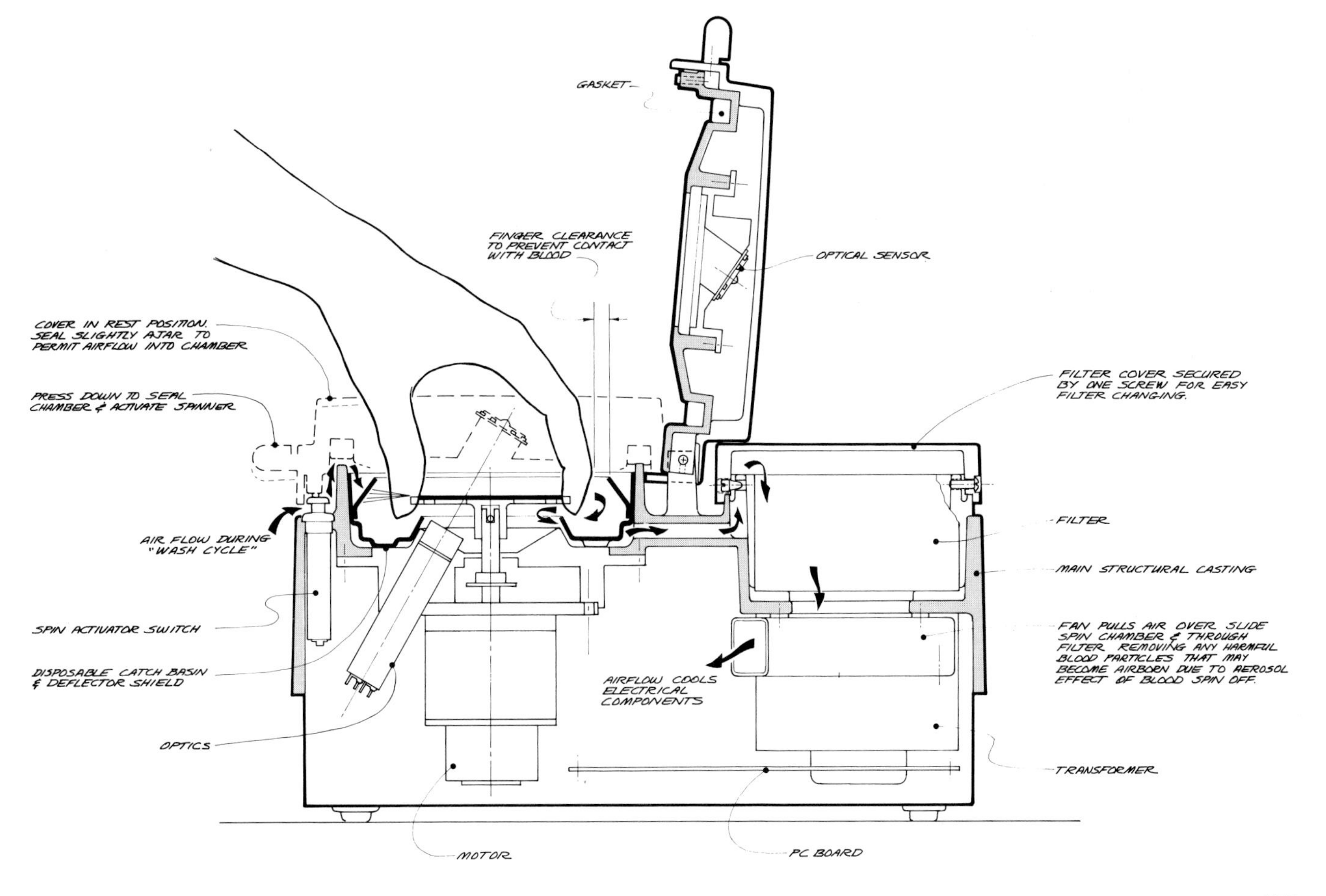

Imed 960 Volumetric Infusion Pump

Used to infuse fluids and solutions into patients, this second generation volumetric infusion pump incorporates new electronic and mechanical technology developed by Imed. The designers handled the project from its initial conception through to the fully working prototypes, with research carried out by the design office within hospitals and medical centers. Newly developed drugs and chemotherapy solutions required equipment that would be hyperaccurate. Technology that is a direct spin-off from aerospace research and developments was used in the pump. Operated by hospital nurses as well as at times by the patient, the pump infuses fluids via disposable cassettes. Fluids are delivered at rates of from 1 to 999 cc per hour at extremely accurate levels. Fully portable, the pump was designed for easy operation and maintenance. Totally sealed switches prevent sticking normally caused by spills of intravenous fluids such as glucose. Controls have been conveniently positioned. The information panel is completely on LCD readout so that the operator is instructed when an infusion is completed, there is air in the line, the battery is not charging, and so forth. The compression-molded SMC fiber-filled plastic case is usually pole-mounted at a height of approximately 40 in. (101.6 cm). The unit weighs 14 lb (6.4 kg) and measures 11½ x 10 x 5¼ in. (29.2 x 25.4 x 13.3 cm).

Materials and Fabrication: SMC fiber-filled plastic is used to form the case by compression molding; it was chosen because it meets UL standards for hospital equipment and because of the strength of the material. Micro switch and Digitran thumbwheel switches were used. Injection-molded polycarbonate is used for the door. Handles are die cast, and seals are of injection-molded polyurethane. The case is painted semigloss white, seals and doors are clear blue tint.

Manufacturer: Imed Corp., San Diego, California.
Staff Design: Oscar Hyman, chief engineer, electronics and engineering; Jon Jenkins, vice president and technical director; Louis Obertreis, senior project engineer; Douglas Rumberger, vice president, sales.
Consultant Design: Designworks: Charles Pelly, owner, design supervisor; Raymond Carter, senior designer.

Detecto Series 7000 Digital Scale
The Series 7000 Digital Scale was developed both for professional use, with standard electrical current to ensure constant power for a high degree of everyday use, and as a consumer product, available in a rechargeable, battery-operated model. Jurors were unanimously of the opinion that as a professional tool the scale's form is handsome and logical, but at a retail price of $300 the scale is out of line for the consumer market. Rigid urethane foam was chosen to make a one-piece, rim injection-molded housing with integral component mounts. The choice of rigid urethane was determined by an initially low production volume and the need for low-cost tooling. Though the savings may not be passed on to the buyer, the choice of materials, according to the designers, results in a low assembly time and reduced labor costs. With an electronic mechanism to compensate for ambient movement on the scale's platform, an instant readout is given with accuracy to .10 lb (45.4 g). The person to be weighed can select a readout in either kilograms or pounds. Weighing in at 40 lb (18.1 kg) itself, the scale measures 35½ x 16 x 22 in. (90.2 x 40.6 x 55.9 cm). The housing is white with a black platform and lens cover.

Materials and Fabrication: Lens cover is injection-molded acrylic. Back is made of cold rolled steel. The housing, rim injection-molded rigid urethane foam, is painted white.

Manufacturer: Detecto Scales, Inc., Brooklyn, New York.
Consultant Design: Samuel Mann Associates: George Horton, vice president, project design manager; Thomas Stevens, assistant designer.

Synerview Computed Tomography System

Extensive human engineering tests were conducted for Picker's entry into the field of computerized tomography. The machine's concept is to offer a combination of body and brain x-raying, with a 30-sec scan time capability. Tests were conducted at a Cleveland clinic and three major hospitals in Pennsylvania. In-house development and testing contributed to the design of the headrest used for brain scanning to ensure the proper angulation for specific scans. The machine functions so that the patient, upon entering the machine's "inner circle," is scanned transversely, and within minutes the section scanned is reconstructed on a CRT with the aid of a computer. As well as providing clear images of areas not visible with other instruments, this method of x-raying eliminates a painful process of air injection in the brain known as "pneumoencephalography." The manufacturer claims a minimal x-ray dosage for safe operation. The Synerview's front center panel, the point of patient entry, is formed of structural foam to lend some warmth to the machine's impersonal bulk and to gain detailing in its design. The other external panels are ⅛ in. (3.2 mm) thick sheet metal. The headrest is made of cast aluminum with a plexiglass headholder. Patients rest on a curved surface made of carbon graphite, crosswoven for strength and dimensional stability. The carbon allows rays to pass through. The computer control panel has been centrally located, allowing operation from either end of the table it rests on. Controls were arranged to create a direct alignment between patient and technician. A minimum of switches causes less distraction to the technician. Two-way speakers in the structural foam panel allow the patient and the control room to be in constant communication.

Materials and Fabrication: A special color system was devised with gray tones used for painted parts. Dimensions for the x-ray box are 80 x 36 x 82 in. (203.2 x 91.4 x 208.3 cm). Carbon graphite table is 81 x 24 in. (205.7 x 61 cm). The table raises from 29 x 40 in. (73.6 x 101.6 cm). Depending upon the equipment used, control room panel varies from 29 x 49 x 26 in. (73.7 x 124.5 x 66 cm).

Manufacturer: Picker Corp., Cleveland, Ohio.

Staff Design: Carl Brunnett, project leader, engineer; Anthony Zupancic, head engineer.

Consultant Design: Richardson/Smith, Inc.: Deane Richardson, director; Lawrence Barbera, senior designer; Keith Kresge, senior designer; David Tompkins, group director.

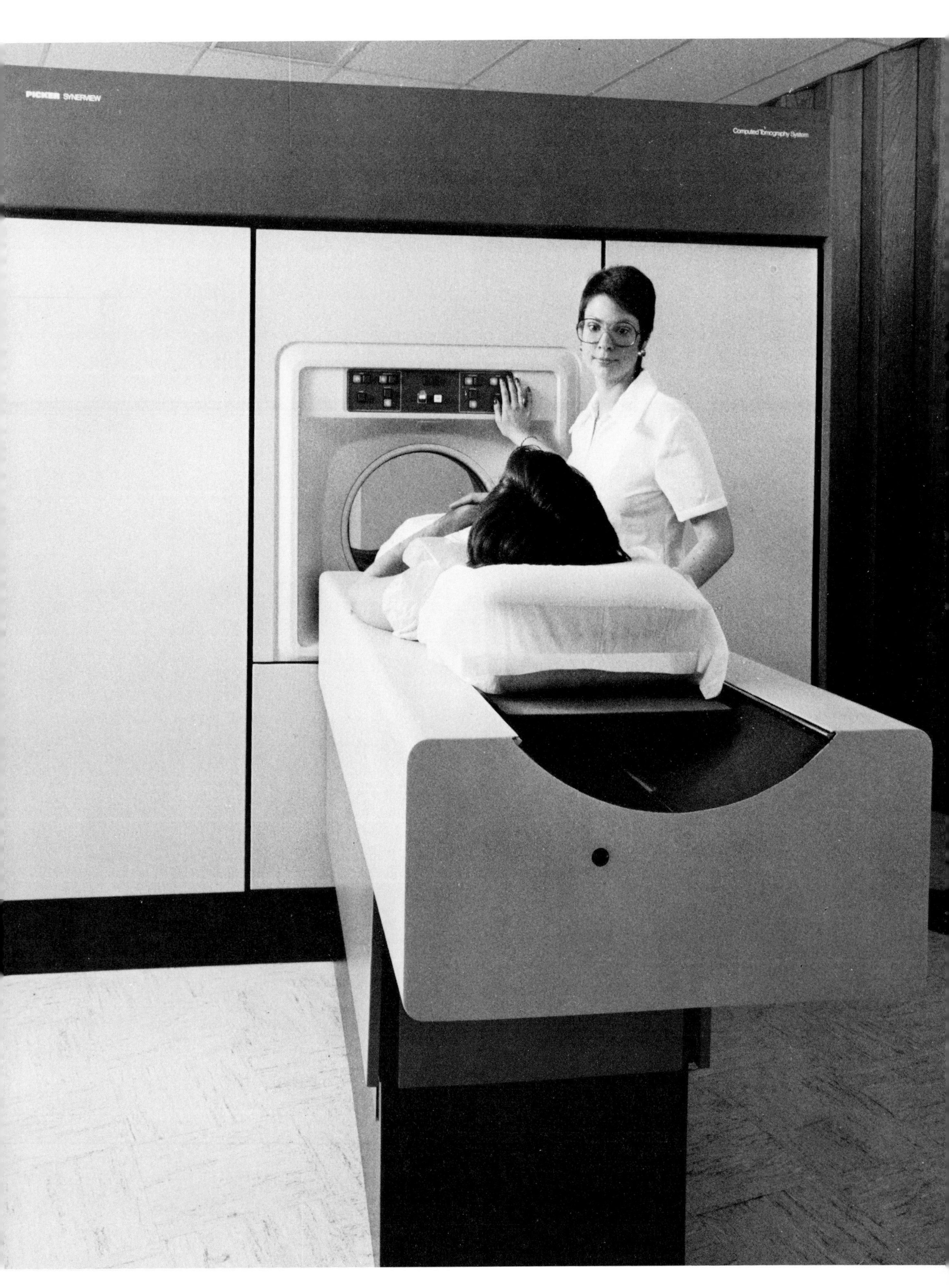
PICKER SYNERVIEW
Computed Tomography System

Visual Communications

BVD Men's and Boys' Underwear Packaging
Packaging System for Remington's Shavers
and Personal Care Products for Men
Packaging for Atra Shaving Systems
Packaging for Sheaffer Writing Instrument Accessories
GAF View-Master Stereo Viewer Package
Series of Four Packages for Hammarplast Housewares
Video Cassette Microphone Package for RCA
Packaging for Project/One, Stereo 100 Headphones
Supreme Paint Brush Line Packaging
Olin Chemicals' Pace® Consumer Line Pool Chemicals Packaging
Package Graphics for Bubblicious Soft Bubble Gum
Package Graphics for Candydent Sugarless Candies
Saks Fifth Avenue Christmas Packaging
Packaging System for Tivoli Ltd.
Berkey's Omega Digital Color Analyzer, SCA 300 Packaging
GAF Draftrace 250 Pads Packaging
Packaging for Gemeni Blood Chemistry Diagnostic Kit
Container Graphics for Bolt Commercial Insecticides
AIGA Packaging 1977 Call for Entry Poster
Stationery Design for BVD
Design of Howard Tech Sheets
Catalog Design for Howard Hardware Products
Instruction Pamphlet and Logotype Design for Ben's Block
Recruiting Book for the Fashion Institute of Technology
Corporate Identity Symbol for Pinkerton Security Services
The Quaker Oats Company 1976 Annual Report
1976 Annual Report for H.J. Heinz Company
Consolidated Foods Corporation 1977 Annual Report
Fluor Corporation 1976 Annual Report
Northrop Corporation 1976 Annual Report
St. Regis 1976 Annual Report

After the exciting design years of the fifties and the sixties, "the seventies are becoming a utility crunch." The safe refuge many designers have found in the international style has made the jurors feel that more whimsy in design would be a welcome relief. The total submissions in this category were up 179 from 145 in 1976. Of these, 31 entries were selected for the 1977 *Design Review*.

Members of the jury panel were Chava Ben-Amos, Penny Johnson, Jack Odette, Louis Rodgers, and Robert Salpeter.

Chava Ben-Amos.

Chava Ben-Amos

Designer-art director with Deskey Associates, Inc., New York, since 1976, Chava Ben-Amos has won numerous awards for designs in both the United States and Israel. Until recently a member of the board of the Package Designers Council (PDC), Ben-Amos has taught both packaging and visual communications at Pratt Institute in Brooklyn. Previously associated with such well-known New York design firms as Schecter & Luth, Sandgren & Murtha, Loewy-Snaith, and Lippincott & Margulies, Ben-Amos studied at the Bezaleh Art Academy in Jerusalem, Israel, before coming to the United States in 1964. She has designed eight different postage stamps for the state of Israel, as well as a number of posters for Broadway shows.

Penny Johnson

With a broad experience in national brand packaging, Penny Johnson became design director in charge of both design and account work for Peterson & Blyth Associates, New York, in 1974. Johnson is currently responsible for the design development of accounts such as American Home Foods, Nestles, General Foods, Pillsbury, General Mills, and Dupont, among many others. She has received numerous packaging graphics awards from the American Institute of Graphic Artists (AIGA), Clio, and various trade organizations for her design work. Johnson earned a Bachelor of Design degree at the University of Florida in Ohio in 1965. She previously worked for eight years with the office of Raymond Loewy/William Snaith in New York, first as a junior package designer, and in her last two years there, she became the staff design director, with the majority of work on the Nabisco account.

Jack Odette

Since his appointment to the position of vice president of communication design at Citibank in 1974, Jack Odette has established the standards under which his department operates. He acts as the communication and design consultant to Citicorp, Citibank, and its subsidiaries. Odette, whose primary involvement is design, also supervises a group of 35 employees in fields ranging from graphics services to photography and audiovisual and visual design. He is a member of the Board of Directors of the American Institute of Graphic Artists (AIGA) and the Design Managing Institute of the Massachusetts College of Art, of which he is a founding board member. He has received certificates of excellence from AIGA and honors from the Art Directors Show, *Communication Arts* magazine, Creativity in 1973, 1974, 1976, 1977, and in 1973 and 1977 from the Mead Library of Ideas International Show of Annual Reports. A member of the Art Directors Club, the Type Directors Club, and the Publication Designers Club, Odette was the owner and designer for Odette Associates, Inc., between 1966 and 1974. Clients included American Express, Planned Parenthood, Head Ski and Sportswear, Time, Inc., the Museum of the City of New York, Westvaco, as well as Citibank. Odette studied calligraphy and design in the evening with Arnold Bank at the Art Students League in New York until 1958 when he worked as the art director and partner to Johns/Odette, Inc., a fashion and promotion agency. Before establishing his own firm, Odette worked for four years as the associate in Maurice Berson's graphic design studio.

Louis Rodgers
As graphics designer in the Graphic Services Division at Marathon Oil Company in Findlay, Ohio, Louis Rodgers' varied responsibilities include work in corporate print advertising, editorial design, corporate identity and sales promotion, display, and design for packaging, point-of-purchase, booklets, and brochures. A member of the Columbus Society of Communicating Arts for the past three years, Rodgers was actively involved in the development, promotion, and exhibition of various art shows of work of Black American artists in conjunction with the Akron Art Institute in Akron, Ohio. He has also taught classes in design and painting. Rodgers was previously associated with the Neighborhood Arts Center in Akron as senior designer/assistant art director and with Scherr and McDermott Designers. In 1970 Rodgers received a scholarship to attend Cooper School of Art in Cleveland, Ohio, where he studied for two years before becoming actively involved in the design profession.

Robert Salpeter
A partner in the firm of Lopez Salpeter since 1971, Robert Salpeter's New York-based firm is involved with all areas of visual communications. The recipient of numerous awards from the American Institute of Graphic Artists (AIGA), the New York Art Directors Club, and the Type Directors Club, Salpeter is an active member of AIGA. He designed all collateral material for the AIGA Federal Design Response, an exhibition sponsored in cooperation with the Federal Design Council to demonstrate current excellence of design in the U.S. government. Also responsible for all graphics in the AIGA 1976 Communications Graphics Show, Salpeter designed the exhibit for the AIGA's 1977 Book Show. Salpeter attended both the School of Industrial Arts and the School of Visual Arts in New York. Previous to his partnership with Richard Lopez, Salpeter was an art director at the IBM World Trade Corporation for ten years, where he was responsible for graphic design. The list of current clients for Lopez Salpeter includes the American Museum of Natural History, IBM, Klopman Mills, New York Telephone, Polychrome Corporation, SCM Corporation, and Sandoz Pharmaceuticals. The firm is also currently involved with a promotional film for Warner Brothers.

Left to right: Jack Odette, Louis Rodgers, and Penny Johnson.

Commenting on the submissions in this category, the jury panelists had the following to say.

Moderator: Would you comment on the state of design in the area of visual communications?

Odette: We're swiftly approaching stasis; by that I mean that we have an equal distribution of taste, talent, money—everything is evenly distributed. There was virtually nothing at the end of the review day that I really remember. That's probably the problem with the state of design today. It's not very memorable. I would say that there's really virtually nothing I can remember clearly, and without trying, which would give me an indication that there are still private visions—those little fairies dancing around with their own ideas of how things ought to be. And that's what troubles me.

Moderator: Are designers afraid of failing, do you think?

Robert Salpeter.

Odette: No, I think it's a triumph of the Swiss school, of the international style. There is virtually nothing else. And every time we come up to it, and we did a couple of times like with FIT [Fashion Institute of Technology] and Quaker Oats, where we had something that was done in a different size, more casually, more artlessly, we certainly didn't welcome it openly.

Moderator: Is there enough fun, whimsy in design?

Odette: I don't think there is any to speak of. If you have ever been to Switzerland, you know that everything there runs on time and it's really clean, and it's very dull to be there for more than three or four days. I think we have emulated that as a style to the exclusion of whimsy. Everything is Helvetica. It's a beautiful typeface. And I find it extremely boring. I enveigle my people, only with partial success, to try to do things that are much more personal—with die cuts and all kinds of crazy things—just to make the reader enjoy the act of turning a page and finding a little surprise.

Moderator: Are you saying that Swiss design is bad design?

Odette: By the eternal principles of design as I understand them, no, it's not bad design. I'm not too sure that it actually communicates anymore. When you look at many annual reports, you see a style repeated over and over again. I think we got a rather good mix here, with good examples submitted.

Salpeter: I think that what has happened with Helvetica is that Helvetica became a stylistic idiom. Originally, from the Swiss concept, it was used because according to their research it was the most readable typeface. I'm not saying whether it was true or not. But the point is that they used it for a very functional reason. Now you have a broad spectrum of areas which designers work in, each encompassing a unique set of functions. You have the packaging, the album covers, and then you have a fire exit sign. Maybe the solution for a problem like the fire exit sign calls for the most readable typeface because it's a matter of life or death. But for a record album cover, that's not the solution. Using Helvetica becomes a style, nothing else. I think the mistake that designers make is that they jump on Helvetica as a style, and when that becomes boring, they just turn it on an angle.

Odette: More than anything else, I think this stuff is safe. Perhaps there is a fear of failing.

Salpeter: In the broad spectrum of design you have the feeling you saw it before. When I look back to the fifties, it was mindblowing. Exciting things were being done. You had people like Doyle, Dane, and Bernbach and Lou Dorfsman starting up. In the sixties there was pretty much more of the same, and you expected that the seventies were really going to do something. And nothing has happened.

Ben-Amos: I think the seventies are becoming a utility crunch. There is no money, magazines are taking on smaller formats, there are smaller budgets for printing, and for everything else. We have to do it for less money and less space—no luxury, no trims. They also don't want to bother people with too much information. Everything has to be very concise and very immediate. People don't have time. They look through things very fast. Time is very precious, money is very precious, paper is precious. That affects the quality of design.

Johnson: There were several big names in the fifties and the sixties. Who is the hero now?

Salpeter: There are no heroes. There are no real pacesetters or groundbreakers.

Johnson: Part of what was happening then was tied together with technological advances in photography and printing capabilities.

Rodgers: I think that what was new and innovative then changed as time went on. Technology changes, people's demands change, society's needs change. I think we see that reflected in the competition here today. The role is different.

Moderator: What is that role? What is being demanded?

Rodgers: Going back to better times. Designers innovated then, and people were willing to accept that. But as time went on those new ways of doing things, the innovations, became old hat as things changed. And along came the turbulent times, economic crises, shortages, the traumatic sixties. All these things shook people up dramatically. They shook up people as much as, if not more than, the design movement did when those innovative changes first took place. The role of the designer has become almost like an aspirin for a headache—to calm and soothe away the woes of the world that are oppressing people. This has a lot to do with the interest that the government's showing now in the design field. They're beginning to realize the importance of this field, as a medicine and as a tranquilizer.

Moderator: Wouldn't some humor help if that's the question?

Johnson: Yes, yes! We seem to be in an area of straightforwardness. No gimmicks. Everybody has had it with the gimmicks, being tricked into buying this or that. Everything is getting to be just nuts-and-bolts, simple, straightforward. We'll have to be with that for a while before we get sick of it, and then some exciting things will begin to happen.

Ben-Amos: Marketing has also become a major criterion. Once it was the gut decision of some people. Today everything is computerized and tested by so many people that everything comes out just like the television shows. It has Nielson ratings written into it.

Moderator: Are they trying to reach the broadest common denominator?

Johnson: That's right. Big companies want to sell to a mass market only. They can't afford to put a new product out unless it sells so many millions. That means it's going to be a watered-down, mass media, mass consumer approach automatically.

Odette: If you don't like the situation, what do you do to change it as an individual or as a corporation?

Ben-Amos: You try to argue, but that's about as far as you can go.

Johnson: You have to try to keep approaching every new project with a fresh mind and not establish no-no's in the back of your mind. That is what I believe is the best thing the designer can do, especially with the big corporations. Keep trying to start fresh and think—what are the possibilities with this, instead of worrying because you know that this particular line is so crazy that they'll never go with it. Have fun and do it, and sooner or later the pendulum will start to swing another way, and people will become interested in variety.

Moderator: Do you believe that, despite the client's consumer testing, the things which you would have chosen over what they chose would sell as well?

Ben-Amos: No, I have doubts. Because, sorry to say, my taste has been educated in a certain way while many other people have been educated in a different way. cannot guess what all the people all over the world do like. The only way to test it really is by asking consumers and checking it. Researchers ask the questions indirectly. They know what they are doing. They ask about the product, they put it into competition with other products, and they ask consumers, "What would you buy and why?"

Salpeter: Are you saying that a well-designed package is mutually exclusive of well selling?

Ben-Amos: Not always. Not to every market. There is a market that will buy good packaging. It's usually 10 percent of the population that has the taste for knowing good design and liking good design.

Johnson: It's depressing to think that the level of taste in middle America is really that bad.

Ben-Amos: They might have good taste in different categories, in different fields. Maybe they love great music. But in general, if you go for the maximum market—and most companies when they come out with a product want to sell as many products as they can—they narrow it down to what will sell.

Moderator: How does designing annual reports compare with packaging?

Salpeter: Annual reports are a lot easier to do than packaging because there's absolutely no research at all. You do it, and the client likes it or doesn't like it. You come up with a system and you know it's going to work no matter what changes they throw at you. There is a different level of communication compared to packages. Number one, you don't have this immediate gauge of whether it's selling or not. They give them away for free to stockholders, so there is no cash register involved. Also, you can't say things outright verbally, and you just design it with a tone in mind. If you have a good working relationship with the client, there's none of the problems related to packaging. At least, the problems are much more minimal.

Ben-Amos: Annual reports are not so easy to do. When I did quite a few of them in the early sixties, there was money. I could go outside and get Art Kane to do the photography. I could get beautiful paper. I could put inserts and cutouts in. Now they cut everything out because the company will have too limited a budget. Another problem is the changes. Usually I got the material after the dummy was done, after everything was beautifully planned. I got the material five days before it was going to close. And then it didn't fit. Then you have to change everything around and cut out some of the most beautiful pages because you cannot add any more pages if you want to and the client has added 20 pages of copy.

Moderator: Why didn't you select much in the area of corporate identity and symbols?

Ben-Amos: I think there were no serious things sent in.

Johnson: I think we all got really sick of corporate identity in the mid-sixties. Every truck now that goes down Broadway has some mark on it. You can only take so many meaningful marks, and then after that they're not meaningful anymore. I think corporate identity has got to be a joke. It's suffered in the last few years. There is not a lot of it being done now.

Rodgers: The annual report is more than likely substituting for the corporate identity, in terms of work for designers. It is more or less an extension of corporate identity because it conveys a company's image. It's becoming a vital force.

Ben-Amos: Some firms are still very busily working with corporate identity. They change clients. Some years ago it used to be banks and big corporations; now it's all the food chains that are changing. All the hotdog stands suddenly got a corporate identity, fast-food places like Nedicks, and there's more of them springing up. There is a lot of work in it.

Rodgers: It's amazing that there are no real dramatic changes in corporate identity in what we've seen here. Likewise, there are no real dramatic changes, nothing really fantastic, in annual reports, I assume that the two are, in fact, connected, linked, an arm from the same body until one or the other changes. You know, they both reflect each other, so if one doesn't change, then how can the other?

Moderator: Do you think it would help if designers were licensed?

Ben-Amos: I think designers should have some kind of a union, but, sorry to say, I'm not going to be the one to start it. I joined the Package Designer's Council [PDC] hoping that we would be able to get credit for designers. I got on the board of the PDC, still hoping that I would have a say. But most of the people in the council are owner-designers. As owners of studios, they are not particularly interested in giving credit.

Johnson: I'll tell you why they are so secretive. They have to protect the hundreds of thousands of dollars they're charging for that one thing. The finished product can't say, "Joe Smith did this at 2:30 on Friday."

Ben-Amos: I once decided that I won't be a design prostitute. I won't just work for money. I will take less money. I took $5,000 less in salary to work for a firm that was very promising and beautiful. And we did nice work for about a month, and then they went out of business. The truth is that there are people like Walter Margolies, of Lippincott and Margolies, who is a genius at selling a good design. He does. The exact same design done by another office may never get through because someone else may not be as successful at pushing a good design. Not everybody can do this. He has a special way of talking to people that makes them feel very unknowing about this whole field, and they feel very insecure and give in. I'm very jealous of that talent.

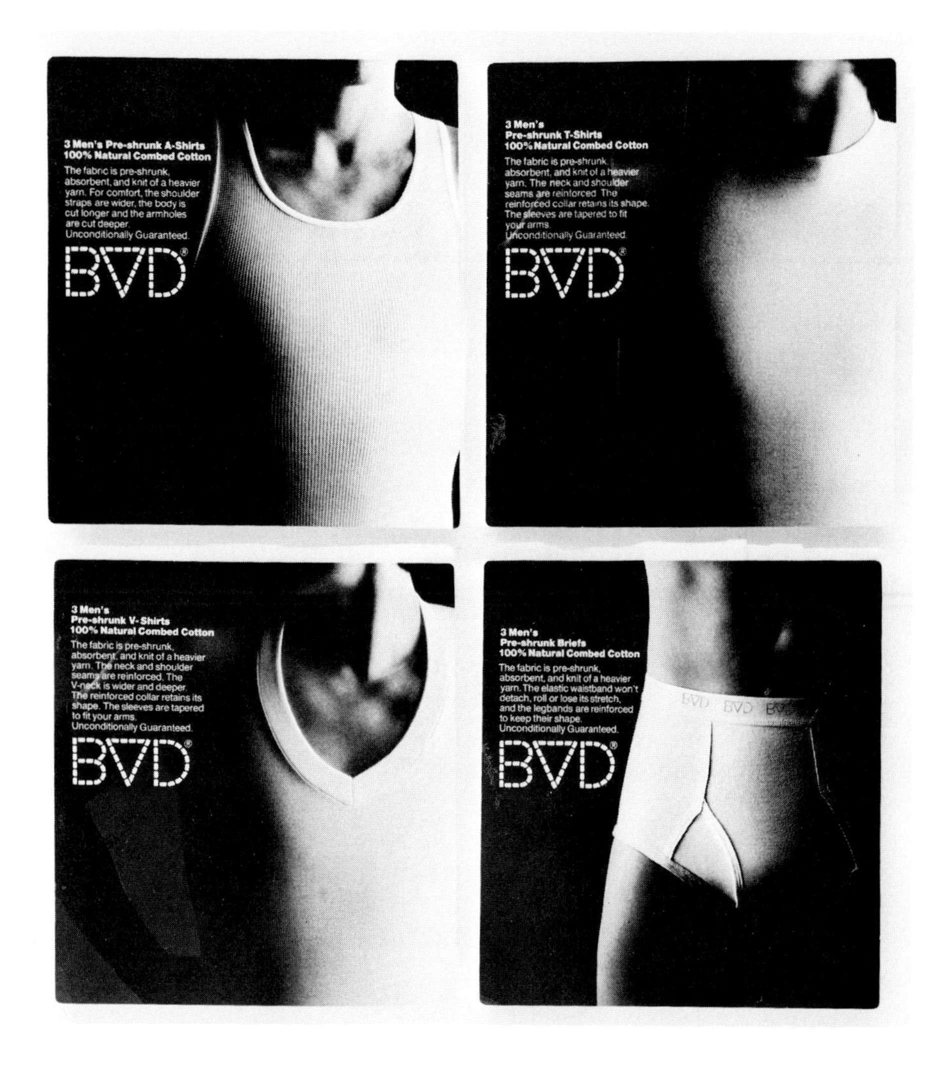

BVD Men's and Boys' Underwear Packaging

The package design for BVD's line of men's and boys' underwear in 22 styles was hailed by all the jurors as the bright spot among the package designs selected. One comment was that the clean quality of the design made the packages easy to understand. The design was also singled out for its logotype. The redesign of this packaging was undertaken to upgrade BVD's image for sales in better department stores. Extensive focus group research was conducted among consumers along with market testings. The rationale behind the use of 4-color photography on the insert card, as offered by the designers, is to allow the customer to see how the garment looks when being worn. The insert card and garment are sealed in a high-clarity polypropylene bag to allow the best possible reading of the photograph inside. The back of the package gives total visibility of the product. A single-item pack contains a card measuring 10 x 9½ in. (25.4 x 24.1 cm), and the three-pack cards measure 11 x 9½ in. (27.9 x 24.1 cm). The background color for the men's basic line photo is blue, and brown is used for the men's fashion line. The boy's line has a background of dark red.

Materials and Fabrication: Insert cards with tapered sides and die cut ends are made of .012 feedcote stock done in 4-color printing on one side with one line tint. Polypropylene bags are high clarity. The back of the extruded and heat-sealed bags are flexo printed in white for fashion colors and black for the all-white basic styles. A 2 mil clear acetate label is used.

Client: BVD Co., New York, New York.
Staff Design: Harvey D. Hirsch, marketing manager, BVD Co.; James Johnston, vice president, marketing, Union Underwear Co.
Consultant Design: Robert P. Gersin Associates, Inc.: Robert P. Gersin, program director; Jan Maakestad, project manager; Ronald H. Wong, graphic designer.

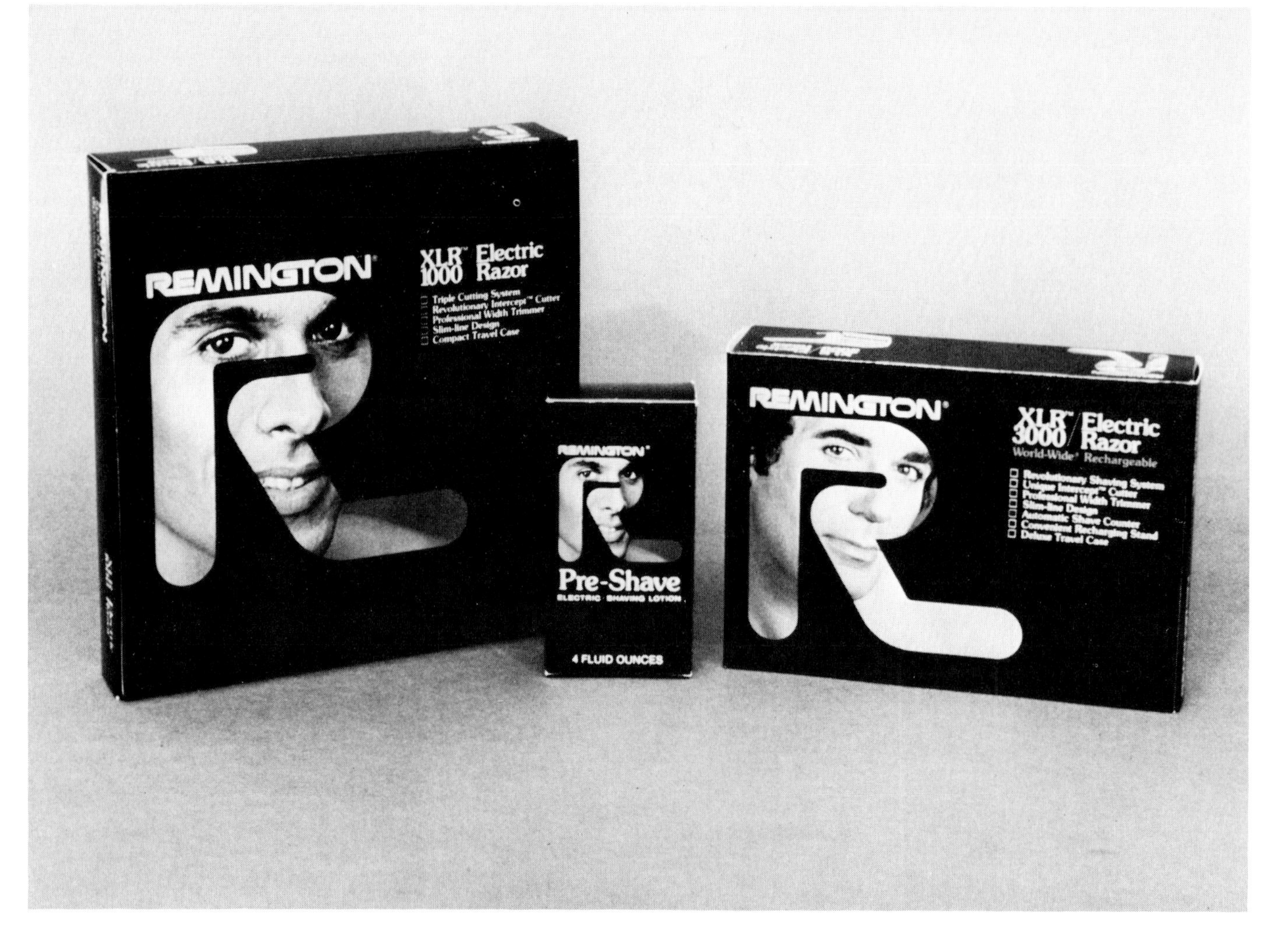

Packaging System for Remington's Shavers and Personal Care Products for Men
The design of this packaging system features the company's brand name on a black background (white is used for the women's product line). Maximum shelf appeal at point of purchase was a design guideline for the packages which are meant to serve as their own display. Some jurors noted that the stylized letter R, stenciled over close-up shots of men's faces, works quite effectively.

Materials and Fabrication: Board type utilized is SBS, with weights from 20 to 24 pt. The windows on some packages use 3 mil acetate. The folding cartons are printed in 5 colors plus varnish.

Client: Sperry Remington, Bridgeport, Connecticut.
Staff Design: Robert Horning, vice president, marketing; Robert McNierney, designer; Robert Tierney, product manager.
Consultant Design: Robert Hain Associates, Inc.: Frederick B. Hadtke, design director; Paul Gensior, graphic design director; Murry Gelberg, graphic designer; Peter F. Connolly, industrial designer.

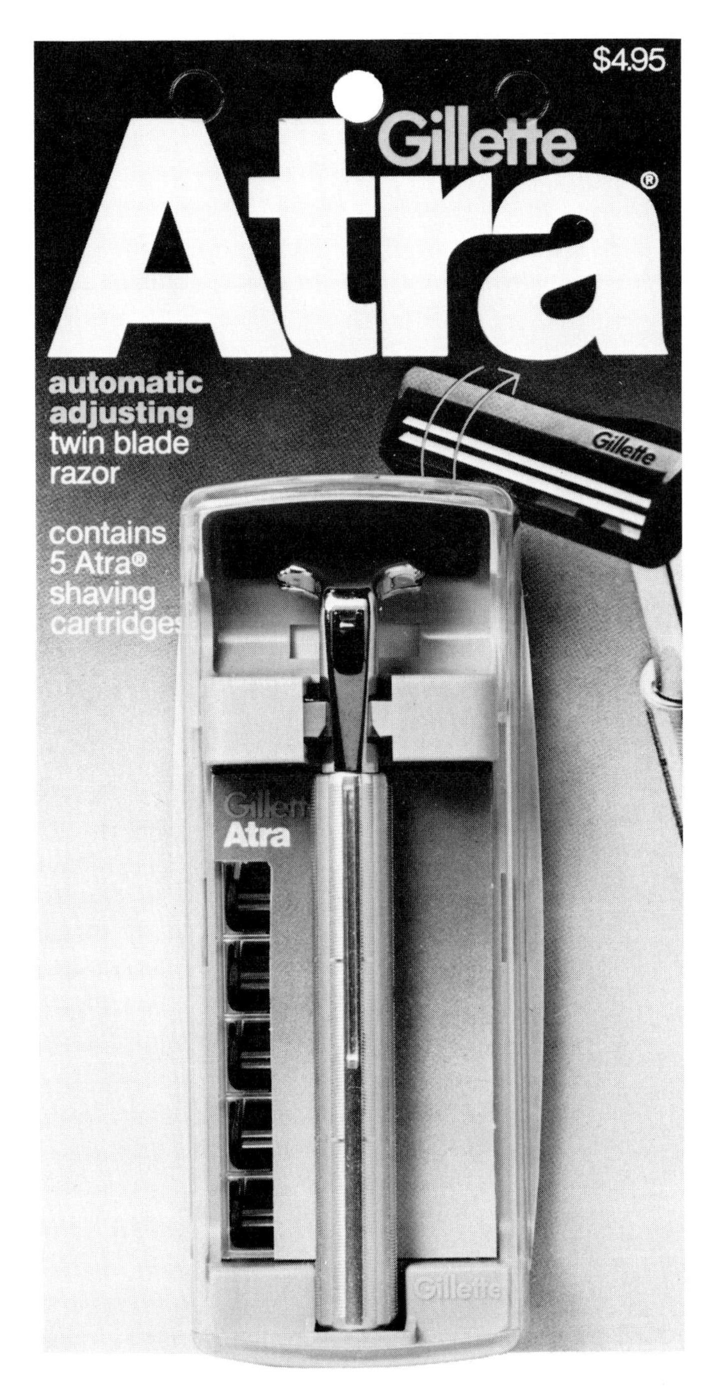

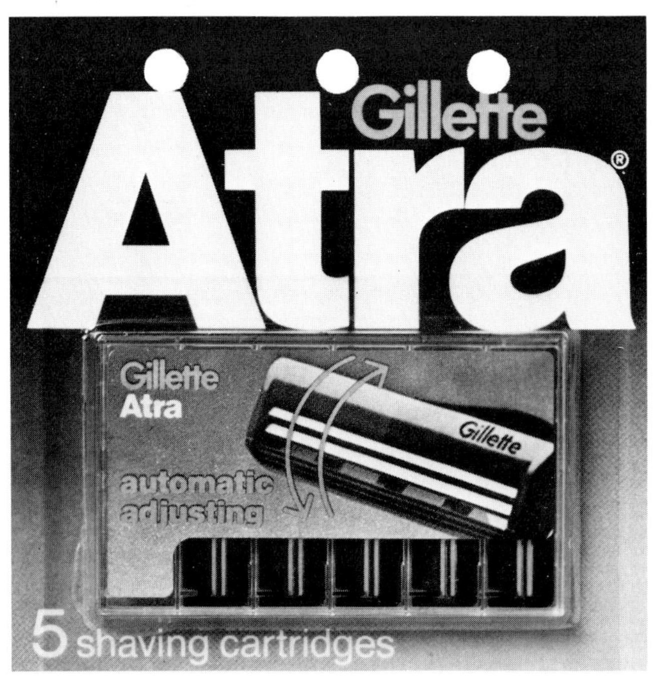

Packaging for Atra Shaving Systems

The package design for this new product relies on a strong presentation of the brand name, printed above a close-up photograph of the razor head. Two swiveling arrow lines in red were applied to the photo, indicating how this razor differs from others. The dark gray cards have the manufacturer's name, Gillette, printed in small red lettering that recedes into a dark background. By comparison the brand name, Atra, stands out boldly in the foreground in large white lettering. The shaded background was achieved in the photography of the razor. Cards for the razor are 4 in. (10.16 cm) by 7½ in. (19.05 cm); blade cards are 4 in. (10.16 cm) square.

Materials and Fabrication: Cards are lithographed. Cases for the razor set adhere to the packaging by means of double-sided tape.

Client: The Gillette Company, Safety Razor Division, South Boston, Massachusetts.

Consultant Design: Morison S. Cousins + Associates, Inc.: James Gager, graphic design.

Packaging for Sheaffer Writing Instrument Accessories
To reduce the cost of packaging and increase sales, Sheaffer's complete line of writing instrument accessories was redesigned. The design process included a complete audit of the company's packaging systems at both the retail and distributor levels. Without any standardization the previous packages used wood, steel, plastic, and paperboard containers. In place of this array of containers a single-sized, new package with three different blister sizes was developed. According to the designers, the new yellow and blue containers are easily prepacked into dozen units. The packages are then wrapped with string in trays for distributor storage and identification.

Materials and Fabrication: Containers employ paperboard and blister packaging.

Client: Sheaffer Eaton Textron, Pittsfield, Massachusetts.
Staff Design: Donald J. Dermeyer, marketing manager.
Consultant Design: Robert Hain Associates, Inc.: Frederick B. Hadtke, Peter F. Connolly, Peter S. Dillon, Paul Gensior, designers.

GAF View-Master Stereo Viewer Package

The panel selected the View-Master package for being a cleverly executed and strong concept which conveys the product with warmth and effectiveness. The package functions to hold the product on peg board or free-standing displays; it also facilitates and encourages prospective buyers to actually pick the unit up to view a demonstration reel and operate the advance lever. The previous packaging was designed to cover the entire product except for protruding eyepieces. Besides allowing access for customer demonstration, the new design gives a full representation of the product's appearance, as well as a visual description of how to hold and operate the viewer. The design parameters for the package were to develop a minimal package, with maximum point of sale impact, that would also help prevent pilferage. In the process, a single bottom self-lock tuck tab was developed. The tuck tab also acts as a platform that holds the viewer in a snug position. This single locking device, the equivalent of two lock tabs plus additional folds required by the previous package's design, consequently saved assembly time and labor, thereby reducing the cost of packaging.

Materials and Fabrication: The package is cut out of 24 SBS box board stock, with four-color printing in red, white, blue, and black on one side. Varnished inks are used to protect the surface. Special die cuts hold the viewer in position for customer demonstration.

Client: GAF Corp., New York, New York.
Staff Design: Paul D. Miller, design services manager; Marc Passy, graphic designer; Larry Shmenco, photographer.
Consultant Design: Harvey Bernstein.

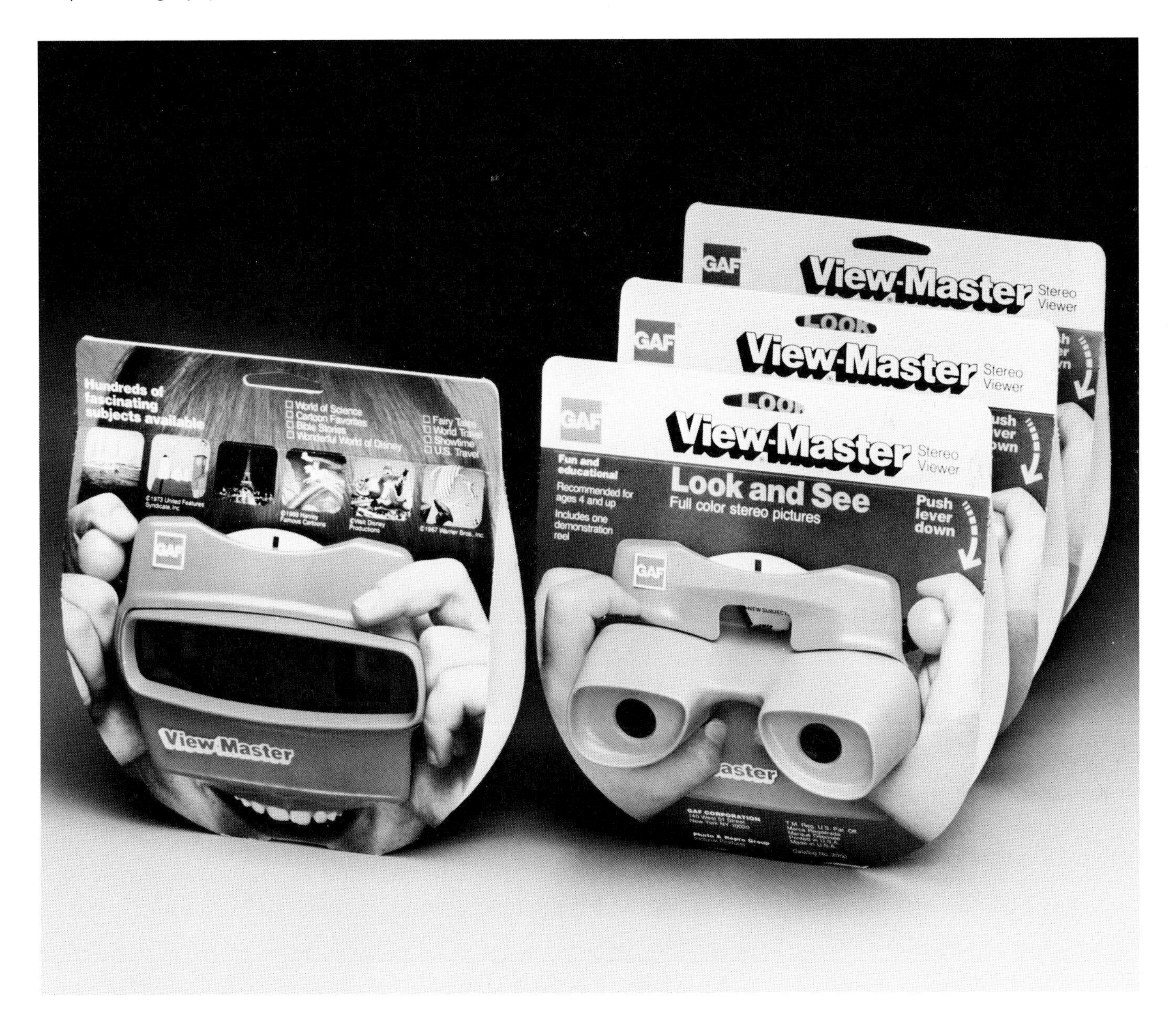

Series of Four Packages for Hammarplast Housewares

The designers of this series had three rather challenging guidelines around which to develop a packaging solution: (1) make nonselling items sell; (2) eliminate the unprofitable situation created by the manufacture of four very different products; (3) unify the appearance of a diversified product line. The panel unanimously agreed that in this case, the designers had come up with the right connections and a successful solution. Though some jurors thought the line a bit uneven in quality, overall they noted the packaging for its simplicity and for a light but firm tone. While surveying existing housewares packaging, the design office also considered problems of store display and ease of handling. The designers studied packages as seen individually, in multiples, and surrounded by other merchandise. With their overriding concern for the effects of packaging on sales at the point of purchase, the designers said, "The photos, and especially the copy, suggest many different ways to use the product. Acetate windows make it possible to see the actual product and its color, which has been found to increase sales over closed cartons. The boxes facilitate attractive store displays for greater point of purchase impact." Among the four products, sold in gourmet shops, houseware outlets, and the houseware sections of large department stores, are three types of storage units—"classy canister," "snappy storage," "anything storage"—and "the perfect pair," a set of salad utensils. Lettering is in either black or white on warm shades of violet, brown, orange, yellow, and white.

Materials and Fabrication: The three folding cartons are made of .020 SBS with acetate windows. Cartons are scored, folded, and glued. The anything storage label is made of .016 SBS. The label is attached to shrink wrapping with a self-stick latex adhesive. Package inserts for classy canister is made of .016 SBS. Printing on all four is 5-color offset with varnish. Dimensions of the anything storage label are 7⅞ in. (21 cm) square. Carton sizes are as follows: classy canister is 13⅝ x 6¼ x 5¼ in. (34.6 x 15.9 x 13.3 cm); snappy storage is 8⅝ x 7¾ x 5⅝ in. (21.9 x 19.7 x 14.3 cm); the perfect pair is 14¼ x 3¼ x 1½ in. (37.5 x 8.3 x 3.8 cm).

Client: Hammarplast, New York, New York.

Consultant Design: Noel Mayo Associates, Inc.: Noel Mayo, president, art director; Virginia Gehshan, director of graphic design, copywriter; Tom Crane, photographer.

classy
canisters
classy
canisters
classy
canisters
classy
canisters
classy
canisters
Hammarplast
snappy storage
snappy storage
snappy storage
snappy storage
snappy storage
Hammarplast

Video Cassette Microphone Package for RCA

The package for RCA's video cassette microphone is among the smallest-sized cartons in a new graphic packaging program for RCA's complete line of video cassette products. The series was designed as a whole to coordinate and unify 16 separate containers with over 10 different sizes into a single product identity. Attempting to make video cassette products synonymous with the RCA identity, the design team set as its goal to wed a strong product identity and product market association with the RCA graphic identity standards. The designers stated that "design participation enabled the strong graphic identity to be carried throughout the variety of products involved. By developing a simple matrix of product/name association, the effective impact was increased while using a simple two-color, cost effective printing approach." Looking the cleanest and least cluttered, the microphone carton stands out as the only one in the series where the product's generic name makes a strong impression by completely filling up one side of the carton.

Materials and Fabrication: Size of this package is 8¼ x 2 x 1½ in. (22.2 x 5.1 x 3.8 cm). All the packaging materials and processes were derived from supplies available in Japan.

Client: RCA Corp., Indianapolis, Indiana.

Staff Design: Tucker P. Madawick, division vice president, industrial design; Pierre Brosseau, manager, TV industrial design; Lawrence L. Mitchell, group leader, industrial design; H. Richard Roudebush, industrial designer.

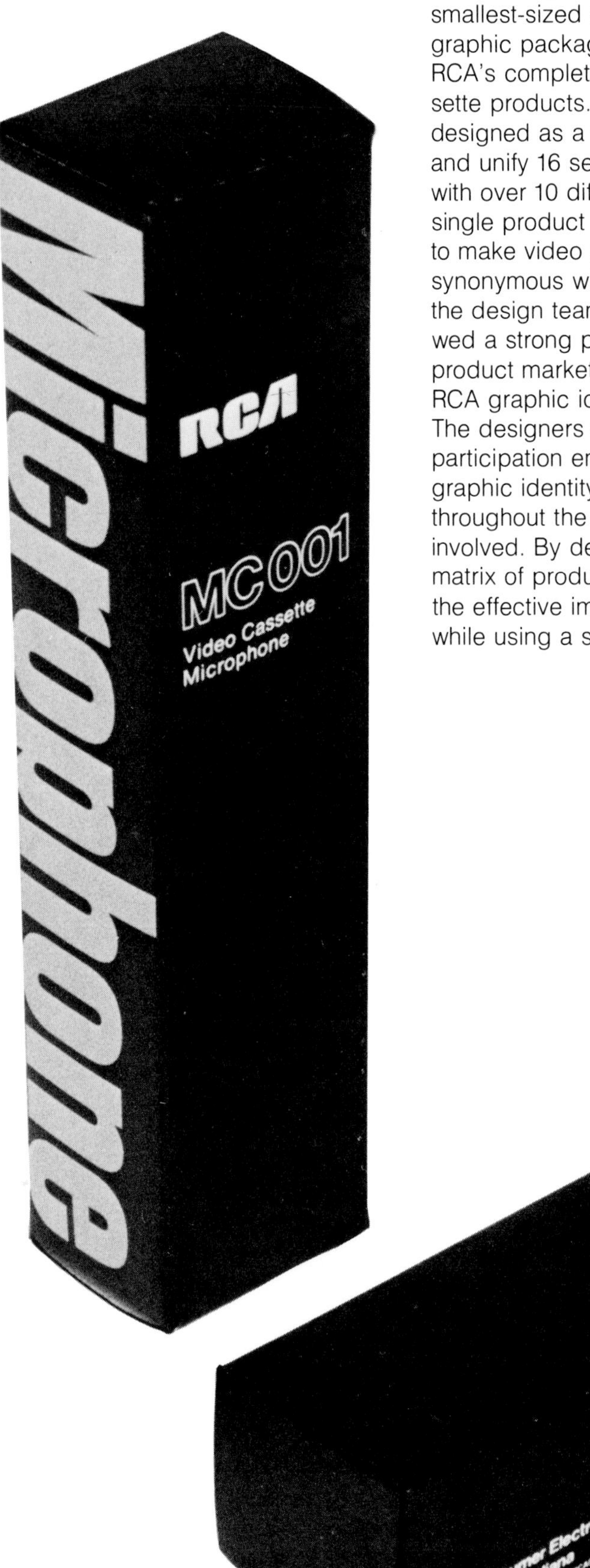

Packaging for Project/One Stereo 100 Headphones

Packages for the Midwestern chain of Playback retail outlets were designed to compete on the shelf by projecting an image that can be quickly identified with the product on a generic basis rather than by a brand name which might be unfamiliar to the average consumer. The Project/One carton measures 6¾ x 6¾ x 2¾ in. (17.2 x 17.2 x 7 cm). The package uses blue and white lettering with a black background on the narrow, end faces. The larger faces, also with black background, are filled with a blue line conversion photo of the headphones. This carton, as well as others in a complimentary series, are designed to be stacked together to form a floor display.

Materials and Fabrication: The corrugated carton has 2-color lithography laminated to it.

Client: Playback, Inc., Oak Brook, Illinois.

Consultant Design: Herbst/LaZar Design, Inc.: Randall Bell, executive vice president, project leader and designer.

Supreme Paint Brush Line Packaging

The jurors agreed that this packaging series is effective for its simplicity and directness. Designed for the retailer as well as the consumer, the packages reflect an effort to provide effective merchandising through quality and service. According to the designers the packaging is "a basic good, better, best program," carried through in white, yellow, and brown colored packages, respectively. Besides deciding from among the line's three levels of quality, consumers must distinguish the type of brush appropriate to the paint being used. To this end packages have a colored arch designed to correspond with the color of the brush handle's tip, indicating one of three brush types—orange for polyester (any paint), blue for nylon (latex paints), green for natural bristle (oil base). The sizes of the cartons vary accordingly. The packaging for the " 3″ " brush, for instance, measures 3⅛ in. (8 cm) wide by ¾ in. (1.91 cm) deep by 7 in. (17.78 cm) high. The package is intended to allow easy inspection of the brushes (if one pushes up on the brush handle) and proper protection of bristles inside the carton.

Materials and Fabrication: SBS whiteboard was chosen along with letterpress printing and varnish in one to three colors.

Client: Supreme Brush Manufacturing Co., Brooklyn, New York.

Consultant Design: Ronald Emmerling Design, Inc.: Ronald Emmerling, Dale Clark, Vicki Mrozowski.

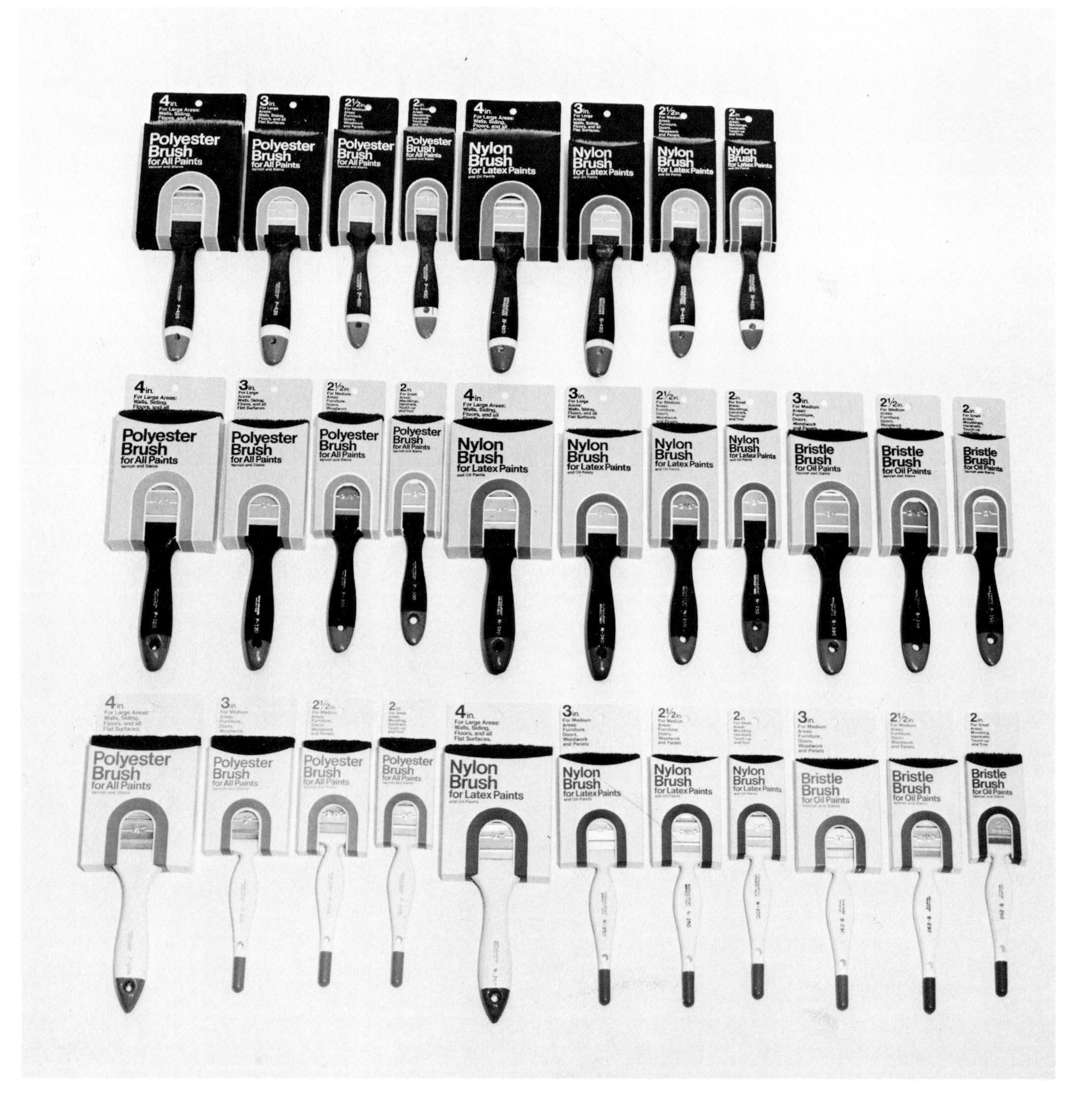

Olin Chemicals' Pace® Consumer Line Pool Chemicals Packaging
This new line of products, developed as an alternate brand to Olin's HTH pool chemicals, is divided into three categories. Since the chemicals require safe handling, each category must be clearly distinct from the others. To accomplish this, color-coded caps are used along with distinguishing illustrations, labeling indicating whether tablets or granules, and cautionary copy. Graphics in yellow, orange, and bright green are meant to create a sunny and clean feeling, as well as impact at point of purchase. To protect them from sun and chemicals, labels have a film laminate.

Materials and Fabrication: Labels are printed lithographically in five colors.

Client: Olin Chemicals Corp., Stamford, Connecticut.
Consultant Design: Gerstman + Meyers, Inc.: Herbert M. Meyers, Juan Concepcion, Vincent Dimino.

Package Graphics for Bubblicious Soft Bubble Gum

A major influence in the design of this product's package graphics that is unique to small-scale packaging is the need to create instant recognition for the product at point of purchase. The designers turned to a selection of strong, if not harsh, colors—acid pink lettering outlined in black on a yellow background. The designers feel that their choice, in comparison with the product's competitors, of bold, attention-getting supergraphics is reinforced by the fact that "most traditional bubble gums have not been supported by advertising." The use of soft, expanded script lettering is meant to reflect the gum's important selling points of soft texture, maximum bubbling, and retention of flavor. While describing the design process, the designers stated, "The importance of 'softness' that is indicated in the design was stressed in initial research . . . that attributed the major portion of growth in bubble gum volume to the new kind of soft bubble gum introduced in 1975. Soft gum was found to be responsible for 75 percent of the bubble gum market generally."

Materials and Fabrication: Packaging is printed in yellow and acid pink and combined in 24-pack counter units.

Client: Warner-Lambert Co., American Chicle Division, Morris Plains, New Jersey.
Staff Design: Saul Heff, art and packaging manager, American Chicle Division.
Consultant Design: Peterson & Blyth Associates, Inc.: Ronald A. Peterson, project director; Gary Kollberg, design director.

Package Graphics for Candydent Sugarless Candies

E. J. Brach & Sons wanted the newly designed packaging for its non-tooth-decaying product to affirm its reposition from the diet food area to the candy sections of stores and supermarkets. Since Brach planned for appeal to children in particular, the designers chose a bold Avant Garde lettering with a bright yellow for package backgrounds. The name is in black, while descriptive copy uses red in condensed lettering. Sections of clear cellophane reveal the candy in both the 4 oz (113.4 g) pouch and the 6 oz (170.1 g) box. Candies are individually wrapped in cellophane with the name printed in white on each. Stripes running across the packages and ending in a cluster of colored circles (purple, yellow, pale green, orange, and red) were designed to portray each of the five flavors (grape, lemon, lime, orange, and raspberry, respectively). For the lollipop package the circles were elongated to reflect the lozenge shape of the candy itself. The cluster and stripe device continues around to the reverse side along with information about the product's ingredients printed in black.

Materials and Fabrication: Pouch and box are approximately 7½ x 5 in. (19.1 x 12.7 cm), and the lollipop pouch is 8⅞ x 5⅞ in. (22.6 x 14.9 cm). Brach chose a lamination of K250-44 cellophane from DuPont on a 75 CB 501 Hercules polypropylene with polyethylene bonding. Packages are printed in rotogravure. Lollipops use paper safety sticks.

Client: E.J. Brach & Sons, Chicago, Illinois.
Staff Design: Robert Urban, marketing manager, new products.
Consultant Design: Peterson & Blyth Associates, Inc.: Ronald A. Peterson, project director.

Saks Fifth Avenue Christmas Packaging

Retailers and department stores in particular have focused more attention in recent years on how they package the items they sell. Considered as an additional means of advertising, packages are carried home through the streets by shoppers and then reused if the bag or box is sturdy and not unattractive. In the metropolitan New York area Bloomingdale's, for instance, is known not only as a department store, but as a lifestyle, complete with its own identifiably "well-designed" brown paper shopping bag. This past year Saks placed its venerable signature on freshly designed holiday packaging. The designer took the traditional Christmas star, stretched it out of its symmetry, and twirled it around to create different effects. The simple white star dances in space above the Saks logo on gift packaging printed with a green, red, or blue background. The star shape was patterned onto the street-level awnings surrounding the store's facade, with strings of incandescent bulbs.

Materials and Fabrication: Collapsible box board packages in various sizes use red, green, and blue ink with a high-gloss finish.

Client: Saks Fifth Avenue, New York, New York.
Staff Design: Doris Shaw, senior vice president, sales promotion manager; Richard Link, purchasing.
Consultant Design: Chermayeff & Geismar Associates: Ivan Chermayeff, designer.

Packaging System for Tivoli Ltd. The design of this packaging system is meant to reinforce Tivoli Ltd.'s retailing image as a sophisticated store oriented towards a European design sensibility. Customers are generally the residents of the surrounding affluent suburb. The store stocks household goods from lines such as Georg Jensen and Royal Copenhagen, which are considered to be of high quality. The system's focal point is actually the creation of a ritual "seal of approval." At the time of sale a Tivoli sticker is applied to the appropriate-sized, blank silver bag or box in a predetermined position. The center of the sticker is red with the word "Tivoli" in white, ringed first by a silver and then a red outer circle. A dark blue arc, with a corresponding inner stripe of orange, swings in from the outer rim of the large red circle. The stickers are 7 in. (17.8 cm), 3½ in. (8.9 cm), and 1¼ in. (3.2 cm). The large range of 20 differently sized bags and boxes needed by the store, with relatively small orders of each size, led to a design solution which allows a high quality 4-color printing at a low-unit cost.

Materials and Fabrication: Stickers are 80 lb, dull enamel, Fasson label stock, with 4-color offset printing in red, orange, blue, and silver. The labels are die cut after printing. Bags and boxes are in a solid silver preprinted paper and box board.

Client: Tivoli, Ltd., Birmingham, Michigan.
Staff Design: Linda McKenney, owner.
Consultant Design: McCoy & McCoy: Katherine McCoy, Michael McCoy, designers.

Berkey's Omega Digital Color Analyzer SCA 300 Packaging
Either amateurs or professionals can use the SCA 300 Color Analyzer, an expensive piece of photography equipment, to set color enlargers. Therefore the designers sought to bring a distinctive, high quality appearance to the type of sturdy corrugated box that can easily look clumsy. Also the package had to make a strong visual statement, whether stacked together forming a pattern with others or standing alone. The carton measures 13⅛ x 9½ x 7¼ in. (33.3 x 24.1 x 18.4 cm). Simple blue and black lettering was placed against a white background for a bold effect.

Materials and Fabrication: White, corrugated folding box, 200 lb test, was used to ensure the safe shipment of individual units. Blue and black ink was chosen for printing with rubber plates.

Client: Berkey Technical Co., Woodside, New York.

Staff Design: Robert Henry, industrial designer; Gary Van Deursen, industrial design manager.

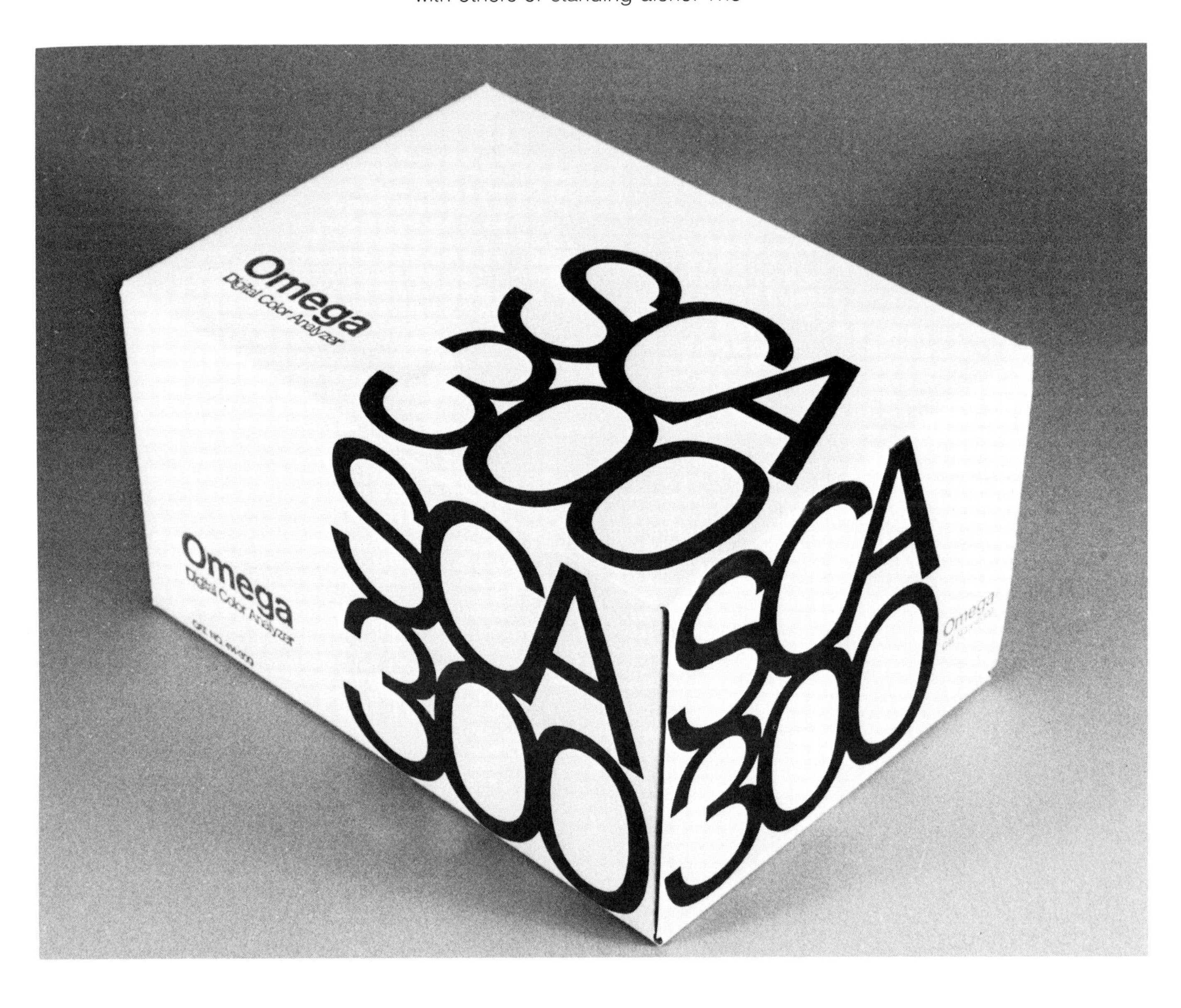

GAF Draftrace 250 Pads Packaging

Another simple, but informative, packaging solution is the updating of GAF's line of professional drawing papers. The pads are manufactured in both metric and inch grids of varying sizes. Each grid type is reproduced on the pad covers within the numeral forms (in this case, "250") of the line's available paper weights. It was felt by the designers that a "clean organization of all elements create strong visual impact."

Materials and Fabrication: One-color offset lithography was used with a glue and tape binding.

Client: GAF Corp., New York, New York.

Staff Design: Paul D. Miller, design services manager; Roger Davidoff, Frank Marshall, designers.

Consultant Design: Ine Wijtvliet.

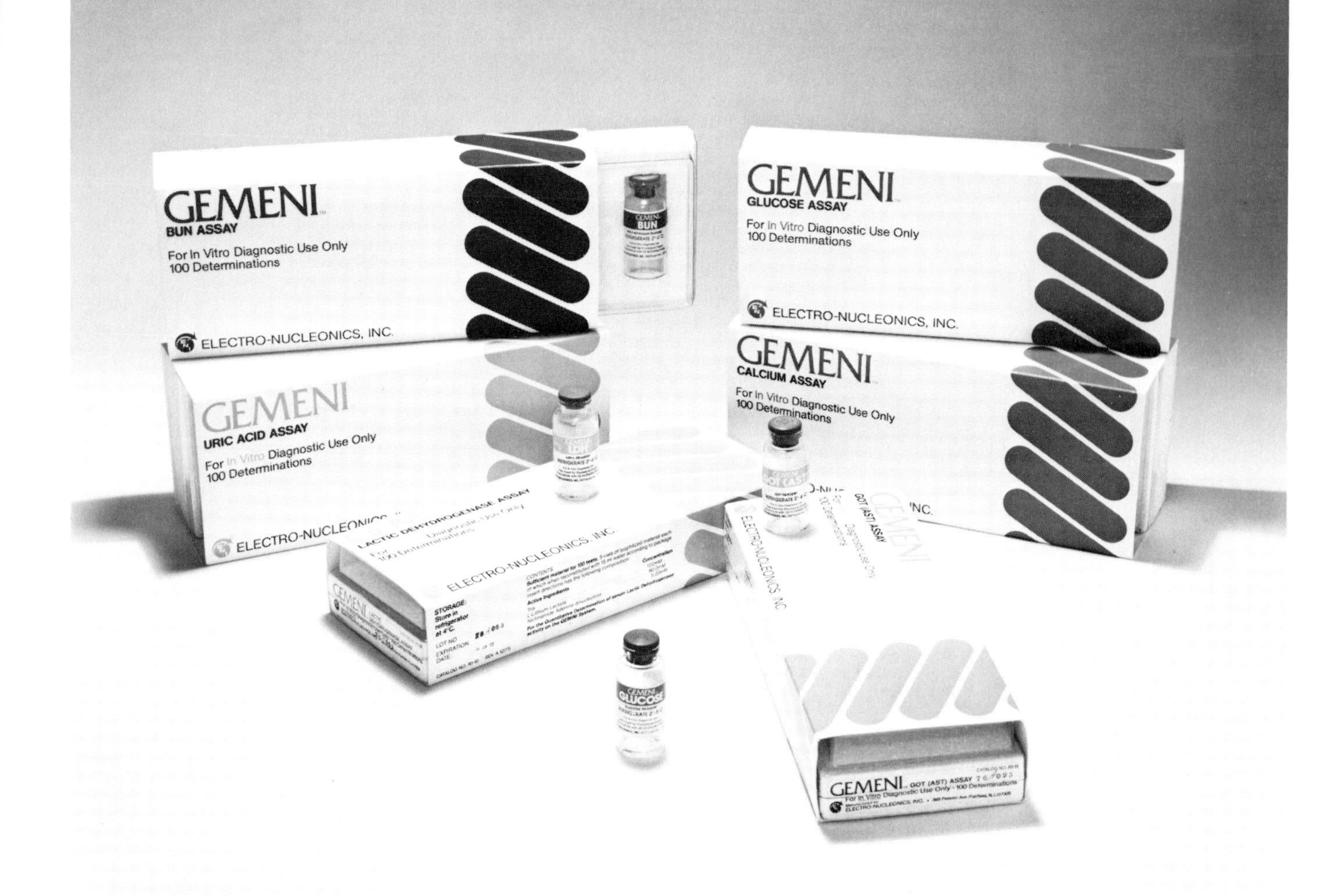

Packaging for Gemeni Blood Chemistry Diagnostic Kit

The jury agreed on the selection of this packaging solution—a new line of up to 20 diagnostic test kits for blood chemistry—because it is a good exception in a market where technical information often has priority over graphics. Gemeni's complete line of diagnostic kits is meant for hospital lab use in conjunction with the Gemeni Blood Chemistry Analyzer. Individual test kits need to be distinct from one another as to procedure and through the use of a color reference code. The bottles of reagent(s) contained in each kit differ from test to test. The reagent(s) are dispensed into a patient's blood serum according to formula, in order to evaluate, for instance, a blood sample for cholesterol level. A bright white, inside and out, was used to give the packaging a clinical, clean appearance and to create a contrast with the various shades of bright yellow, blue, purple, violet, red, and so forth used in the lettering and product graphics. The designers stated that "The clean, crisp colors used for each test kit are in marked contrast to the color schemes used by other test kit manufacturers, which tend to use their corporate color(s) in conjunction with alphabetic differentiation. The design input intended to give each test kit its own easily recognizable identity within a system of up to 20 kits or more. It was also intended that a level of consumer graphic appeal to be instilled in a commercial area where sales are not usually generated by esthetics."

Materials and Fabrication: Package sleeves and bottle labels are varnished and printed in specified PMS color designations for each of the test procedures. The package sleeves are 18 pt. SBS printed on letterpress and varnished. The bottle labels are 60# paper that is bright white and varnished. Sleeves are die cut, glued, and shipped flat. Bottle labels are printed, die cut, and supplied on rolls for use with a bottle-filling operation.

Client: Electro Nucleonics, Inc., Fairfield, New Jersey.
Staff Design: Daniel Chowanec, marketing manager; Maureen McGowan, director of creative services; Lawrence Shack, Gemeni system manager.
Consultant Design: Robert Hain Associates, Inc.: Peter F.. Connolly, vice president of industrial design; Paul Gensior, vice president, director of graphic design; Miro Barulich, Connie Venable, designers.

Container Graphics for Bolt Commercial Insecticides

Considering the poor quality of graphics which exist in this particular product line, to some extent due to the large amount of cautionary and instructional copy required for safety in handling, the jurors selected these containers as a job well done. Design, in this case, was aimed at giving the product a more professional look through a use of graphics which clearly communicate to the end-user (maintenance personnel in commercial institutions) the difference in use of each item within the pest control line. The designers engaged in extensive field interviewing from which they derived a direction for the graphics. Among those interviewed were company sales personnel, distributors, and end-users. The containers utilize a combination of symbols showing the type of insect to be controlled and color coding in red, black, and green on caps and in the graphics and lettering.

Materials and Fabrication: The printing process is basically lithography on aerosol cans: 1 and 5 gal (3.8 and 18.9 l) cans for liquid application and 55 gal (208.2 l) drums.

Client: S.C. Johnson & Son, Inc., U.S. Industrial Products Division, Sturtevant, Wisconsin.
Staff Design: Stanley Cairns, vice president, U.S. Industrial Products Division; Michael Coyle, product manager; John Rizzo, advertising and promotion director.
Consultant Design: Blau/Bishop & Associates: Alan Van Cleven, senior vice president, design coordinator; Donald B. Weber, president, account supervisor.

AIGA Packaging 1977 Call for Entry Poster

From among the six posters submitted, this year's panel selected AIGA's 1977 call for entries to the "What's Real in Packaging?" exhibition. With text in brown, black, and orange lettering, the poster's graphic focus is blue lines of varying thicknesses angled to form an illusory edge, with the exhibition's opening date cut in to reinforce the visual illusion. Exploring the conflict between fantasy and reality was a part of the show's intention. Text on the poster includes entrant information such as theme description, the jury, design categories, submission rules, crediting information, fees, and a membership application. The poster measures 38 x 19 in. (96.5 x 25.4 cm) wide.

Materials and Fabrication: Champion 80 lb paper was offset printed in 4 color.

Client: AIGA, New York, New York.
Consultant Design: Robert P. Gersin Associates, Inc.: Robert P. Gersin, design director; Kenneth R. Cooke, graphic designer; Jan Maakestad, project manager.

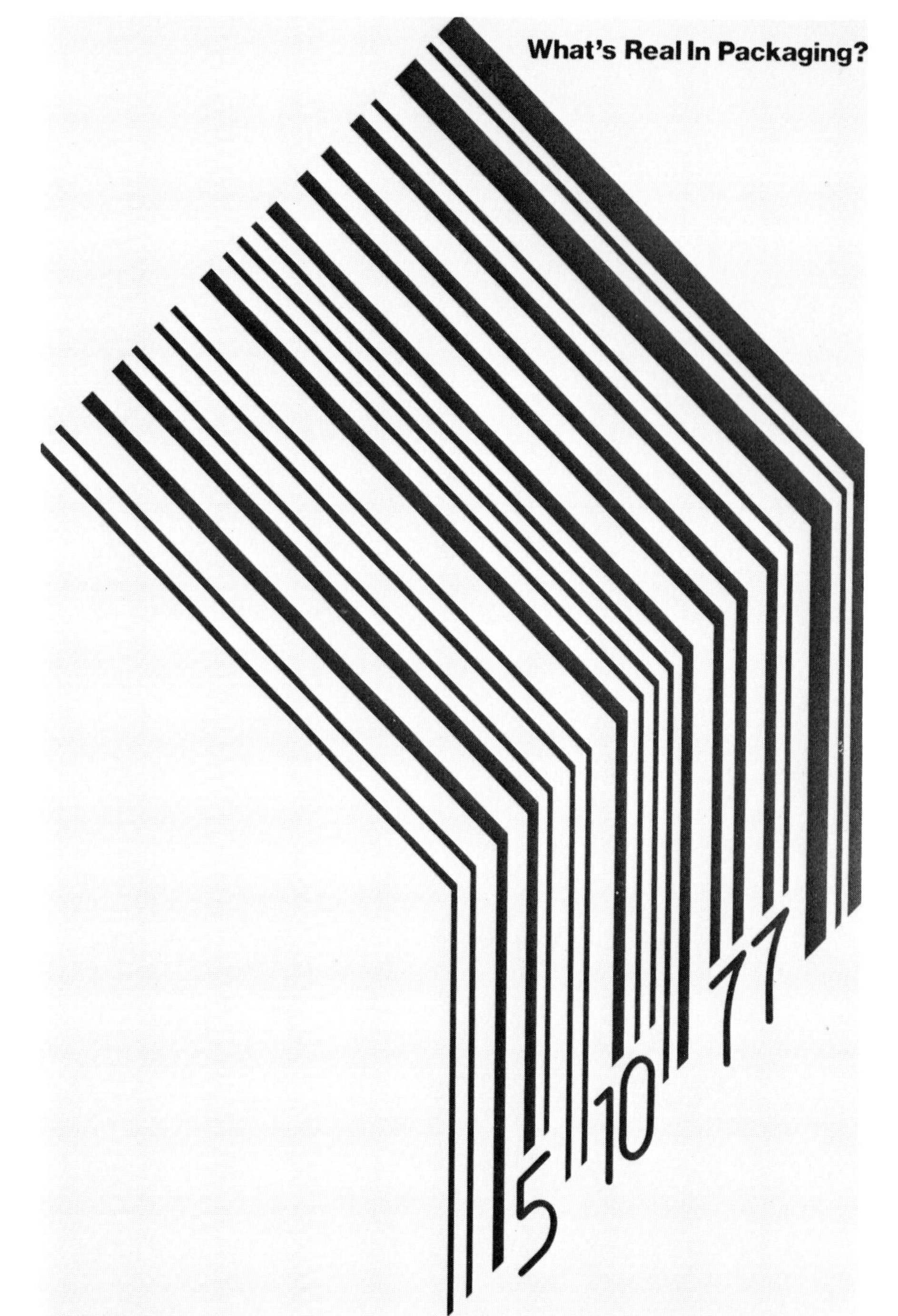

Stationery Design for BVD
Individual placements of logotype, copy separated and structured simply with minimum typefaces, carries through the level of consistently good design that is also evidenced in the packaging for BVD's men's and boys' underwear lines. A whole new packaging and fixtures program dictated the new corporate image for BVD. Standard stationery items include envelopes, mailing labels, and business cards.

Materials and Fabrication: Letterheads and envelopes are printed on Strathmore fluorescent white wove 24 lb stock. Labels are Mac Bac pressure sensitive. Business cards are printed on Hammermill radiant white 65 lb cover. All are nonengraved, printed 2 color with PMS 430 and 287 colors.

Client: BVD Co., New York, New York.
Staff Design: Alan Szydlowski, advertising, sales promotion, Union Underwear Co.
Consultant Design: Robert P. Gersin Associates: Robert P. Gersin, program director; Jan Maakestad, project manager; Alea Garrecht, Ronald H. Wong, graphic designers.

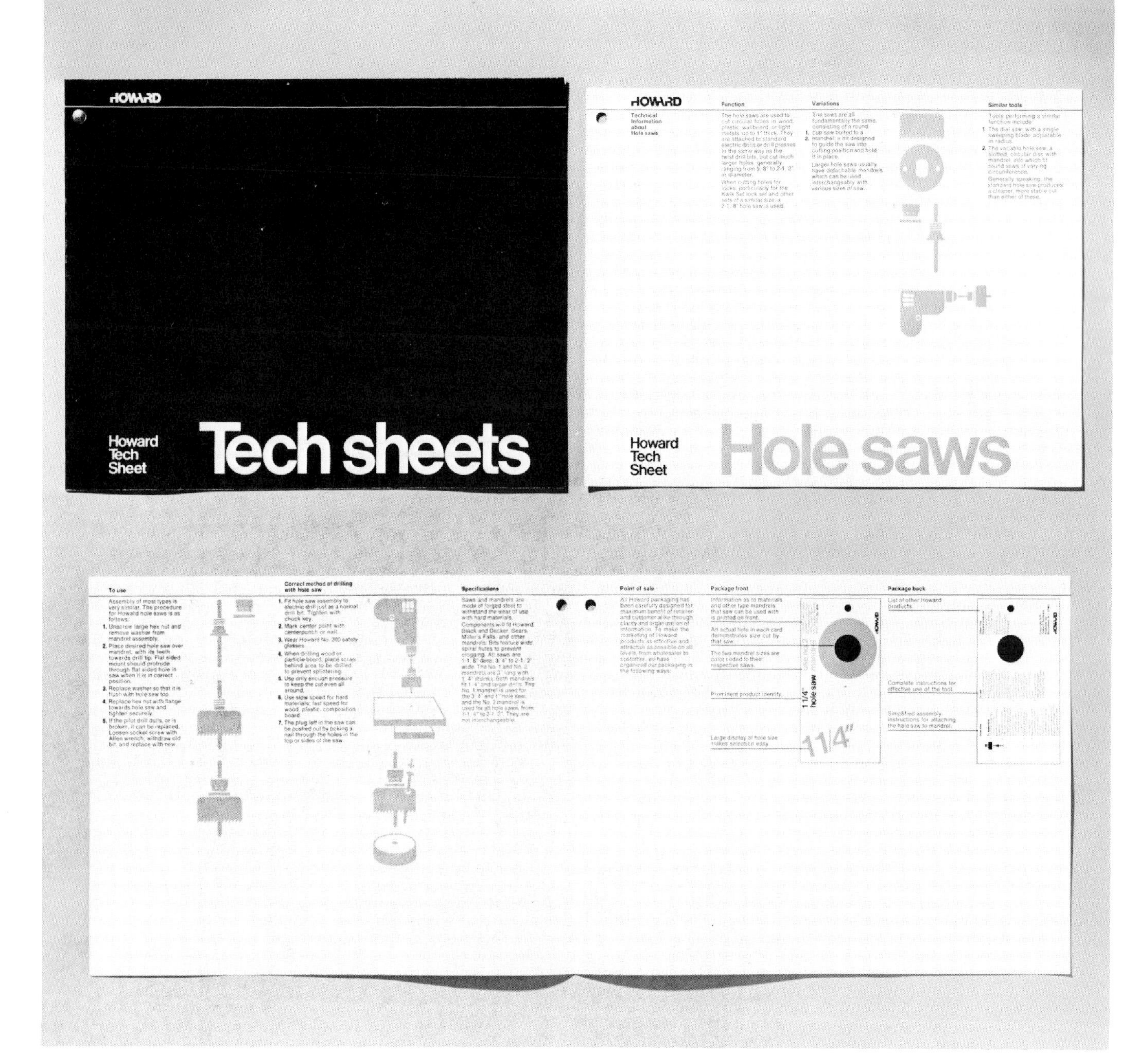

Design of Howard Tech Sheets
Howard Hardware Products decided to develop a series of technical information sheets to describe their line because they felt store clerks too often are not as knowledgeable as they could be about the products they are selling. Besides providing thorough product information, the brochures describe sales aids which relate to Howard's carefully thought-out retail packaging. Stylized graphic drawings illustrated each product and how it functions. The technical sheets utilize a format similar to the Howard catalog, but here text columns are interspersed with vertical rows of illustrations. Brochures measure 8½ x 11 in. (21.6 x 27.9 cm) when folded.

Materials and Fabrication: The vintage velvet stock is printed in a 4-color process, with offset lithography. Kromekote is used for the cover.

Client: Howard Hardware Products, Bloomfield, New Jersey.
Consultant Design: Morison S. Cousins + Associates: James Gager, designer; Johann Schumacher, illustration design.

Catalog Design for Howard Hardware Products

The newly designed catalog sheets for the Howard Hardware Products catalog are uncluttered and to the point. The catalogs are intended for use by salespeople when showing the Howard line to buyers and are to be kept by buyers as a reference to the line. The sheets are designed to measure 8½ x 11 in. (21.6 x 27.9 cm) when folded. The cover page for each tool section has the Howard logo in black, an appropriate symbol for the tool(s), and the section title in red lettering. The reverse side has a black background with orange and white lettering for the text. Here the symbol for each tool is shown in white in an enlarged view detailing the tool's form. The remaining pages contain text running in four columns from the top, with photographs below that illustrate the actual retail packaging for each item. The 4-color process used is offset lithography.

Materials and Fabrication: Vintage velvet stock is printed in 4-color by offset lithography.

Client: Howard Hardware Products, Bloomfield, New Jersey.

Consultant Design: Morison S. Cousins + Associates: James Gager, designer.

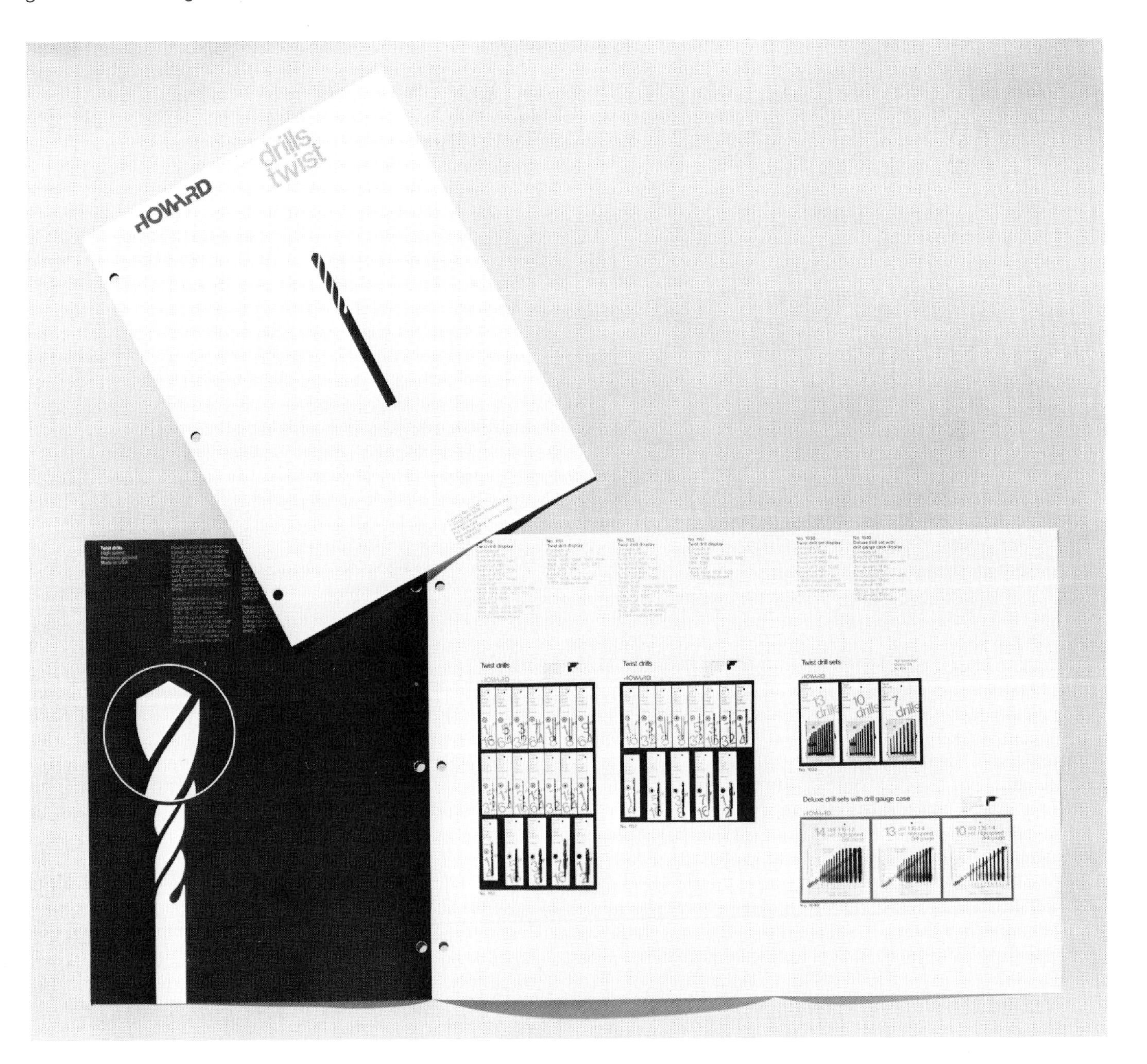

Instruction Pamphlet and Logotype Design for Ben's Block
Both the instruction pamphlet and logo printed in three different weights of the same type on the triangular wooden block were developed to explain and help clarify to the user how Ben's Block aids in the relief of head and neck tensions. The basic concept for the logotype was to symbolize the block's triangular shape by using it in the form of an apostrophe in the word "Ben's." Because each of the block's three edges is distinct in function from one another, the designers chose Helvetica bold for the dull edge, Helvetica medium for the intermediate edge, and Helvetica light for the sharpest edge. The end surfaces of the blocks are equilateral triangles, 3¼ in. (8.3 cm) on a side. End to end the block is 8¼ in. (21 cm) long. The instruction pamphlet's format was determined by the three progressive steps in the therapy. The accordion folded pamphlet, measuring 8 x 32¼ in. (20.3 x 81.9 cm), is photographically illustrated and printed on one side for use as a hand manual or poster. Shrink-wrapped with the block, the pamphlet is first seen by the potential buyer as a part of the packaging. Design of the instruction pamphlet conveys a healthful, clean, and relaxed image for the product.

Materials and Fabrication: Paper used for the pamphlet is 80 lb, which is offset on one side and accordion folded. The logo is wood burned onto the block along the adjacent edge. Colors used are red PMS 185 and brown PMS 497.

Client: Relaxation Tools, Inc., New York, New York.
Staff Design: Ben Benjamin.
Consultant Design: Robert P. Gersin Associates, Inc.: Robert P. Gersin, program director; Barbara Daley, designer.

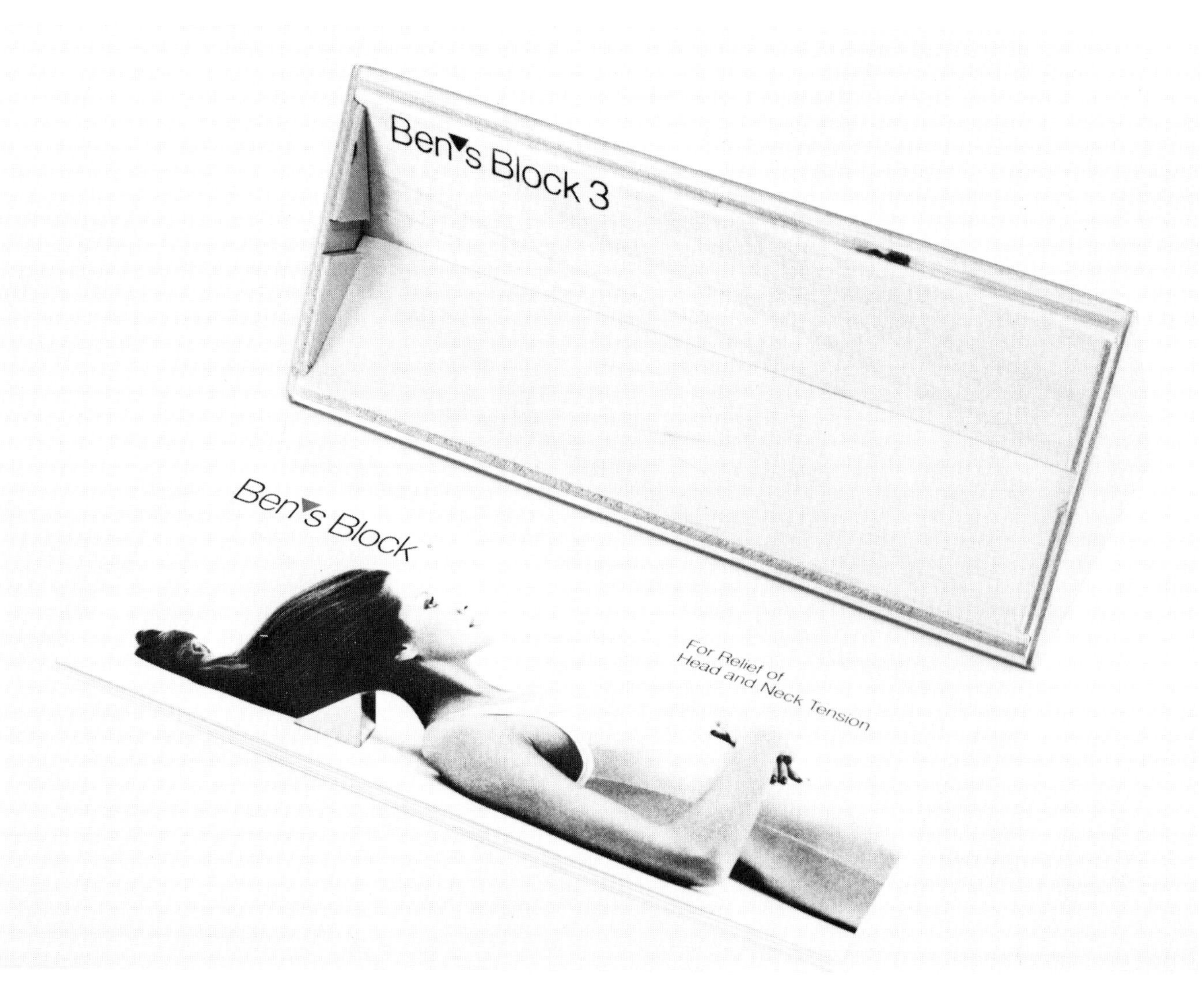

ment to the highest professional standards in career education.

In the United States, there are almost 1,400,000 people employed in apparel design and production, with close to 200,000 of these in New York City. There are nearly 1,000,000 Americans employed in textile design and production. The figures are equally impressive for the fashion-related interior design and home furnishings industry. New York City, designated "Fashion Capital of the World," is the nerve center for the fashion industries. The biggest apparel and textile firms make their headquarters here. Buildings along Seventh Avenue, also known as "Fashion Avenue," Sixth Avenue, Madison, and Broadway, house the thousands of companies that turn out clothing for men, women, and children, and the fibers and fabrics used for apparel and home furnishings.

All the members of the F.I.T. technical faculty come directly from industry, bringing to their teaching the immediacy of their continuing professional activity. In addition, the college draws on the expertise of professionals presently working in industry to serve as critics, lecturer-consultants, and as teaching fellows.

New York City is the jumping-off point for big business. The realm of high finance is dominated by Wall Street and The New York Stock Exchange. Major corporations keep their home offices in New York. The vast communications field finds a focus in the city; there are thousands of advertising agencies, photographers, graphic designers, publishers, and printers. Hundreds of art directors, illustrators, interior designers, creative people from the worlds of theater, dance, opera, film, call New York home because it is a scene of ceaseless excitement and vitality.

The little boutiques, the big department and specialty stores, hundreds of art galleries and antique shops, more than forty museums, make New York the world's greatest cosmopolitan bazaar. Walking the streets of New York is an effortless learning experience. You can take in the fantastic diversity of a city which is not like anyplace else precisely because it has absorbed so much of the culture, so many of the people of the rest of the world. To be a student in New York City is to add a giant plus to a college education. New York lets you stretch yourself because it makes the best of everything accessible, a part of daily living

Recruiting Book for the Fashion Institute of Technology

Compared with the clean, well-organized, almost barren feel of the Swiss approach so prominent in graphic design today, this recruiting brochure for the Fashion Institute of Technology (FIT) appears to come alive with a noisy clutter of eclectic images. Student work—silhouetted, turned on its ends, and sometimes overlapping each other—creates a collage of images taken from illustrations, drawings, photographs, graphics, and filmstrips. The panel cited the brochure for effectively conveying an accessible, hands-on image for FIT. Outsized for a school brochure, the book measures 11 x 14 in. (27.9 x 35.6 cm).

Materials and Fabrication: Printing and typography were done by Crafton Graphic Co., Inc. and Cardinal Type Service, respectively. Northwest matte sheet was printed in 4-color, offset lithography, including the black and white images.

Client: Fashion Institute of Technology, Office of College and Community Relations, New York, New York.
Consultant Design: Danne & Blackburn: Richard Danne, designer.

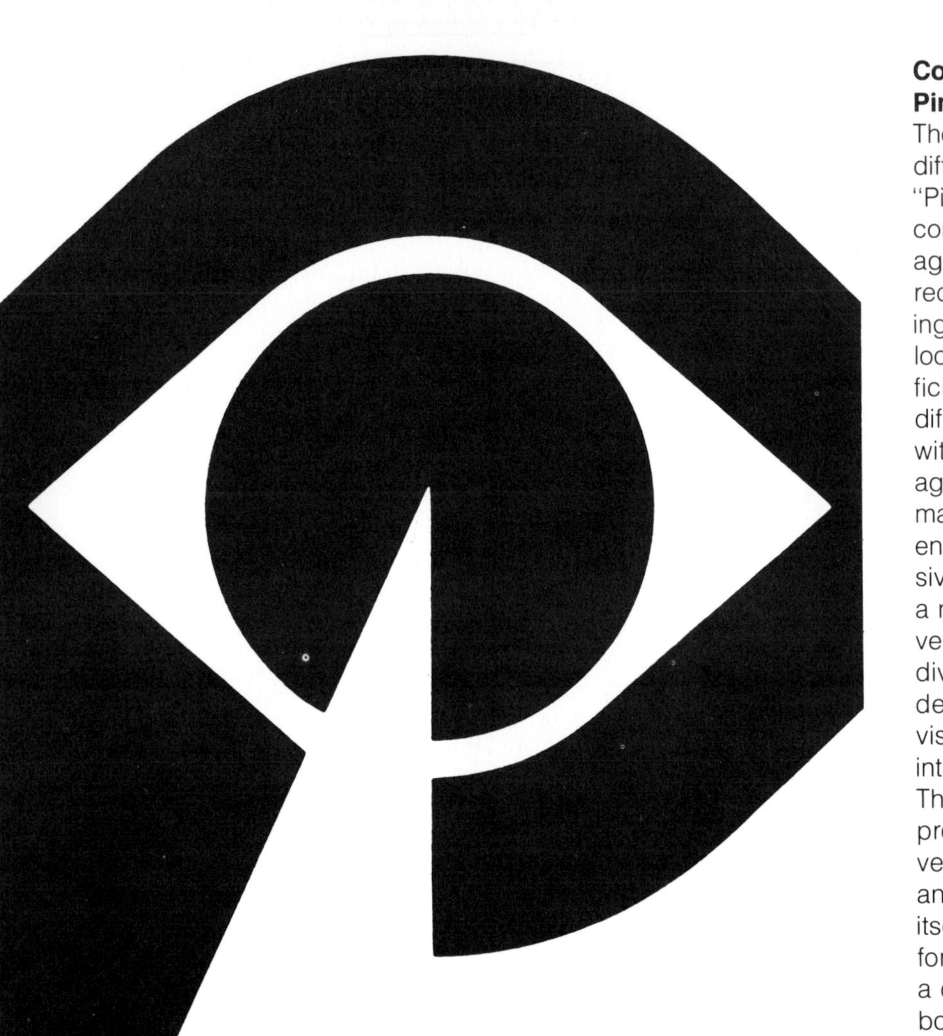

Corporate Identity Symbol for Pinkerton Security Services
Though few people would have difficulty equating the name "Pinkerton" with high security, the company felt that its symbol was aging badly. The old mark didn't reduce well, receded in advertising, and projected an overall dated look for the company. Pinkerton officials also felt that there is a different public to communicate with than the one of a 100 years ago. It was decided to relate their many years of professional experience with a youthful and progressive outlook. Based on this attitude a new identity program was developed for the corporation, its divisions, and subsidiaries. Prior to design input in the new symbol, a visual audit was taken along with interviews of Pinkerton personnel. The outcome is a corporate identity program which covers uniforms, vehicles, advertising, stationery, and financial reports. The symbol itself is the initial P abstracted to form an eye. The use of the eye is a carryover from the previous symbol, a stealthy eye which stared straight back at anyone who dared. Those were the days when the image for "private eye" was something to be taken literally.

Materials and Fabrication: The materials and the method of fabrication vary with the application. In most cases, the symbol is blue.

Client: Pinkerton's, Inc., New York, New York.
Consultant Design: Selame Design: Joseph Selame, president, designer.

The Quaker Oats Company
1976 Annual Report

Quaker's competently designed annual report is done in full color with an eye-pleasing blue as the main color theme on a grayish paper. Appropriate to the company's humble image, the report is small sized, measuring 6 x 9 in. (15.2 x 22.9 cm). The blue cover has a die-cut square at its center, which when the page is turned, reveals the familiar Quaker man from head to toe.

Materials and Fabrication: The report is printed in the 4-color process.

Client: The Quaker Oats Co., Chicago, Illinois.
Staff Design: David Mishur, manager, corporate communications; John Rourke, director, corporate public relations.
Consultant Design: Graphics Group: Steven Keller, partner, art director; Susan Johnson, designer.

1976 Annual Report for H.J. Heinz Company

Heinz's 1976 annual report did not include any sumptuous photos of ketchup slowly oozing from its bottle or any of the other well-known Heinz products for that matter. The designers attempted to provide a different, low-key approach by creating a separate photographic portfolio. The result is a rich photographic essay, shot by Art Kane, with text about America and its cultural background.

Materials and Fabrication: Format size is 8½ x 11 in. (21.6 x 27.9 cm). The cover uses 10 pt Wedgewood gloss, and the text is on 100 lb Quintessence enamel. Gloss varnish was used on all photography and text sections. Printing is offset lithography throughout, 4-color process.

Client: H.J. Heinz Co., Pittsburgh, Pennsylvania.
Staff Design: Thomas McIntosh, director, corporate public relations; Oscar Shefler, conceptual development, writing.
Consultant Design: Harrison Associates: Peter Harrison, design director; Jay Tribich, designer.

Shasta Beverages

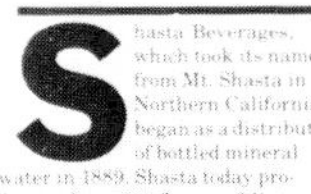

Shasta Beverages, which took its name from Mt. Shasta in Northern California, began as a distributor of bottled mineral water in 1889. Shasta today produces a line of 14 flavors of diet and regular soft drinks. Shasta achieved national distribution in 1976 and will complete geographic expansion throughout all of Canada in 1978. The company operates 22 plants in the U.S. and in Canada.

The carbonated soft drink market has estimated annual sales of more than $10 billion. Growth has been steady due to increases in both population and per capita consumption, although there was a temporary slackening following both the cyclamate ban and the dramatic sugar price increases in 1975.

1977 Results

In fiscal 1977 Shasta achieved record sales of over $180 million with earnings up appreciably from the prior year.

Shasta's Business

Shasta is unique among soft drink companies in several important respects. It is the only carbonated soft drink company that offers a full-flavor line of both regular and diet formulations on a nationwide basis.

Shasta also is distinguished from the other major national brands because it is fully integrated, producing its own syrup and bypassing the franchised bottler distributor. In consequence, Shasta enjoys significantly lower ingredient costs than other major brands. In addition, Shasta distributes most products through chain and wholesale warehouses instead of using the more costly route-truck method. As a result, Shasta can provide equivalent quality beverages to consumers at significantly lower everyday prices than its national competitors.

The Future

Like other soft drink manufacturers, Shasta faces several unknowns. One concern is possible legislation favoring or requiring returnable containers. Shasta, while maintaining its position in cans, is in the process of introducing returnable bottles in several of its major markets on a test basis to counter this possibility and, as well, to take advantage of growing consumer preference for returnable packaging.

Another unknown is the future of saccharin as a sweetener in diet soft drinks. The FDA proposed a ban on saccharin following Canadian experiments that link saccharin to bladder tumors in the offspring of rats which received massive doses over an extended time. Saccharin has been in use in food products for over 80 years. Numerous tests have been conducted, but the Canadian study was the first to suggest that saccharin might be a carcinogenic. Because of the need for a non-caloric sweetener by diabetics and those concerned about weight control and because of the absence of definitive studies, Congress presently is considering an 18-month delay in any ban until further tests can be conducted.

Shasta is committed to meeting consumer demand for low-calorie soft drinks. This is the fastest growing segment of the soft drink market, and it is a segment in which Shasta is particularly strong. Shasta will continue to manufacture diet soft drinks using saccharin as long as available scientific evidence supports its safety. In the event saccharin is banned, Shasta is prepared to introduce other diet products, although all currently available sweeteners contain more calories than saccharin.

Shasta recently entered the food service industry as a supplier of fountain syrup with encouraging initial responses. Shasta is well positioned to compete successfully in this nearly $2 billion segment of the overall soft drink market. Also, Shasta will continue exploring new packaging opportunities, such as "Short" Shasta, an 8 oz. container, introduced this past year.

10

Sales for Business Group

Percent of Total Sales

Shasta's newly designed packaging has strong eye appeal and offers significant potential for exciting shelf displays. In the center row (below) are Shasta's new "Shorts." Short Shasta contains only eight ounces rather than the normal 12. Consumer acceptance in test markets is excellent.

The Value Litre returnable bottle is successfully marketed in Oregon and certain California markets. The new container responds to the trend in some areas toward returnable containers.

Named after Mt. Shasta in Northern California, Shasta Beverages offers a full line of 14 flavors in diet and regular, including the ever popular Cola. Shasta completed nationwide expansion in 1976 and will complete its geographic expansion in Canada in the coming year.

11

Consolidated Foods Corporation 1977 Annual Report

Consolidated Foods is made up of a diversified group of products ranging from a broad spectrum of foodstuffs to institutional food service, restaurants, home furnishings, clothing, toiletries, and vacuum cleaners. Each product category is covered in a double-page spread, one after the other, with close-up product shots silhouetted along with blocks of type on a white background. Three different stocks of paper were used with full color. Dimensions of the book are 8½ x 11 in. (21.6 x 27.9 cm).

Materials and Fabrication: Cover is 10 pt Warren Lustercote stock. Text stock is 80 lb Warren Cameo dull with Weyerhaeuser Andorra. Printing of the text is 4-color process, with web offset lithography, and the cover was printed by sheet-fed offset lithography.

Client: Consolidated Foods Corp., Chicago, Illinois.

Staff Design: Curtis Linke, director of public affairs, project coordination and copy.

Consultant Design: RVI Corp.: Bart Crosby, vice president, design director; George Bosek, photography.

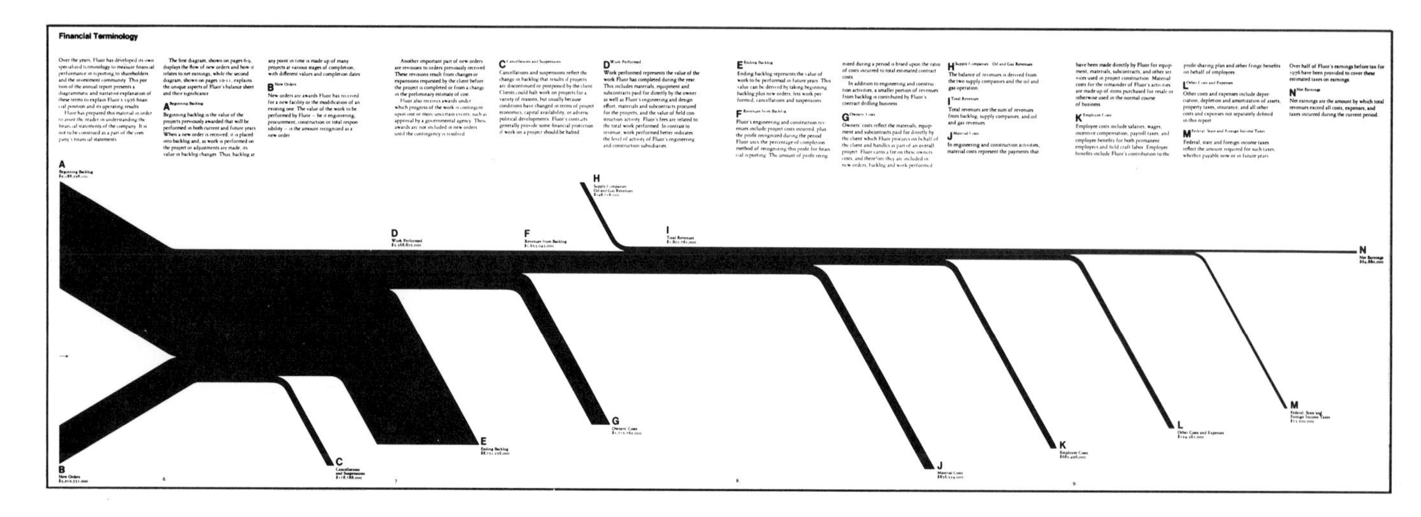

Fluor Corporation
1976 Annual Report

The design of the Fluor report was cited by the panel for its chart graphics, especially the fold-out financial graph done in a soft green with black lettering on a white background, although the jurors did feel that because of its positioning it could be easily overlooked. The highly readable chart has a linear form with off-shoots for each cost data organized by letters of the alphabet. Varying line thickness is used to denote the relationships between each of the costs. Soft shades of color in mustard, brown-orange, green, and violet blue predominate in the various charts and graphs throughout the report.

Materials and Fabrication: Printed with color lithography, the book measures 8½ x 11 in. (21.6 x 27.9 cm). Paper used throughout is 100 lb Kromekote text.

Client: Fluor Corp., Los Angeles, California.
Staff Design: Paul Etter, vice president, corporate public relations, copywriter.
Consultant Design: James Cross Design Office, Inc.: James Cross, art director; Emmett Morava, designer.

Northrop Corporation
1976 Annual Report

This report is of special interest because although the book contains color, all photographs are full-page black-and-whites. These photographs are extremely effective in conveying a serious, high-quality, almost ominous tone throughout the report. To quote from the letter to the shareholders, Northrop serves "the defense and foreign policy interests of the United States and the compatible needs of other nations."

Materials and Fabrication: Measuring 8½ x 11 in. (21.6 x 27.9 cm), the book has Quintessence dull cover 80 lb stock for the cover and Quintessence 100 lb for the text; Kilmory text is the additional stock. Printing is offset lithography, with black and three match colors and a dull varnish.

Client: Northrop Corp., Los Angeles, California.
Staff Design: Les Daly, vice president, corporate affairs; Judith Wheeler, manager, editorial services, copywriter.
Consultant Design: James Cross Design Office, Inc.: James Cross, art director; Andrew Nawrocky, designer; Robert Horton, Ronald Scott, Marvin Silver, Per Volquartz, photographers.

St. Regis 1976 Annual Report

Visually lush, this annual report was selected mainly because of its well-chosen and carefully cropped images. St. Regis is involved in the printing field as a manufacturer of publishing papers, packaging and related materials, and specialty reprographic papers. At first glance the bold graphic images seem not to relate to the data they are interspersed with. A second look reveals high-quality reproduction of product images, such as a roll of paper viewed from its edges, which have colors and shadings difficult to reproduce sensitively, especially in full color.

Materials and Fabrication: Four-color process used in an 8½ x 11 in. (21.6 x 27.9 cm) format.

Client: St. Regis, New York, New York.
Consultant Design: Cook and Shanosky Associates, Inc.: Roger Cook, Donald Shanosky, designers.

Graphics for Marketing Impact. *In the dazzle of today's supermarket, what makes the shopper in a hurry pick one product out of a thousand—such as our customer's frozen peas—to put on the dinner plate? The package is one of the keys. Its color and shape. The distinctiveness and realism of the illustration. The stimulation of the word message. St. Regis knows buying psychology and how to design and print a package that sells at retail, be it a frozen food overwrap or other flexible food package, a folding carton, a consumer bag, or even a corrugated box, which can now be printed with new visual appeal. What assistance can the company offer a customer in the creation of a hard-selling package? The St. Regis marketing and design team can research his product and marketing rationales and develop ideas for graphics—rough at first and then fully refined. These ideas are matched to production capabilities, and finally, St. Regis can generate the artwork and finish the complex preparations for printing and converting the package.*

Bag Packaging. The Bag Packaging Division still felt the effects in 1976 of the overheated economy of 1974—a time when many users of multiwall bags, consumer bags, blown film, and other packaging products accumulated inventories. The year 1975 saw weakening of demand and eroding prices as inventories were adjusted during the recession. In 1976, volume picked up strongly in the first half, fell off in midyear, and then moved up again in the closing months. But prices, though higher at year-end, have not kept pace with cost increases. As a result, profit from operations was 16 percent below that of 1975.

Folding Cartons. Sales of folding cartons in 1976 moved up in line with increased consumer spending for nondurable products. However, price competition was extremely vigorous. As a result, the Folding Carton Division could not offset steadily rising costs of paperboard and other materials. This, combined with the non-recurring costs of reestablishing the former Pensacola plant in a new, more efficient facility in Atlanta, affected the business, and profit from operations declined 89 percent.

Laminated and Coated Products. Resurgence in demand for the diverse packaging and protective products of the Laminated and Coated Products Division was the main factor behind a sharp turnaround in this division's results. It gained 92 percent in operating profit from the extremely depressed year of 1975. A very strong market in 1976 was the automotive industry, which was a substantial buyer of the division's inner wrapping materials for parts packaging. There were several new products that broadened the division's line of masking papers, as well as added items in its line of release-type papers. An important new paper used for image transfer in copy-machines became fully commercial.

Consumer Products. Extremely good business in both paperware and school supplies was offset by difficulties in the envelope operation, which was adversely affected by a falloff in volume and by operating problems at a newly relocated plant. Profit from operations was off 22 percent. In paperware, the division benefited from a better product mix and distribution pattern, as well as from more selective selling. In school supplies, the principal factor was the achievement of national distribution through a number of well-known retail chains. Plans were announced to build a new plant at Phoenix to serve southwestern and western markets.

11

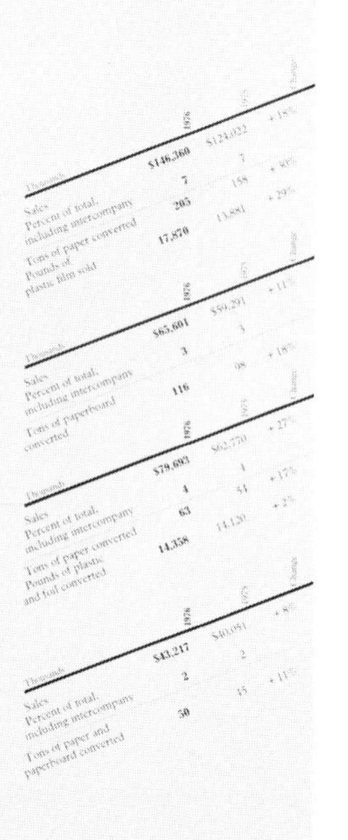

Thousands	1976	1975	Change
Sales	$146,360	$124,022	+18%
Percent of total, including intercompany	7	7	
Tons of paper converted	205	158	+30%
Pounds of plastic film sold	17,870	13,881	+29%

Thousands	1976	1975	Change
Sales	$65,601	$59,291	+11%
Percent of total, including intercompany	3	3	
Tons of paperboard converted	116	98	+18%

Thousands	1976	1975	Change
Sales	$79,693	$62,770	+27%
Percent of total, including intercompany	4	4	
Tons of paper converted	63	54	+17%
Pounds of plastic and foil converted	14,358	14,120	+2%

Thousands	1976	1975	Change
Sales	$43,217	$40,051	+8%
Percent of total, including intercompany	2	2	
Tons of paper and paperboard converted	30	[illegible]	+11%

Environmental

Artsite, Traveling Museum for Original Works of Art
MAN TransFORMS/Aspects of Design Exhibition,
  Cooper-Hewitt National Museum of Design
Exhibit Components of the Participatory Learning Environment,
  Brooklyn Children's Museum
Lever House Exhibition, Design Education at Pratt Institute
Corning Housewares Exhibit
Citicorp Center
Brookstone Retail Store
Lutheran Medical Center
Squash/1
One Fifth Restaurant Design
Meadowlands Racetrack Lighting, New Jersey Sports Complex
Coordinated Architectural and Environmental Graphics Program
  for North Central Bronx Hospital
Interior Design of Elevator Cabs
Site Markers and Trailblazers for New York City Heritage Trail
Signage Program for Central Ohio Transit Authority (COTA)
Zoo Graphics System, Animal Information Signage

The number of submissions in this category was 66, of which 16 were selected by the panel. It continues, along with the Contract and Residential category, to be the most undersubmitted category in the review. The entries submitted formed the following groupings: exhibition and trade show design, environments and interiors, transportation and special use vehicles, street furniture and public amenities, environmental graphics and signage programs.

Members of the jury panel were Bruce Burdick, David Pesanelli, Davad Rice, and Judith Stockman.

Bruce Burdick.

Davad Rice.

Bruce Burdick
Founder of the Burdick Group in San Francisco, Bruce Burdick strongly believes in finding the design solution to fit the environmental situation. His firm has sought out innovative resolutions to design problems, most notably in the field of exhibition design. A 1960 graduate of the Rhode Island School of Design, with a degree in industrial design, Burdick plans his exhibits with effective display techniques and audiovisual aids so people can interact with them. Some examples of recent designs include the Food of Life Exhibit, sponsored by Swift Eastmark at the Museum of Science and Industry in Chicago (Burdick and his team developed a computer access system capable of providing personalized information on more than 200 foods to visitors, based on their height, weight, age, and sex); the California Edison Exhibition for the Museum of Science and Industry in Los Angeles, with a 12-ft (3.7-m) communications tower that talked to viewers about the energy crisis; and the development of a concept for the new San Diego Zoo.

David Pesanelli
As the principal of David Pesanelli Associates, a Washington, D.C., firm working in print graphics, exhibitions, audiovisual, signage, and some industrial design, David Pesanelli has also been engaged in designing some specialized environments for Amtrak. A total environment package that includes a control room and city ticket center system, it can be used in any of the spaces Amtrak leases. An innovative approach that his firm is developing is formative and summative evaluations supported by a consulting psychologist. Pesanelli is a member of the American Institute of Graphic Artists and the Washington Art Directors Club. The firm has received awards from both groups. Pesanelli received his BFA from Rhode Island School of Design in 1960 and worked for three years on automotive design with the Ford Motor Company. Over a five-year period he was involved in designing corporate exhibits. In 1969 Pesanelli became a partner in Tasi Gelberg Pesanelli, Inc., which was reorganized into its present form six years ago.

Davad Rice
Nexus Design, Inc., founded by Davad Rice in Detroit in 1972, lists among its clients the city of Detroit, Detroit Edison, the National Bank of Detroit, Detroit Bank and Trust, and Manufacturers National Bank. Now in the process of designing an exhibition in collaboration with photojournalist Ed Bailey for the Ford Motor Company, Nexus Design was cited in the January 1978 issue of *Progressive Architecture* for its involvement in graphics and signage design for an environmental street furniture manual which was developed along with another firm. Other current work ranges from corporate identity programs to a line of designer T-shirts. Rice, who established the Organization of Black Designers in 1975, is a member of the Society of Environmental Graphics Designers. He received his BFA in industrial design from the Center for Creative Studies in Detroit in 1971. Before opening his own consulting office, Rice freelanced for a year and a half and spent a brief stint with Ford and Earl Associates in Warren, Michigan.

Judith Kovis Stockman
A principal of Stockman & Manners

Associates, Inc., in New York, Judith Stockman's work covers all facets of design for corporate headquarters, banking facilities, restaurants, hotels, and exhibits. Stockman's design philosophy is strongly rooted in marketing. Accordingly, she believes good design must not only solve the client's functional requirements and be esthetically pleasing, but also project a strong identity. Recent examples of her firm's work, all in New York City, include The First Women's Bank, GAF Corporation offices, Cafe des Artistes restaurant, La Potagerie restaurant, and preliminary designs for the proposed New York City Convention Center. Stockman & Manners has received awards from the Illumination Engineering Society of New York, *Institutions* magazine, the Art Directors Club, and Print Casebooks. A graduate of Pratt Institute's department of interior design, Stockman has lectured at the Smithsonian Institution, Washington, D.C.; Parsons School of Design, New York; Pratt Institute, Brooklyn; and for the Institute for Business Designers.

Following is a general discussion of the submissions in this category.

Moderator: Would you comment on why two submissions, Art Site and Brookstone Hardware Stores, both by the same designer, Murry Gelberg, were selected?

Pesanelli: It's because Murry has a feeling of totality about things. When you've looked at so many projects and find the exhibition part of it is nice, or the science part of it nice, but the logo stinks—it's not a wholly satisfying design. But Murry has one of the most unique feelings for the nature of things. He really gets inside it and is able to express the concept, not so much in analytical terms, but in the essence of the thing—the personality, the character, all that. He incorporates an analytical character too, but that's not generally the direction he comes from. He just understands the nature of things very well and is able to put a project together as a total thing.

Moderator: That word "personality" has come up a number of times in the judging. There is a lot of criticism about the lack of it in design, that everything is so sterile, so similar. There's very little that says, "Hey! I'm something special and I'm good design as well."

Burdick: I'm fairly certain that Gelberg's experiencing the encounter himself with the objects, and that he's designing out of that encounter because both things have a very real encounter experience to them. You are inside them in many ways from the way that he's handled them.

Left to right: Judith Stockman and David Pesanelli.

Stockman: Part of that comes from the fact that he really projects who the user is. You can see this especially with the tool shop [Brookstone], the fact that he let the design be very much in keeping with the use that the tools have. The detailing and the materials are both in keeping with what those materials are used for and who uses those tools. The type of person who is interested in his tools will also be interested in their design.

Moderator: One wonders if this area that you're judging isn't one of the only areas where it's easier, in fact, to project those aspects, as opposed to packaging or consumer products which are highly researched and go through endless handling and testing before they're distilled down to the broadest common denominator.

Burdick: The problem of greater numbers is inherent in them. Whenever you begin to design a greater number, you are immediately entrapped in that problem. The world is divided up into 5 percent markets. A Chevrolet is designed for the greatest number, the Porsche is not. It's designed for the 5 percent who may want a Porsche. Those tools are not designed for any great number; they're designed for the 5 percent.

First off, I think that you have to design for yourself, because that's the only input that you have. That's the reason that the Brookstone thing is so successful. Gelberg designed it for himself. And then you have to hope that some other people like what you have done.

Moderator: Do you think designers can solve any problem, that they can be in touch with any market, or must they have an affinity with what they are designing?

Burdick: It depends on what they're bringing with them. For instance, with Henry Dreyfuss's group of elements, he could not have helped but design the telephone any other way than how it was designed. It's homogenized milk, it has no cream in it. It has no personality. It has nothing, but it functions well.

Moderator: If that phone had been designed today, would you include that in *Design Review*?

Rice: That's a difficult question. Are you implying that the design has a particular classical longevity, or are you talking about its appropriateness to the problem that has to be solved? Since problems shift, I would assume that solutions would also shift.

Moderator: Let me give you another example. Are you familiar with Polavision? Would you include that in *Design Review*?

Burdick: It depends on what you ask from the things around you. If you ask for them to enrich your life, then I think that hopefully they do some enriching. They may have an appropriateness to you on some level other than its function. For instance, a styrofoam cup holds wine, so does a wine goblet. So as far as the basic function, the styrofoam cup fulfills that function in terms of holding a liquid. But we have other functions that we put upon the serving of wine. So the question is what functions one puts upon the products that one uses. Most of us put very little requirement on the telephone except to dial it. It is completely neuterized. It is distilled water drippings. You don't want, I don't think, too many things neutralized.

Pesanelli: I'd like to continue a little further by asking if someone with Gelberg's type of perception, for example, could apply the quality of design he accomplished in that store and exhibition on a larger scale. Knowing him pretty well, I feel that, as a person, he likes to be in control of everything his work encompasses. I think that that's what he's doing very well, working at that scale. Those are not very large projects. They have a discreet quality to them and definite limits. In the Artsite exhibition, he controls everything beautifully. It defines its own space, it clears up the floor, it gets rid of extraneous structure, it shows everything well with a lot of visibility. But it's only 15 x 20 ft [4.6 x 6 m] and retains a sense of an intimate, personal statement.

Moderator: Do you think that environmental projects lend themselves more to the designer's "soul"?

Stockman: I think that they do in that people experience them on so many more levels. And a designer can express him or herself on so many more levels. There are more ways to communicate with people than simply the functional level that one is restricted to with products, literature, or promotional graphic products.

Rice: You're consciously dealing with more dimensions. And that in itself generates more excitement. It's like being a juggler.

Burdick: As an example, one of the difficulties in teaching is that if you use the word "emotions," and this is really the expression of the designer, that can release a lot of students to say, "Okay, I'm going to do my thing." But that thing has to have a verbal matrix that it moves through, otherwise it's awful trite when it comes out. Murry hits a lot of levels. Other design that we've looked at here doesn't reach those levels.

Rice: I like to think of a designer, in a sênse, as an actor. An actor brings himself to many roles. There are some roles where you'll see a guy and say he is miscast. He might have done a credible job, his enunciations were good, his emotions were good, but for some reason, he did not come off in that role. I have a feeling that, discounting the economics and what have you, a designer can be successful in most things that he does, based upon how well he knows himself. I think that when you know yourself, you are more secure about what you attempt, regardless of what the constraints are.

Pesanelli: I had the feeling after going through all the projects here that I kept seeing too many times what I had seen before. There was not very much spirit with an experimental attitude or of an adventurous nature. I think that designers have basically found a visual way of communicating between themselves. They have found a way of getting the approval they want by staying very much within certain forms and by offering a limited number of experiences to the public. A lot of design is not oriented to an audience, whether it is the 5 percent audience that Bruce talked about or the 80 percent audience. It is really designers speaking to themselves in their own visual vocabulary. Maybe it's also designers finding approval among their clients with a visual vocabulary that clients can relate to. What's showing up may be good business, not creative design. As I was going through the entries, I felt that a lot of times I was lowering my standards by accepting some of them. A lot of the work comes out in a sort of office style. Yet, you would expect more diversity because of the heavy use of freelance talent, especially in New York City. But it doesn't show up. What I really think is that I didn't expect all the work to be super-creative and adventuresome or out on a limb, but I didn't see very much of that at all. I think that the design firms which are doing very well, profitably, should be the ones to exercise leadership there—that they can afford to do it more than they do.

Moderator: What is it that's missing in the education process that doesn't help develop more designers with some depth?

Pesanelli: What is missing, first, is four years of a liberal arts education before a student starts design school. It's not that you can't get awareness and sensitivity without the educational exposure, but very few people do. So we have a relatively shallow head in operation, and relatively shallow heads produce relatively shallow work. Our total educational system is turned around a technician base. Only the classic professions of law and medicine escape that.

Moderator: Are you saying that designers are more attuned to being technicians than to being creative people?

Burdick: I'd be willing to say that.

Rice: I've done some teaching and I've seen some fairly good technicians. I see a lot of people with what I like to call a passion for design, who are maybe not good technicians, but who I know will eventually become good technicians. You can teach technical expertise, but you can't teach that passion. That passion has to be there. I think that's an in-depth feeling and respect for what you are doing and knowing why you are doing it, not just to make a living. I think you have to have a certain kind of ego in there that says, "I am trying to make a statement and I'm being honest with myself about it." A lot of schools are now teaching people how to make money and how to use cliches, but they're not really instilling that sense of personal integrity that says, "When you go out to design, have some passion."

Pesanelli: A lot of what we looked at in this review just wasn't creative. It looked like people who had been at it for 5 or perhaps 10 years and had become very good technicians. The creativity was lacking. In one sense you can define creativity as just being first, but there weren't a lot of firsts. There were a lot of 25ths and 28ths and 100ths.

Rice: I say take one guy with so-called good taste, or let's say a passion or a good feeling for design. It's hard to teach that, some of it has to come inbred. But you take that guy and give him five technicians, educate him in what the technicians are capable of doing in relationship to his job, and he is going to be a damn good designer. He is, in a sense, the creator, although it doesn't take anything away from the people who are working on the technical level. It's a hierarchy and it's unfortunate that a lot of guys and gals are not coming out with almost that sense of Renaissance-man feeling. Maybe we're overspecialized. I think, that breeds sterility.

Burdick: That passion is inbred. I hate to think that, but I don't believe it's teachable. I think it comes from having gods. That is perhaps an unpopular idea, having gods, but I mean having some heroes to pursue. I doubt if there are enough designers around of heroic proportion now. Maybe there's a lack of heroes at a particular time period that occurs.

Moderator: Is there anything that you feel is really going to have a strong impact on the kind of design that's done in the future?

Stockman: I find in my business that the costs of construction and the difficulty of finding skilled labor make it harder and harder to do things. Almost everything becomes out of reach. You are forced to do things in standard building types of ways. The kinds of details that really make a difference in the way things fall together are becoming harder and harder to obtain.

Rice: I think the economic situation is going to have a lot of impact on what we do. On one end of the spectrum, it's going to make us a lot more creative, and on the other end, it's going to make us a lot more mundane. The energy situation and the economic situation and the lack of skilled personnel, in terms of poor execution, might contribute to the design vocabulary getting even smaller. You might end up with very few, very fine solutions, but when you get them, they're going to be super solutions. But I think we're still going to end up with a lot more "blah." The only way we're going to overcome that is for designers to become a lot more versatile. There are going to be a lot more demands made of us and I think that's going to take us out of the category of specialization. I see the spiral going the other way now.

Pesanelli: It is a matter of survival, of not being too specialized, unless you're absolutely the best in your city or your area or your region. Then you can be specialized. But if you're not absolutely the best, then you have to do a number of things rather well in order to survive as a business. It's going to be very expensive to be a small business, with Social Security taxes going up, with Workmen's Compensation going up, all of these practical matters. We've constantly got that struggle between the business aspect and the creative aspect that is getting tighter and tighter all the time.

Artsite, Traveling Museum for Original Works of Art

The panel selected this self-contained traveling exhibit with unanimous raves. One juror thought it the best solution in the entire category. Another juror added that it "defines its space, clears the floor of legs, feet, and panels, while still making structural sense." A traveling art gallery for the Neuberger Museum located at the State University of New York in Purchase, the demountable exhibition system can contain a gallery room full of art. The structural bearing beams disassemble into eight separate sections. The beams are sheet-formed aluminum, lacquered white. Each of the seven cases is a self-contained package hanging off the structural beams. There are a number of different configurations for the cases to accommodate the changing subject matter from show to show. The total area measures 7½ x 12½ x 16 ft (21.1 x 3.8 x 4.9 m). The character of this "community outreach" module incorporates and contrasts the classical feeling of an ancient Roman building with the bright white metal quality of a contemporary minimalist sculpture. The outline of the beams creates the sense of an enclosed room with interior-lit cases further suggesting a self-contained environment. Security programs were researched in consultation with the Metropolitan Museum of Art, New York. This resulted in the design of hidden locks, special hardware, and the utilization of ½ in. (12.7 mm) thick plastic, mechanically fastened. The project's total cost amounted to $12,800. Aluminum was chosen for the structure because of its quality, light weight, and ease of assembly and because it is able to span the 16 ft (4.9 m) required and still hold the 7,000 lb (3,175 kg) of art suspended in the seven cases.

Materials and Fabrication: Structure is breakformed 10 gauge aluminum. Plastic cases, ½ in. (12.7 mm) thick, are 30 x 40 x 35 in. (76.2 x 101.6 x 88.9 cm). One title case is 8 x 30 x 35 in. (20.3 x 76.2 x 88.9 cm).

Client: The Neuberger Museum, State University of New York at Purchase, Purchase, New York.
Staff Design: Jeffery Hoffeld, concept; M. Susan McTigue, art selection; Jacqueline Sheinberg, educational consultant.
Consultant Design: Murry Gelberg, design director; Robert Berge, engineer; Stephen F. Gordon, design coordinator; V. Lorenzo Porcelli, consulting form designer.

MAN TransFORMS/Aspects of Design Exhibition, Cooper-Hewitt National Museum of Design

The exhibition which marked the reopening of New York's Cooper-Hewitt Museum in October 1976 as the Smithsonian Institution's National Museum of Design was a collaborative effort by an international team of ten artist/designers. As a presentation of the museum's philosophy, the exhibition was designed to create an awareness in the general public of the scope, complexities, and potentials of the design process. This was accomplished through a series of exhibits which confronted visitors with the familiar and the ordinary in unexpected and cogent contexts meant to amuse and inspire the visitor into fresh insights. Among the exhibits, which ranged from film and slide shows to games and environments, was a lively exposition of cloth transformed from shelter as a tent, to transportation as a sailboat, to energy as a windmill, to flag, semaphore, altar cloth, and towel. Breads from around the world were displayed in their various forms. Shapes were explored as elements in natural and man-made design. One environment imprisoned those who entered in a gilded cage with an angel in a room walled with blue skies, bare tree tops, and white puffs of clouds. Another room juxtaposed daily routines from the toilet to the TV. An extensive, 172-page catalog complemented and expanded upon the exhibits' scope through essays and photographs, drawings and graphics taken from the show itself. Short film series

also acted as extensions and footnotes to many of the exhibits. The exhibition was sponsored by the Johnson Wax Co.

Materials and Fabrication: Lumber, plastic, steel, and cloth were used as appropriate. Many rooms were sheathed in fabric. Based on standard construction techniques, as well as sewing, other elements included standard exhibit cases, panels, mannequins, models, 14 audiovisual areas of mainly super-8 mm film loops, and some slides. The exhibition occupied approximately 10,000 sq ft (928.9 m²), or 2½ floors of gallery space.

Client: Cooper-Hewitt National Museum of Design, New York, New York.
Exhibition Staff: Dorothy Twining Globus, exhibition coordinator; David Lerner, production supervisor; Lucy Fellowes, research assistant; Hermann Czech, project assistant; Madeleine Jenewein, project secretary.
Consultant Design: Hans Hollein, director of exhibition design; Nader Ardalan, Peter M. Bode, R. Buckminster Fuller, Murray Grigor, Arata Isozaki, Richard Meier, Karl Schlamminger, Ettore Sottsass, Oswald Mattias Ungers, exhibition design; George Nelson, catalog design; Hillary Harris, George Melies, Frank Mouris, National Film Board of Canada, additional films.

Exhibit Components of the Participatory Learning Environment, Brooklyn Children's Museum
The panel thought the exhibit components designed for the Participatory Learning Environment at the Brooklyn Children's Museum created a fascinating assemblage, an engaging and lively looking environment. That is just what the designers intended when they placed their emphasis upon tactile experience with objects as a learning technique. Exhibits are organized according to the historical division of physical reality into earth, air, fire, and water. These elements are arranged so that their interdependence can be understood. Water from a stream running through the space can be put in a freezer or boiled in a steam engine to produce usable energy and demonstrate the various, changing states of the element. The exhibits, including a windmill, hydraulic lift, and a gigantic plastic model of a diamond's molecular structure, stand as fully articulated forms executed in a scale meant to lure the visitor into discovery and learning. No distinction is made between natural and manufactured objects, between scientific thought and artistic feeling. It is the designers' intention that throughout the environment the spirit of discovery remains of primary importance, as opposed to the categorical distinctions which come later on in the learning process.

Materials and Fabrication: Components include: greenhouse with soil mixture area; running stream bed with child-operable controls and surrounding neon helix; portable freezer and ripple tank; steam engine, boiler, and condenser; windmill; air lift; circus wagon and restored calliope.

Client: Brooklyn Children's Museum, Brooklyn, New York.
Consultant Design: Saville Design: Brent Saville, project designer; Leonard Berta, Kenneth B. Smith, designers; Peter Pearce, Synestructics, Inc., design of curved space structures.

DEMPSTER
BEATRICE
U.S.A.

Lever House Exhibition, Design Education at Pratt Institute
Developed to demonstrate the interdisciplinary characteristics of Pratt Institute's undergraduate and graduate-level programs in the graphic, industrial, and interior design fields, the exhibition's main focal point is four topologically undulating "exhibit landscapes." Designed as a display device that unifies a variety of objects, the topological modules provide a contradiction of their own to the formal, hard-edged environment of the steel and glass Lever House office building on Park Avenue in New York where it was on view. Also included in the exhibit were a separate display area approximately 15 x 25 ft (4.6 x 7.6 m), for environmental projects; eight 4 x 8 ft (1.2 x 2.4 m) freestanding surfaces for two-dimensional design; and a slide show presenting a cross section of design work on three 5 x 7 ft (1.5 x 2.1 m) screens. Three hollow core doors were assembled to form each topological module. With corrugated cardboard, eliptical domes were formed in the style of egg crates, and flat disks were adhered. Foam rubber sheets, 1 in. (25.4 mm) thick, were stapled in place around domes and disks. Stretch fabric was then applied over this as an outer skin. Panels covered with white cotton were fastened to the periphery of each module. All projects were color-keyed to their appropriate graduate or undergraduate programs. With student help the total cost was $4,000.

Materials and Fabrication: Structure of topological modules was made of: corrugated cardboard eliptical domes; hollow core doors; stretch fabric; 1 in. (25.4 mm) thick foam rubber sheets. Typeface used was Futura Light.

Client: Pratt Institute, Brooklyn, New York.
Staff Design: Ann Kone, exhibit coordinator.
Consultant Design: Etan Manasse Associates, Inc.: Etan Manasse, designer; David Freedman, Steven Lee, design assistants.

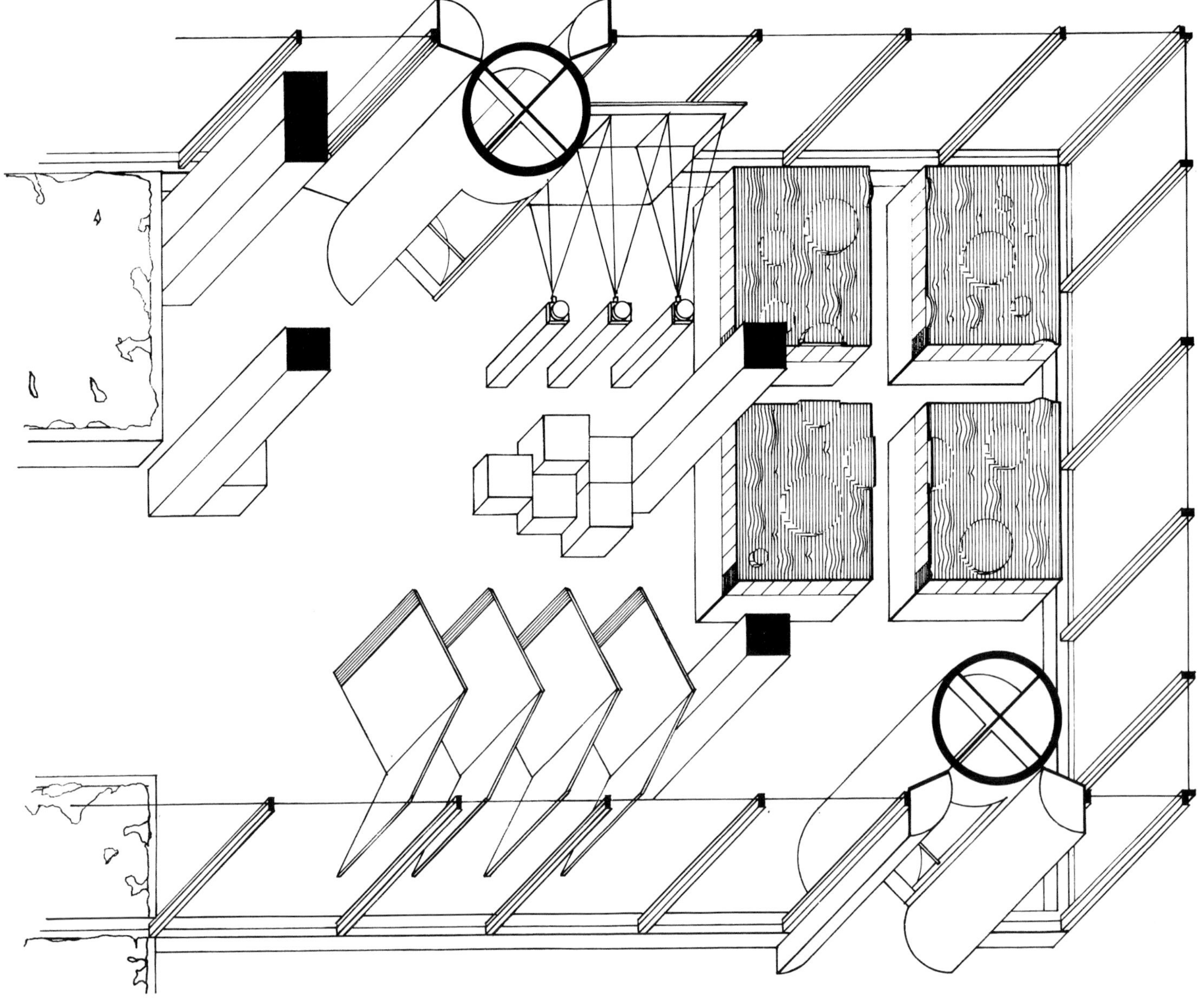

Corning Housewares Exhibit
The panel was impressed with the degree of restraint evident in this clean-lined solution to the problems which beset any trade show, such as excessive noise, visual clutter, and competitiveness. Shown in January at the National Housewares Manufacturers Association in McCormick Place, Chicago, the low-profile, soft-sell of this exhibit is perhaps a reflection of the confident stance of a leader in its field. The designers' approach was to illustrate how the Corning products are used in every part of the home throughout the day by every member of the family. An illusion of reality was built up through photographic reproductions of appliances and furnishings to show the products in use in their natural environment. Contributing to the illusion were real products, appliances, furnishings and the architectural details of a house. Specific information for any new products introduced in the display was organized in one location. The exhibit was designed to be set up easily by exhibit hall trade union members and to be easily modified when the display's theme is changed biannually.

Materials and Fabrication: The booth was constructed of hollow-core Masonite panels with an overhead aluminum grid and supporting members. The overall structure was lacquered white as a neutral backdrop for the theme. Space measured 30 x 70 ft (9.2 x 21.3 m).

Client: Corning Glass Works, Consumer Products Division, Corning, New York.
Staff Design: Robert Bruce, project director, designer; Kenneth LeVan, designer.
Consultant Design: Davin Stowell, designer; Victor Scocozza, photographer; Warren Displays, builder.

Citicorp Center

Since its recent dedication in October 1977, Citicorp Center, a condominium office complex and Citibank's new corporate headquarters in midtown Manhattan, has stirred up a lot of criticism, most of it quite favorable. Comments from the panel ranged from "dynamic concept" and "exciting, corporate intimidation" to "some ground scale problems" and "difficult access and poor visibility of retail spaces." Of course, a project of this scope creates opinion because of its high potential for influencing the environment one way or the other. Probably no one foresaw the possibility that chunks of accumulated ice could slide off the tower's unique wedge-shaped top, forcing the street below to be closed for a day in January. No one was hurt, though, and it seems that any minuses are far outweighted by the benefits which the center provides for its immediate surroundings, as a distinctive addition to the city's skyline, and for interesting design and engineering features inside and out. Encompassing a one-block site, the center is comprised of office and commercial spaces and a freestanding church on its original corner site, St. Peter's Lutheran Church. The tower is raised off the site by four 112-ft (34.1-m) supercolumns. Sitting beneath three sides of the tower's base is a terraced eight-story retail/office building. An open-air plaza is positioned below street level at Lexington Avenue and 53rd Street. Silver reflective glass alternates for 914 ft (278.6 m) with encircling bands of brightly finished anodized aluminum coordinated in color and reflectivity to provide a uniform surface appearance. Among special energy conservation features are a heat reclamation system for utilization of heat normally wasted during the winter cycle; use of 100 percent outside air for cooling in intermediate seasons; the proposed use of special air filters to reduce the amount of outside air necessary for conditioning; double glazing with reflecting glass to reduce energy

consumption; and special single tube, low-brightness fluorescent lighting fixtures to reduce electrical needs. The double-glazed thermal glass covers only 46 percent of the office and commercial building exteriors. The remainder of the building's skin is insulated aluminum, with a highly reflective light color to reduce solar gain. Though the low-rise structure has conventional elevators, the tower utilizes an innovative double-deck elevator system. With a single unit in a single hoistway, the system permits two floors to be served simultaneously, thereby reducing waiting time. Use of diagonals as part of the building structure, enclosed within the glass line and exposed to view from the offices' interiors, creates larger open office spans and increased flexibility for interior layouts. The sense of openness throughout the design of the building is also evident in the plaza level galleria, accessible from the street. The focal point of the mid-

rise building, the galleria rises seven stories to a skylighted roof. The designers hoped to create a sense of the marketplace for shoppers moving around any of three shopping levels which form a U-shape around the galleria's escalator-linked 65,000 sq ft (6,038 m^2) of retail space. Activity within this area is visible from the street through glass-enveloped facades surrounding the plaza. The 24 sq ft (2.2 m^2) 10-story high columns lifting the tower above create a soaring sense of space and distance when passersby stop to look up from beneath the outer perimeter of the tower's belly.

Materials and Fabrication: Principal structural material is steel. Floors are cellular steel topped with concrete. Tower frame utilizes chevron bracing, with its structure carried down to solid rock approximately 50 ft (15.2 m) below grade. Cooling towers within sloping top. Tuned mass damper tested by Simpson, Gumpertz, and Hager. Curtain wall tests were by A.S. Sakhnovsky Construction Research Lab. Wind tun-

nel tests by Alan Davenport, University of Western Ontario. Solar energy study conducted by Energy Laboratory of MIT. Exterior glass is 1 in. (25.4 mm) thick thermopane by LOF, silver # 114. Exterior aluminum is 3/16 in. (4.8 mm) thick, with a bright anodized finish.

Client: Citibank, New York, New York. **Consultant Design:** Hugh Stubbins and Associates, Inc.: Hugh Stubbins, designer; W. Easley Hamner, project architect; Howard E. Goldstein, project manager. Associated Architect: Emery Roth and Sons: Julian Roth, administration; Richard Roth, construction documents. Structural Engineers: LeMessurier Associates, SCI: William J. LeMessurier, designer; Stanley Goldstein, project manager. Office of James Ruderman: Murray Shapiro, project manager. Mechanical and Electrical Engineers: Joseph R. Loring and Associates: Joseph R. Loring, partner-in-charge; Joseph Felner, mechanical; John van Deusen, vertical transportation. General Contractor: HRH Equity Corp. Vignelli Design Associates, graphic and interior design for St. Peter's Lutheran Church; Halcyon Marketing, project development; Design International, market design.

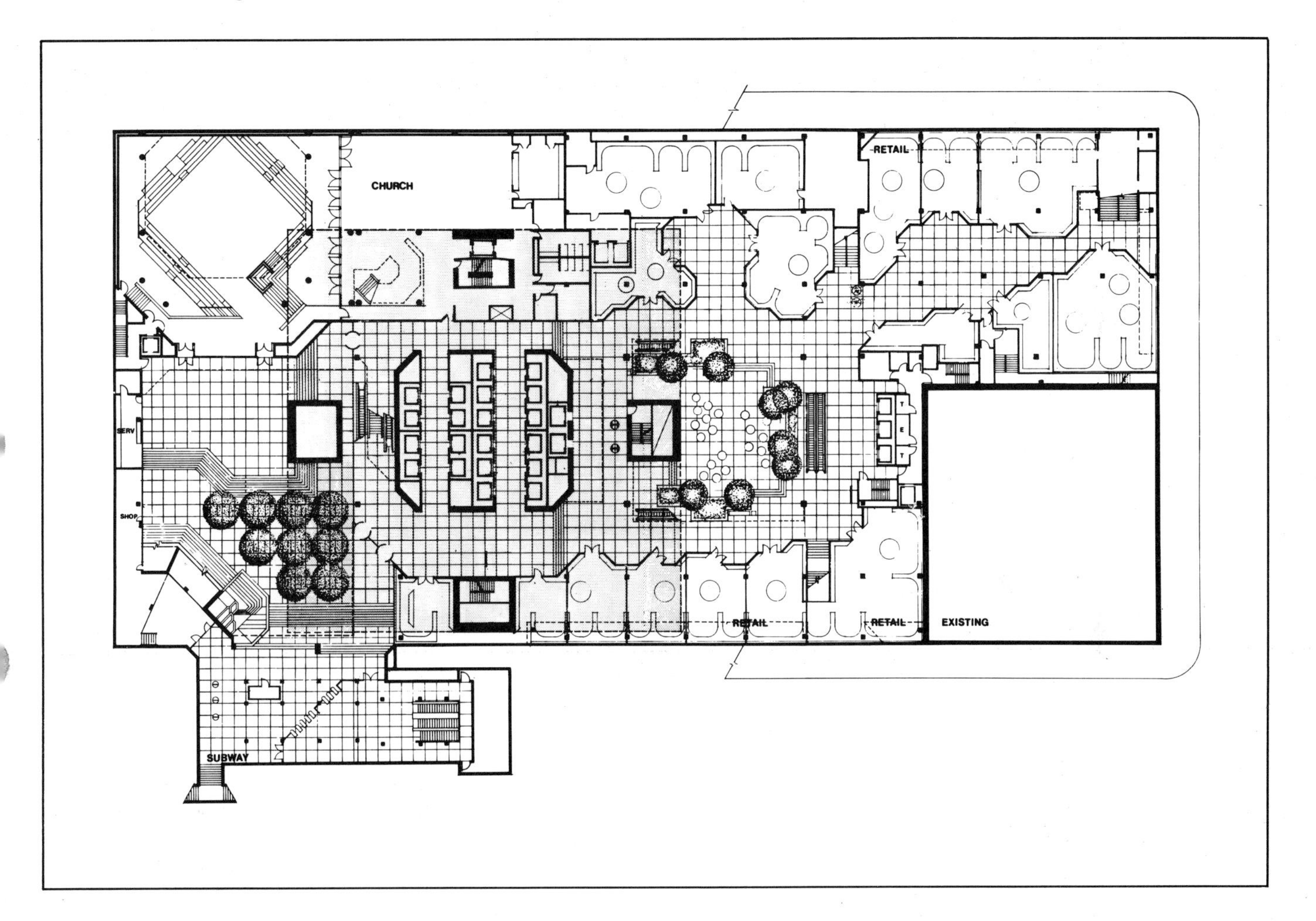

Brookstone Retail Store

This design provides the prototype retail environment for a company previously doing a strictly mail-order business. Since its successful opening in downtown Boston, the company has opened a second outlet in Philadelphia, and more are being planned. The designer was concerned with creating an environment that would truly reflect the low-pressure, New England style of business for a company selling high-quality hardware and food preparation and lawncare tools with full guarantees on any items sold by a knowledgeable staff. Brookstone wanted the stores to be able to compete in the urban environment with a space plan that would flow easily and create a comfortable enough feeling to sustain either a 15-min or a 2-hr stay by customers. The result is three furniture systems, signage, door pulls, clipboards, and sales counters that can be utilized in stores measuring from 1,500 sq ft (139.3 m²) to 4,000 sq ft (371.6 m²). Needing only reoiling for proper maintenance, 2½ in. (6.4 cm) thick birch was chosen for all these elements because it can take constant falls of heavy tools, as well as set a background tone that reflects the feel of a wooden workbench. The windows of the Boston store, located on the Freedom Trail, are highlighted by a "museum of tools that built America" as a community amenity for the trail. Interior sections are defined by a bold box joint furniture system with wide plank construction of from 8 in. (20.3 cm) to 16 in. (40.6 cm). With variable plug-in wooden pieces, the system displays the range of items available. Peg-and-plank walls and low A-frame units act as supplementary display areas. The stockroom is equipped with a conveyor system that delivers written orders in 3-4 min.

Materials and Fabrication: Select, hardwood birch, finished in natural penetrating oil, is used throughout. Box joint tables and sales desks measure 4½ x 2 ft (137.2 x 61 cm) by either 28 in. (71.1 cm) or 32 in. (81.3 cm) high, and 8½ x 2 ft (259.1 x 61 cm) by either 28 in. (71.1 cm) or 32 in. (81.3 cm) high. The A-frame measures 50 in. (127 cm) high, and the wall system's height is either 50 in. (127 cm) or 6 ft (182.9 cm). Also specified is hemp rope carpet, metal lights with wire guards, rubber and hardwood flooring. Total cost of wood is $15,000; woodworking is $35,000.

Client: Brookstone Co., Peterborough, New Hampshire.
Staff Design: Steven Tytel, marketing program.
Consultant Design: Murry Gelberg, designer.

Lutheran Medical Center

Probably the first major health facility to be recycled from a deserted factory, the Lutheran Medical Center is housed within the shell of the abandoned American Machine and Foundry Company Plant in Brooklyn. Besides bringing a new hospital with advanced medical care to a blighted neighborhood, this recycling project has brought along some hope of revival for that neighborhood. In terms of construction, with the total cost less than $43 million, the decision to use recyclable architecture rather than build from the bottom up saved approximately $10 million. The cost for the project overall is at $63.5 million. The 600,000 sq ft (55,735.5 m²), five-floor concrete shell of the old building was left almost intact. New boilers, emer-

Before.

gency power, radiant heat for patient air-conditioning, and heat recovery wheels were installed, as well as the adoption of the sprinkler option in the 1973 Life Safety Code. Windows, with individual segments left operable, were reglazed with mirror glass and blocked inside to reduce heat loss. New to the structure, the front entrance and circulation core are serviced by eight elevators and two escalators.
A monorail was installed on both the first and fifth floors, with five vertical connections to provide efficient materials handling throughout the facilities. An expansive lobby, one level above the street, is intended as a dramatic central focus for the building's interior. Six medical and surgical units occupy the top three floors, along with 80 percent double rooms. Other facilities include ten major operating rooms, two cystologic operation rooms, four delivery rooms, two special procedure operating rooms, an extensive ambulatory care unit, and ten radiographic and fluoroscopic rooms. Nursing stations and the rooms they service use distinctive color schemes for identification. Bold and cheerful colors are used throughout to aid orientation in what is a very large structure and to create a reassuring and hopeful environment. The panel unanimously agreed on the overall success of the solution to a tough, potentially dull architectural space.

Materials and Fabrication: Reinforced concrete structure, with Amelco reflective glass panels, utilizes steam absorption refrigeration system with radiant ceiling heating and cooling panels. Monorail is by Amsco. Chairs are from Atelier and Herman Miller. Carpeting is Seamloc throughout. Floorings used are Armstrong Excelon, Dexotex, and Flintokote. Peter Pepper pamphlet racks are used in the outpatient clinic. Vinyl graphics are by Belt Painting, and vinyl wall coverings are from Columbus Coatings. Also used were Paraline ceilings, L&B Products' stools and tables, and Westinghouse desks and panels. Exterior signage was done by Art Craft; interior signage by The Other Sign Company.

Client: Lutheran Medical Center, Brooklyn, New York.
Consultant Design: Rogers, Butler & Burgun, architects; J. Armand Burgun, partner-in-charge; William Adkinson, project architect; Stephanie Mallis, Michelle Zoller, interior designers. Balsey & Balsey, landscape architecture. V. L. Falotico, Inc., electrical, mechanical, and sanitary engineering. Purdy & Henderson Associates, structural engineering. Turner Construction Co., construction management. Cini Grissom, food service consultants.

Squash/1

The industrial qualities of a steel fabrication plant built in the 1950s were borrowed from and enhanced upon in the process of renovating the plant into a squash club, which has turned this game, traditionally played behind closed doors, into a social and spectator sport. Long-span, column-free construction and 27-ft (8-m) high ceilings provided an ideal space for conversion into five regulation-size courts and a balcony area overlooking three of the courts that are opened up for viewing through the use of glass back walls. Encompassing approximately 4,500 sq ft (418 m²), besides the three open and two private courts, a pro shop and the men's locker room are located downstairs, while the women's locker room, a combination lounge and children's play area, and the manager's office have been placed upstairs. Like the existing steel, the new structural steel was left exposed and sprayed white. New ductwork, highlighted by chrome yellow paint, is also in view. All solid interior walls are painted white in contrast to a neutral warm gray carpeting and ceramic tile and the wooden court floors. Colorings of wood are brought into the pro shop with maple furniture and a custom-designed butcherblock counter. The club's graphics echo predominating interior colors of blue, used in lounge seating, wall murals, and the men's lockers, and yellow, used for ductwork, balcony railings, and women's lockers. The strong interior colors reappear on all corporate materials. Because the project was designed to serve as the prototype for future clubs, establishment of a strong visual identity for the concept was a priority. The glass back walls for three of the playing courts were custom designed and fabricated for Squash/1. The back wall system makes straightforward use of readily available materials, as is the case with all other major design elements. According to the designers, the glass-walled courts are always the first to be taken by players. Overall cost for the project, including all fees and interior furnishings, was $170,000.

Materials and Fabrication: Balcony railings are of 1½ in. (3.8 cm) steel pipe, with inset panels of clear Plexiglass fastened with stainless steel acorn nuts and bolts to steel tabs welded onto the pipes. Glass back wall system consists of ½ in. (12.7 mm) tempered glass walls and bracing fins joined by stainless steel clips, hinges, latches, and acorn bolts. Clear silicon is used to seal the various assemblies at their joints. Other court walls use fiberglass-reinforced plaster over conventional block, finished smooth.

Client: Squash/1, Mamaroneck, New York.

Staff Design: Rodney Brent, partner.

Consultant Design: Gordon/Spencer Architects, architectural, interior design; Michael Dalton Associates, mechanical engineering; Marjorie Katz Design, Inc., graphic design; Arne Thune Associates, structural engineering.

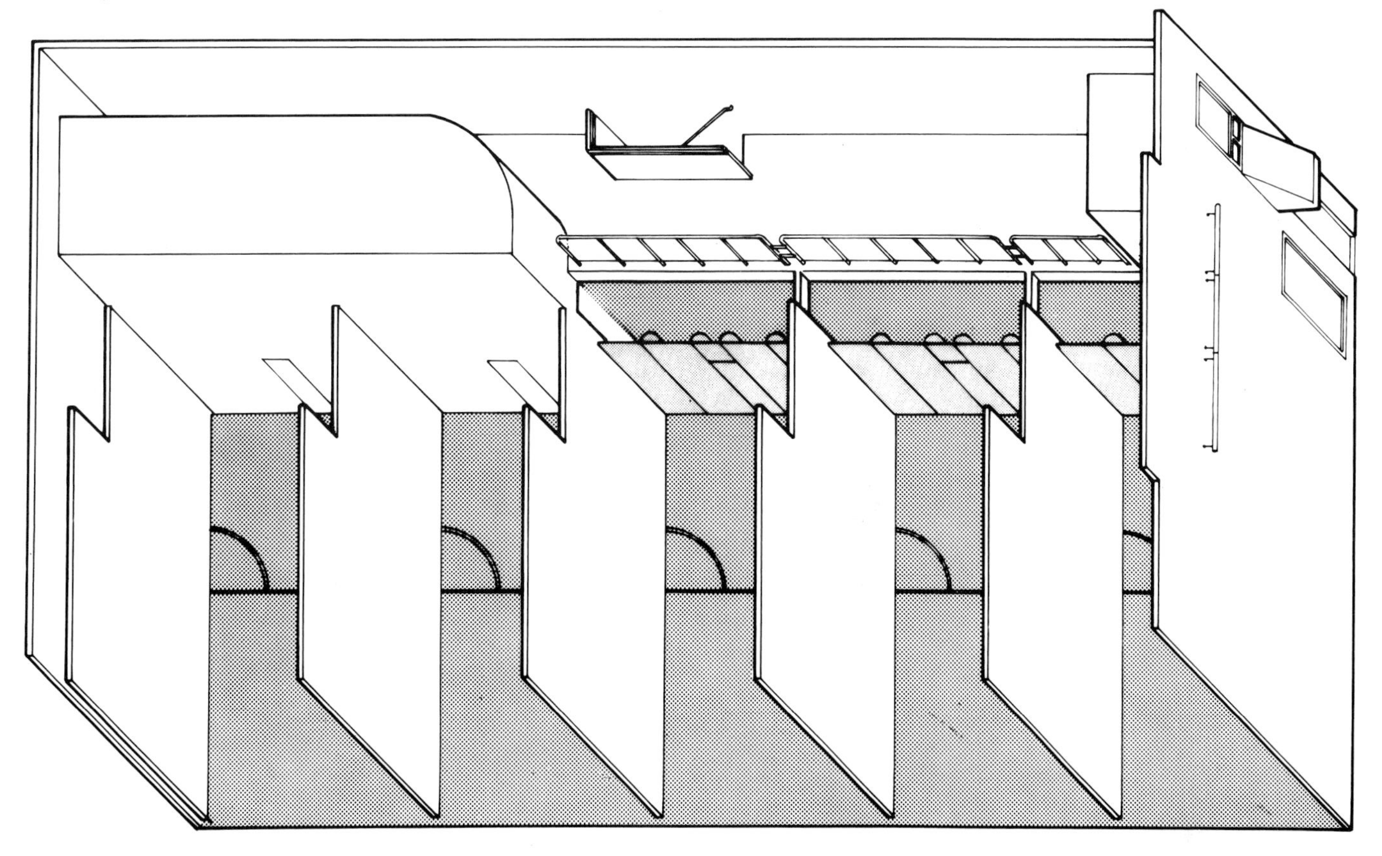

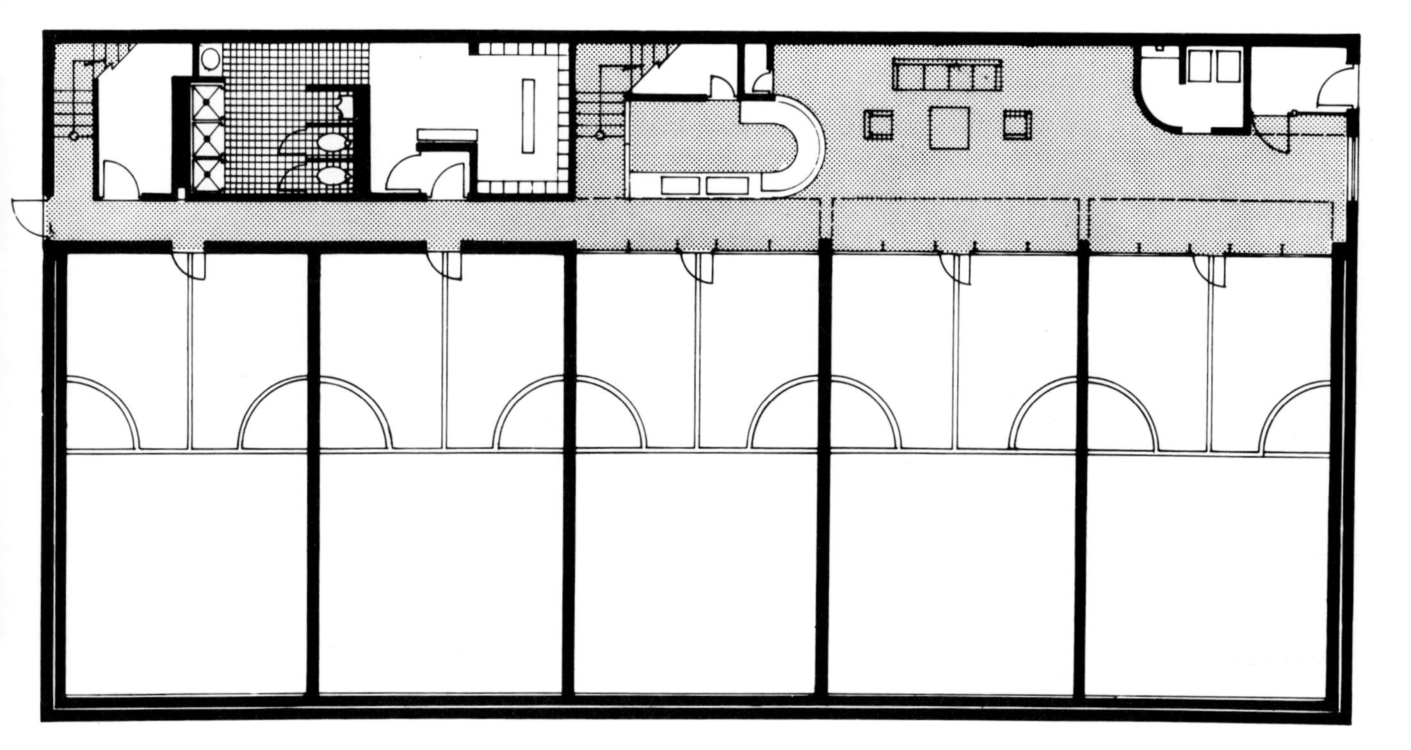

One Fifth Restaurant Design
Located at One Fifth Avenue, New York, in an older, once-elegant, recently renovated apartment building at the corner of Eighth Street, this street-level restaurant space mixes some newly designed elements with a majority of authentic period 1930-style furniture and fixtures. Much of the materials, which went into creating the restaurant, bar, and clam bar, with an occupancy of 290 guests, came from the sunken remains of the *S.S. Coronia.* The bar and clam bar, as well as Art Deco chairs and a dessert cart, were found in Hoboken, New Jersey, just across the Hudson River. With columns and floor covered in a modern white Italian tile, the main dining room uses the ship's window frames above each of the tables placed along the wall. Inside the frames are salmon-pink silk curtains, behind which is mounted a sepia print by Ernst Haas of an ocean wave. Also recycled from the *S.S. Coronia* are pink mirrors, sconces, brass railings, and cove lighting. Near the clam bar a painting by Winold Reiss sets a 1930s mood. The restaurant's space measures 150 x 50 ft (45.7 x 15.2 m) and cost $75,000 to remodel. A host of accessories were designed to cinch the image being developed. Among these are a set of dishes with the restaurant's symbol centered in either a red or blue double-ringed border, ashtrays, reservation cards, matches, tablecloths, white on navy blue T-shirts, a white captain's tie with black printing, a black waiter's tie with white printing, as well as a line of stationery with the logo. The jurors felt that all the elements fell together quite well with the proper spirit achieved without an overly designed feeling. The break up of spaces to accommodate a variety of uses for both day and night dining was favorably commented upon by the panel.

Materials and Fabrication: Mostly handmade in England, the materials were recycled from the *S.S. Coronia* and a bar in Hoboken, New Jersey. Modern white Italian tiles cover floors and columns.

Client: Goupole Restaurant, Inc., New York, New York.
Consultant Design: Kiki Kogelnik, designer.

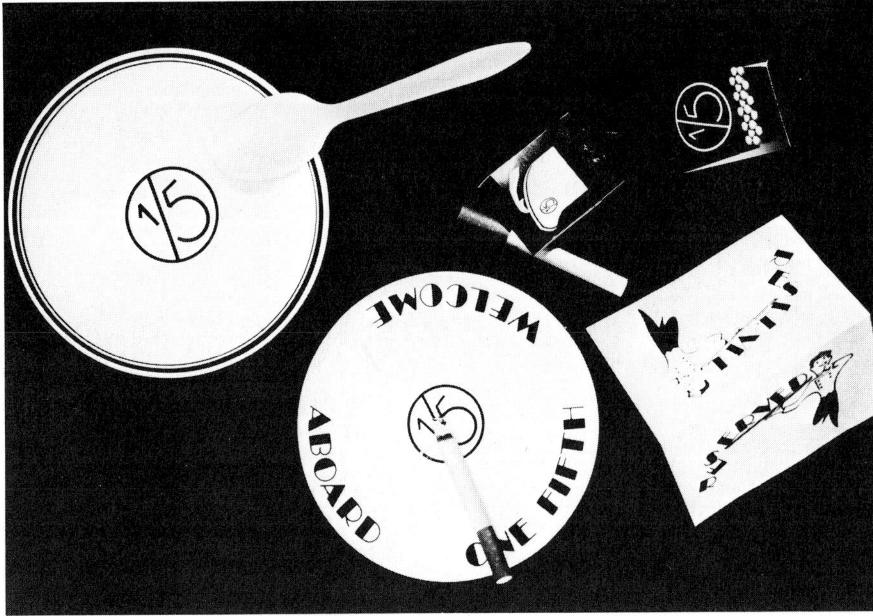
WELCOME
ABOARD
ONE FIFTH

Meadowlands Racetrack Lighting, New Jersey Sports Complex
Literally reflecting the excitement of the sport, the lighting design at the Meadowlands Racetrack is the medium for creating an atmosphere of eventfulness. With a variety of lighting levels from dusky to high illuminations, the building uses less than 2 watts per sq ft (9.2903 dm^2). The low construction cost of the lighting design is sustained by a low cost of maintenance. Standard industrial fixtures are used throughout to complement the exposed purlins, ducts, and conduits that give the large minimal structure its industrial character. Lighting is used inside and out to define areas, establish character, and clarify circulation paths. Lighting in public areas such as the restaurant and grandstands is incandescent. Fluorescent lighting is used only in business areas. Foot traffic through the complex is guided by long strips of neon lighting, sometimes swinging around corners or swooping up escalators. Upon visits to numerous racetracks, which helped in the development of the lighting concept, the designers found that while the lavish tracks did not need much in the way of lighting to create atmosphere (horse racing creates its own excitement), the tracks which had simple enclosures were depressing as a place of assembly.

Materials and Fabrication: Standard industrial equipment used throughout the project was reinforced by neon used as both an illuminant and a graphic element.

Client: Ewing Cole Erdman Eubank/ Claus & Nolan, Architects/Planners, Philadelphia, Pennsylvania, for the New Jersey Sports Complex.
Consultant Design: Howard Brandston Lighting Design, Inc.: Lawrence Kirnon, associate-in-charge; Interspace Design Associates, interior design, ticket window booths; Peter Muller-Monk, graphic design, banners; Synergo, Inc., engineering.

Coordinated Architectural and Environmental Graphics Program for North Central Bronx Hospital
North Central Bronx Hospital is a new, large municipal facility, encompassing 18 floors and 700,000 sq ft (65,024.8 m²). A primary orientational system was developed as components of the interior architecture to facilitate the hospital's operation. With the total facility divided into logical areas and location designations assigned to each, information of concern to visitors and patients was given the major visual emphasis while staff and service functions were visually subordinated. Those primary location designations remaining constant are applied to cross-corridor fascias. Specific, changeable functions are presented on modular plaques. Special attention was given to primary public areas in the hope that graphic components would not only solve the information requirements, but would also play a part in creating an environment softened by noninstitutional elements. With a total construction cost of $160,000, graphic elements included sculptural units, murals, cross-corridor fascias, directories, a plaque system, and modular directory strips. Full-scale mockups of the major components and the modular system were studied by the designers at the site.

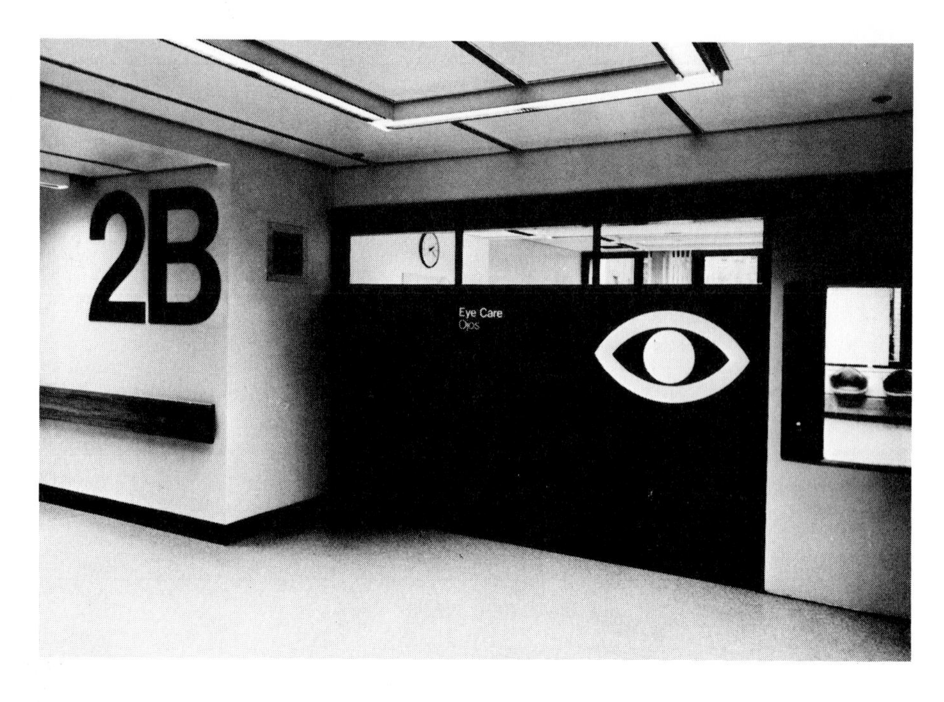

Materials and Fabrication: Canopy and suspended fascias were made of ⅛ in. (3.2 mm) aluminum. Fiberglass, 3/16 in. (4.8 mm) thick, was used along with ⅛ in. (3.2 mm) aluminum for all major sculptural units. Major wall units and murals utilize 3/16 in. (4.8 mm) fiberglass with molded returns. Fascia identification is die-cut vinyl letterforms. Major numbers and the plaque system are made from subsurface acrylic lamination. The elements measure: 11 murals are 8 x 16 ft (2.4 x 4.9 m); 6 ft (1.8 m) sculptural units and diagonal wall units; 8 x 1 ft (2.4 x 30.5 cm) cross-corridor fascias; 3 ft (91.4 cm) high large number designations; 3 ft (91.4 cm) square, and 3 x 9 ft (91.4 x 2.7 m) directories; 6 in. (15.2 cm) to 18 in. (45.7 cm) square plaque system; modular directory strips of 2½ x 18 in. (63.5 x 45.7 cm). All metal units are welded with mechanical constructions and are mechanically fastened. Fiberglass and acrylic units are molded with an adhesive construction and then adhesive mounted. Finishes are duranodic and baked enamel, semigloss for aluminum and P-94 semigloss for all plastic materials.

Client: New York City Health and Hospitals Corp., New York State Facilities Development Corp., New York, New York.
Staff Design: Robert Rohrich, director of interior design; Tina Liu, designer, New York City Health and Hospitals Corp.; William Herman, graphic coordinator, New York State Facilities Development Corp.
Consultant Design: E. Christopher Klumb Associates, Inc., graphics consultants: E. Christopher Klumb, director of design; Michael Clemens, designer. Mason, Da Silva Associates, architects and planners: Peter da Silva, principal in charge.

Interior Design of Elevator Cabs
The design concept of the latest installations for the 12 elevators in the 26-story office building at 77 Water Street, located in lower Manhattan's financial district, is lower Manhattan itself. The simple approach focuses on sights such as a view from the Staten Island ferry and birds and seagulls circling the area's well-known sites, like the Statue of Liberty and the Verrazano Bridge. The elevator cabs measure 6 ft (1.8 m) square x 8 ft, 6 in. (2.6 m) high. The photos, converted to halftone screens and enlarged, are easily read from outside the cabs. Upon entering a cab the dot pattern emerges as large and graphically abstract. Photos are covered with clear Plexiglass in a bright stainless frame, for easy maintenance. The total project cost for the 12 cabs was $24,000.

Materials and Fabrication: Side walls are white plastic laminate panels with bright stainless frames. Ceiling and wall areas are painted out with black. Carpeting is red.

Client: William Kaufman Organization, New York, New York.
Consultant Design: Pamela Waters Studio, Inc.: Pamela Waters, designer.

Site Markers and Trailblazers for New York City Heritage Trail
The Heritage Trail was commissioned to provide a self-guided tour connecting significant historic sites in lower Manhattan and thereby creating a permanent outdoor museum composed of buildings, open spaces, and monuments which have played key roles in the early economic, social, and political development of New York City and the nation. Serving as an educational tool, as well as a valuable public relations amenity, the trail provides a continuous set of visual and written messages which, together, give a sense of cultural and political growth in the city. The system consists of an identifying symbol, site markers, a stanchion displaying historic information at each site, and the trailblazers—curbside displays including the symbol along with explicit messages to guide pedestrians along the trail. The site marker is a monolith fabricated from a custom-designed aluminum extrusion with a wall thickness of ⅛ in. (3.2 mm). The profile of the extrusion prevents postering and inhibits graffiti. A dark-bronze two-color, architectural-grade duranodic finish is used to relate the marker to both contemporary and older buildings along the route, and it was also chosen because it can withstand exterior abuse. Tempered glass glazing expedites cleaning. Markers may be used either as free-standing, two-sided displays or reduced in height and wall hung. The trailblazer, finished with red, white, blue, and black porcelain enamel, displays the symbol pointing downward toward the trail. The 66 trailblazers and 18 site markers installed cost $40 and $1,800 each, respectively. Flag mounted 9 ft (2.7 m) above the pavement, the trailblazer measures 9 x 36 in. (22.9 x 91.4 cm). Site markers measure 96 x 20 x 6 in. (2.4 x 50.8 x 15.2 cm). The entire panel slopes inward from the top face of the unit to reduce background glare.

Materials and Fabrication: Site markers are bolted to vertical steel mounting reinforcements cast in a below-grade concrete footing. A tempered glass sheet is sealed to the display panel with a self-adhesive gasket for added protection. Markers are made from a 6 in. (15.2 cm) wide, custom-extruded module, welded and riveted to form a hollow rectangular box and coated with duranodic #313 on a bright bronze anodized base. Continuous tone pictorial material was reproduced with 133 line resolution. The trailblazer uses a 16 gauge steel sheet and is finished in red, white, blue, and black porcelain enamel.

Client: New York City Bicentennial Corp., succeeded by Friends of the New York City Heritage Trail, New York, New York.
Manufacturer: Universal Unlimited, Inc., Glen Cove, New York, site markers; Forrest Engraving, New Rochelle, New York, site marker graphics.
Staff Design: Susan Shaw, coordinator for New York City Bicentennial Corp.; New York City Mayor's Office of Development, project administrator; American Express Co., sponsor.
Consultant Design: Samuel Lebowitz Design: Samuel Lebowitz, principal designer; Peter Musgrave-Newton, graphic designer; Nicholas Polites, editorial consultant.

Signage Program for Central Ohio Transit Authority (COTA)
A complete graphic identity program, including maps, corporate identity, bus graphics, uniforms, and other public image materials was part of a federally funded grant to upgrade the public's awareness and impressions of the mass transit system in Columbus, Ohio. Though the panel agreed that some elements needed refining (for instance, the sign panels seem too easy to steal), the jurors felt it important to encourage participation from designers in this type of project. A single sign panel is the basic recommended signage at each stop location. The 14 x 18 in. (35.6 x 45.7 cm) sign is bolted, flag style, from a 2 in. (5.1 cm) square post perpendicular to and away from the roadway. Keeping a minimum 7 ft, 3 in. (2.2 m) above finished grade, panels can be added when additional route information is necessary. Each sign panel is divided into two graphic areas: the upper half displays an orange-colored bus and man pictogram on a white reflective background; the lower half is used to identify two routes by number and name, levels of service, and the COTA telephone information number. White nonreflective lettering is used on a gray background for the lower half of the sign. The system can expand from the basic two-route sign up to signage for 10 routes per stop. Additions are made with either a 14 x 9 in. (35.6 x 22.9 cm) or 14 x 18 in. (35.6 x 45.7 cm) sign, or combinations of both. The designers wanted to create a simple, direct system of signage for an urban environment cluttered with existing signage to the point of confusion.

Materials and Fabrication: Based on combined cost appearance and strength characteristics, aluminum and 1/25 in. (1.02 mm) structural steel tubing were chosen for panels and signposts, respectively. Dark bronze DuPont Durepox epoxy paint was used on signs and posts. Silk-screened orange pictograms are set against a white background of 3M Scotchlite reflective. White die-cut vinyl transfer letters are used for route information. Fabrication and installation costs per average is $20.

Client: Central Ohio Transit Authority, Columbus, Ohio.
Staff Design: Walter Daggett, executive director; Donald Moore, purchasing manager.
Consultant Design: Dave Ellies Industrial Design, Inc.: Gregory Crook, senior product designer; Steven Degnen, vice president, design director; Mark Denzer, senior graphic designer.

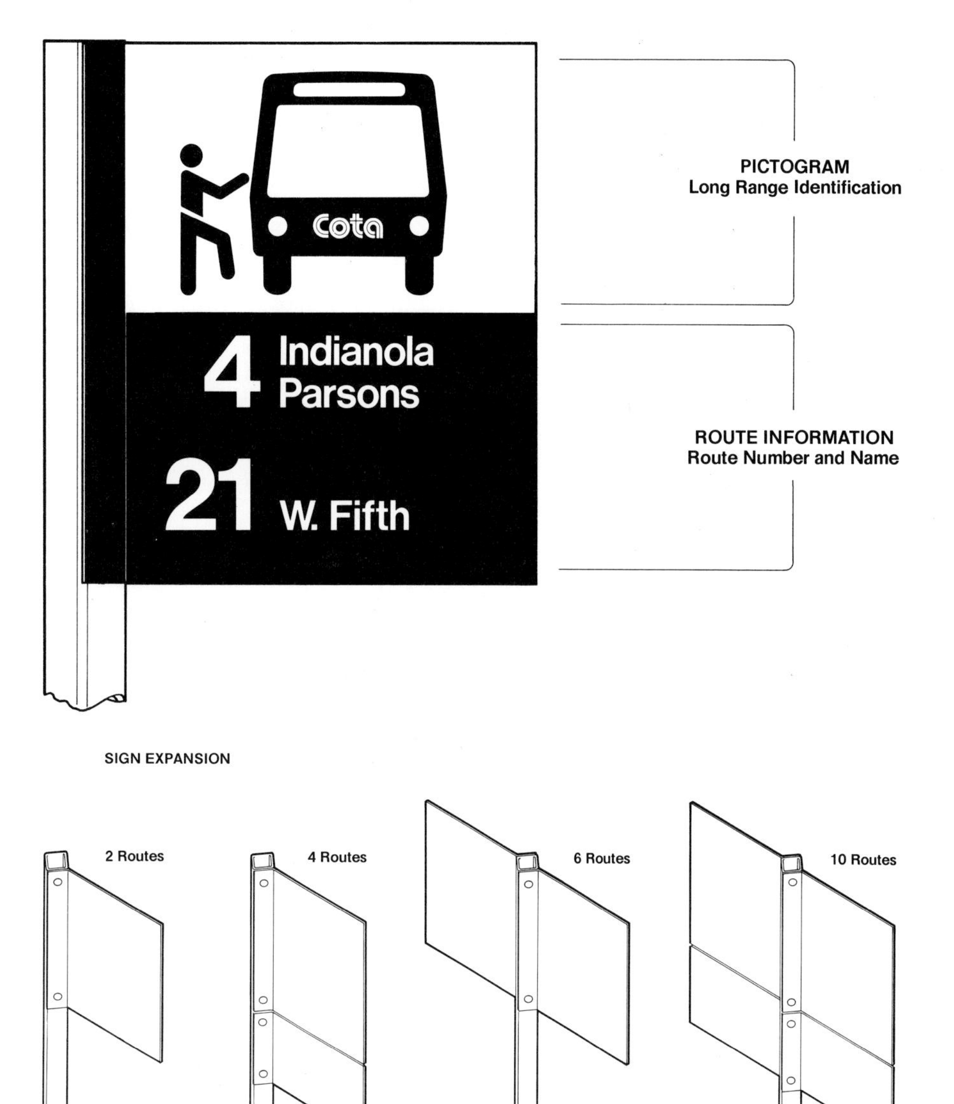

Zoo Graphics System, Animal Information Signage

Children and international visitors comprise between 80 and 85 percent of the people entering the Knoxville Zoological Park. For this reason the universal language of symbology, specifically pictographic representation, was chosen for its ability to communicate more effectively than traditional, lengthy verbal communication. The pictographs were abstracted by a children's illustrator to emphasize each animal's peculiar characteristics. Besides providing educational information about food, habitat, range, and the animal's name, the zoo requested a signage system that would be safe from mischief and vandalism and easy to maintain. Consistent with the zoo's architectural program, this subset of the information signage system led to color coding to define exhibit areas and their geographical location. The open land planning of the park is coordinated by color-coded directional signs to facilitate movement of visitors through all areas. A Cor-Ten steel standard, designed for color dot coding, supports each sign as a structure independent of each animal's enclosure. Cor-Ten was chosen for its ability to weather to a maintenance-free earthy color and texture. At 45 lb (20.4 kg) installed, the sign is awkward to steal. The standard is only 18 in. (45.7 cm) high to permit a child's viewing and touching. The sign's graphic face is tilted back at a 30° angle from the vertical, allowing a comfortable adult view. This arrangement allows all sizes of visitors to see and read the 16 in. (40.6 cm) square sign without the sign blocking a view of the animal in its enclosure. The art is silk-screened between two ⅛ in. (3.2 mm) pieces of nonglare Plexiglass. The diagonal positioning allows water to run freely off the flat surface. Though the project was cancelled due to lack of funds, the designer thought up a concept whereby a by-line would be added in appreciation of sponsorship, and the signs could be sold one by one. Based upon this individual sales program, as opposed to contracting with a single client and producing at a lower cost, the total cost for the 86 signs of the Animal Information Subset, including design, art production, fabrication, sales commissions, and installation, is approximately $220 per sign.

Materials and Fabrication: Cor-Ten steel stand, ¼ in. (6.4 mm) thick, is bolted into a concrete pad. Sheared and formed, the sheet of steel measures 14 x 36½ in. (35.6 x 92.7 cm). This length provides a 4½ in. (11.4 cm) horizontal base in which two holes are made to receive bolts, plus 18 in. (45.7 cm) for the color code area and 14 in. (35.6 cm) for the attachment of the sign face at a 30° angle back from the vertical. The steel's finish is a natural patina color. A black-and-white Helvetica typeface was used with art encapsulated between two ⅛ in. (3.2 mm) thick, nonglare Plexiglass panels. Silicone adhesive is used to attach sign to stand, providing flexibility between steel and Plexiglass in varying temperatures.

Client: Knoxville Zoological Park, Knoxville, Tennessee.

Consultant Design: Handprints: Birney L. Hand, principal, designer; Lois Ehlert, graphic illustrator; APCO Graphics, Plexiglass sign fabricator.

Credits

Photographers are listed below according to the pages on which their work appears.

28–29, 73, 92–93, 114–115, 152–153: Denis Larkin

36, top: Roger Marshutz Photography

55: Mel Goldman Studio

56: Ernest Pappas

69: Mario Carrieri

86–87, 124–125: Tom Crane

158, 164–168: Norman McGrath

160–161: Saville Design

178–179: Robert Perron

Directory of Products

Directory of Designers

Consumer Products

Contract and Residential

Equipment and Instrumentation

Visual Communications

Environmental

Index

Edited by Sarah Bodine and Susan Davis
Designed by James Craig and Jay Anning
Set in 10 point Helvetica Light